Presented To

Bitsy

From

Mom - A. on my 53 birthday.

Date

_2016_

BECAUSE
YOU
BELIEVE

CHRISTIAN ART
PUBLISHERS

Originally published by Christelike Uitgewersmaatskappy
under the title *Omdat jy glo*

© 2010

English edition
© 2010 Christian Art Publishers
PO Box 1599, Vereeniging, 1930, RSA

First edition 2010
Second edition 2015

Translated by Mairi-Ann Bonnet

Cover designed by Christian Art Gifts

Images used under license from Shutterstock.com

Set in 12 on 15 pt Palatino LT Std
by Christian Art Publishers

Printed in China

ISBN 978-1-4321-1391-9

Dedication

With gratitude to Piet Smit:
A dedicated follower of the Master;
Distinguished gospel singer;
Faithful friend.

Foreword

The Word of God emphatically teaches us that Jesus came, lived, suffered, died and rose again to give us true life. "In Him was life, and that life was the light of men" (John 1:4). And also that, "I will show you what he is like who comes to me and hears My words and puts them into practice" (Luke 6:47).

✳God's Word repeatedly declares that true life can only be given to us by Jesus Christ.✳There is no hope for a true life without Him. However, there is certainty of abundant life through faith in Him. The early disciples always emphasized the resurrection of Christ, because without the Resurrection there would not have been a church of Christ.✳But the Resurrection proves that God is alive and invincible; that He is the God of life and death and that He is eternal. Behind Christ stands God and therefore nothing can stop His power to change people's lives.✳There is no limit to what the living Christ can do in a person's life, if we would only follow and obey Him.

May the Holy Spirit lead you in your reading of these devotions and may this devotional not only guide you as you ponder on what you read, but also inspire you to act on it; in order to bring you to the living Christ who wants to be your Guide to the only true life; until you reach a point where you can say, "I can do everything through Him who gives me strength" (Phil. 4:13).

✳"Whoever believes in the Son has eternal life, but whoever rejects the Son will not see life, for God's wrath remains on him" (John 3:36).

Soli Deo Gloria!

~ *The Publisher*

Contents

January

Gathering the Flock

"I am the good shepherd.
The good shepherd lays down
His life for the sheep."
~ John 10:11

Without a shepherd, sheep are not a flock.
~ Russian Proverb

*L*oving, timeless God of yesterday, today and tomorrow,
to You all praise, honor and worship
as we venture out on unfamiliar paths.
We thank You for being our Savior to show us the way.
Thank You, Lord Jesus, for coming to this sin-torn world to
lead us from our wandering back to the Father's House.
Help us to follow You not only when we can clearly see the
road before us, but also when we go through dark valleys.
Grant that our faith in Your guidance will never falter.
Thank You that You were sent to make us part of God's flock;
that You are the Good Shepherd who wants to lead us beside
green pastures and quiet waters. Let us start this month with
our hand firmly in Your loving hand and grant that we will
willingly and obediently follow wherever You might lead us.
In the name of our Savior and Master.

Amen.

God Gave

Read John 3:1-21

"For God so loved the world that He gave His one and only Son, that whoever believes in Him shall not perish but have eternal life." (John 3:16)

To truly and intimately know someone, you need to meet with that person, speak to him and even live with him. There are people who have pen pals in far-off countries. Having a pen pal means that you tell him all about yourself through the letters that you write.

You might send a photo of yourself so that your pen pal can get to know you better. If you are able to phone each other you will get to know each other's voices. If you know of someone who is going to visit near where your pen pal lives, you might ask that person to visit your pen pal or to deliver a gift for him. Your pen pal will continually gather knowledge about you. Hopefully the day will come when the two of you can meet face to face and then you will truly and intimately know each other.

> *Jesus did not come to make God's love possible, but to make God's love visible.*
>
> *~ Richard Baxter*

When Jesus came to earth, God Himself arrived. Messages were no longer necessary. It was now an individual, face-to-face, interpersonal relationship. Jesus did not only come for Peter, James and John, but for every person in the universe.

When Neil Armstrong landed on the moon, he said, "We came in peace for all mankind." When Jesus Christ came to earth, God's message for humanity was, "I come in love for all mankind!" A cardinal truth became known through this event: God is pure, sincere, self-sacrificing love! This is the greatest truth the world will ever experience.

Wonderful God of grace, let all of humanity come to know Your undying love. Amen.

God's Love Becomes Visible

Read John 3:1-21

For God so loved the world that He gave His one and only Son, that whoever believes in Him shall not perish but have eternal life. (John 3:16)

If you study the people of Israel in the Old Testament you will discover that a fear of God is reflected. Scripture tells us about individuals who tried to flee from God and hide from the mighty Jehovah. Their lives were filled with a fear of His wrath. We discover that Abraham was willing to sacrifice his son, not only because he was obedient to God, but because he feared Him.

Nothings binds me to my Lord like a strong belief in His unchanging love.
~ Charles H. Spurgeon

Through Jesus Christ, God affirmed that He is not only a God to be revered and feared, but that He is, in essence, a God of love. Jesus brought the love of God to humankind through His life and sacrificial death. He banished fear and paved the way for a new relationship with the holy love of the Almighty God.

Even today people find it difficult to accept that God is not simply a feared Judge who has various ways to punish our transgressions. As a result their spiritual lives become dead and their worship is ruled by fear rather than a true desire to worship.

Even though we will all be held accountable for the way we lived our lives, Jesus Christ came to this world to bring God's love to you and to lead you into a personal, loving relationship with Himself. Live unceasingly from within the source of His love and experience the abundance of life through Jesus Christ (see John 10:10).

Holy Lord Jesus, in Your love I find fulfillment in life and hope for the future. Amen.

How Far Does Love Reach?

Read 1 John 3:11-17

This is how we know what love is: Jesus Christ laid down His life for us. And we ought to lay down our lives for our brothers. (1 John 3:16)

Human love is often a case of, "I'll love you as long as you love me." Even the love between parents and children can be strained, especially when the child is the "black sheep" or when the parents let the child down.

Through Jesus Christ, God's love reached new depths. Before Christ, people knew that God loved them and expected them to keep His commands. But before Christ, they didn't know *how much* God loved them.

Jesus taught people what the love of God meant. His parables about the Prodigal Son and for-

> *The love of God is like the Amazon River flowing down to water one daisy.*
> ~ Charles H. Spurgeon

giveness of the guilty speak about this. His deeds revealed God's love: His healing of the sick, feeding of the hungry and love for the outcast. Through these acts, the love of God was demonstrated.

But it was Jesus' death on the cross that proved that there are no boundaries to God's love. With this one sacrificial deed God said to humankind, "This is how much I love you. As unlovable, rebellious, weak and unfaithful as you are, I seek to save you and to win your trust through this act of unrequited love. You deserve death and your sins separate you from Me. I died in your place. Won't you repent, believe and love Me in return?"

God's love is not sentimental. It sets the final standard of love. How is this standard of love being upheld in your life?

God of Love, grant me a love as endless as Yours. Amen.

Sent to Save

Read John 3:1-21

"For God did not send His Son into the world to condemn the world, but to save the world through Him." (John 3:17)

Jesus Christ came on a mission to save and He was sent for this specific purpose. His coming to this world, His service and teaching, His healings and friendships, and His death and resurrection were all for one single purpose: He came to save!

In what respect must you be saved? Firstly, you must be saved *from* sin. This means that you must first receive forgiveness for your sins. Confess that you have sinned and wandered away from God, and then accept God's forgiveness. You will then enter into a living and permanent relationship of trust and submission to Jesus. You will also seek His help and inspiration to fight and overcome the sinful things you were involved in before, and to lead a sinless life as far as possible.

> Salvation is the work of God for man; it is not the work of man for God.
>
> ~ Lewis Sperry Chafer

Then you must be saved *to* a new life of honoring and glorifying God, of accepting His leadership, and of becoming actively involved in serving your fellow man. Your experiences with other believers will encourage you and so you will be united with the community of believers.

You were saved by Jesus to serve Him. You then become an agent in the saving work of Jesus, which you yourself received. You have been saved to a life which must grow in the likeness of Christ, spiritual maturity and perfect love.

Ask yourself honestly before God: *Have I been saved?*

Gracious God, thank You for the salvation that Jesus brought.

Amen.

True Life

Read 1 John 4:7-20

This is how God showed His love among us: He sent His one and only Son into the world that we might live through Him. (1 John 4:9)

When you are young you are encouraged to study so that you can use your talents and accumulate knowledge to help you get the best out of life. Young people often wonder, "Will I be successful? Will I be happy? Will I be rich?" They believe that this is what life is about.

The Christian faith suggests something completely different. It regards success, happiness and wealth as secondary goals. But if you follow these goals alone, you will miss the really important things in life, namely to know and to serve God. The Christian faith tells you that God's view of life is so important that Jesus came to live and die to make it available to you.

I asked for all things that I may enjoy life. I was given life that I may enjoy all things.
~ Anonymous

His life was "true life" in contrast to mere "existence," because His life was driven by love. Love originates in God and God loves us. This love is made personal through Jesus Christ, "I have come that they might have life, and have it to the full" (John 10:10). We receive this life and then pass it on to others.

Christ's way of life is also a source of joy. The certainty of knowing that we are loved is the source of a positive feeling of joy, praise and worship. This kind of life enables us to handle the dark side of life. It offers forgiveness and redemption to the guilty, healing to the sick, and the prospect of a new life after death. For human weakness He offers His strength. In the darkness He gives light. It is truly an enriching "life" that God grants us through Jesus Christ.

Lord Jesus, thank You for the enrichment and improvement of my life. Amen.

A Godly Initiative

Read 1 John 4:7-21

This is love: not that we loved God, but that He loved us and sent His Son as an atoning sacrifice for our sins. (1 John 4:10)

We all think that we know precisely what love means. Even so, human love is a strange mix of wonder, sympathy, selfishness, lust, caring and sacrifice. In our love relationships we experience mere glimmers of what God's love is like.

God's love always supersedes our love. He loved us before we loved Him. He loved us before we were born. He loved our parents before He loved us. He loved humankind before He brought it into existence.

> *It is not after we were reconciled by the blood of His Son that God began to love us, but before the foundation of the world.*
>
> ~ John Calvin

Humans became living beings through God's love. We didn't ask God to love us, He took the initiative. All other loves come from His love and they are brought to life through His love.

Our love for God and each other is molded on His love. Despite His great love for us, we hurt and neglect Him. By doing this, we distance ourselves from Him.

But God loved us even more and His great desire to win our love led Him to offer His Son. Through this sacrifice we are forgiven.

When we accept that God has adopted us, unworthy as we are, then His love becomes the most valuable thing in our lives. It saves, heals, restores, motivates and enables us to grow in the likeness of our Savior, Jesus Christ.

How do you respond to God's great love?

Holy Father God, how can I ever thank You enough for taking the initiative in loving me? Amen.

Abundance or Want?

Read John 10:1-10

"I have come that they may have life, and have it to the full." (John 10:10)

Many people don't live life to the full; they simply exist. Howard Rutledge, a United States air force pilot, was shot down over Vietnam during the early stages of the Vietnam war and spent several years in a Vietnamese prison cell. There he discovered how little he had to cling to. Before the war he had been "too busy" to spend time with God. He said that, "It took time in prison to make me see how empty my life was without God."

The essential reason why Jesus came to this world was so that people who trusted and followed Him could experience life in all its fullness.

Faith in Jesus brings joy; not a superficial, carefree life without depth, but a deeply rooted, quiet joy that meets the harsh realities

> *The value of life lies not in the length of days, but in the use we make of them; a man may live long yet live very little.*
> ~ Michel de Montaigne

of this world with a calm confidence borne from the knowledge that God is in control.

Faith in Jesus gives you purpose because you know that you are important to God, that He loves you, and wants to travel with you on life's journey. Faith in Jesus gives you hope when circumstances are difficult and demanding. Faith in Jesus helps you to get your life in order when you otherwise would have fallen apart. Faith in Jesus motivates you to love others and to overcome the self-centeredness that would otherwise dominate your private world.

Do you want to live a life of abundance or want? Jesus is the answer – and the choice is yours.

Lord Jesus, I plead that You will give me the fullness of life that was Your purpose in coming to this world. Amen.

How Do You React to Life?

Read John 10:1-10

"I have come that they may have life, and have it to the full." (John 10:10)

People react differently to the stresses and demands of life. Some see life as an intense battle and become aggressive, others are apathetic and quietly accept everything that comes their way without rejoicing or moaning. Most people react emotionally to life and live imprisoned by their attitudes; they allow their feelings to rule their lives.

It's your responsibility whether something that happens in your life will bless you or hurt you. When painful things happen, the emotional and spiritual scars can remain and you can lose your faith in God. But with God's help you can control your reactions and strengthen your faith, patience and endurance.

> *Each small task of everyday life is part of the harmony of the universe.*
> ~ St. Theresa of Lisieux

Don't approach life with an attitude of self-pity, frustration, impatience or anger. Life does not get hurt through these things – but you do.

Different age groups react differently to life. Young people seem to react with a naïve charm, while older people often react with self-reproach and a pervasive glumness. But everyone reacts to life – in one way or the other.

As a Christian you know that you have been made in the image of God and are of priceless worth. Because you and the Father are one, you should be filled with self-confidence and live in peace with Him and in harmony with yourself. With this blessed inspiration, faith and spiritual peace, you will be able to react to life with the strength and wisdom of Jesus and the Holy Spirit. This is the reason why Jesus came.

Savior and Master, I praise and thank You for equipping me with the Holy Spirit, to react to the demands of life. Amen.

Live United with Christ

Read 1 John 2:18-27

See that what you have heard from the beginning remains in you. If it does, you also will remain in the Son and in the Father. (1 John 2:24)

Many things can cause you to backslide in your faith. Sickness and depression might make you feel that God has rejected you. Family issues might discourage you. Failure in a business undertaking might make you doubt God's goodness. Conflict in your congregation can gnaw at your faith. Doubts about whether God even exists can slip into your life. In situations like these your faith in God can wane.

It is essential that you be aware of any inclination or temptation that can rob you of your faith. Don't allow these things to cause you dismay. Be firm in your faith

> *Temptation usually comes through a door that has deliberately been left open.*
> ~ Anonymous

and cling to it like a drowning person clings to a life buoy. In the end you will be thankful you did. Remember Paul's words to the Romans, "I am convinced that neither death nor life, neither angels nor demons, neither the present nor the future, nor any powers, neither height nor depth, nor anything else in all creation, will be able to separate us from the love of God that is in Christ Jesus our Lord" (Rom. 8:38-39).

Believers have good and bad days, just like everyone else. They have to make it through testing, stress and pressure. It's the same for you and me, no matter how strong our faith is or how long we have held fast to it for. Regardless of situations you should always stay in Christ Jesus; He will never forsake you. He knows your every circumstance and intercedes for you with the Father. He prays for you today, tomorrow and till eternity. Praise the Lord!

Lord Jesus, hold me in Your love so that I might never lose my faith in You. Thank You for interceding for me with the Father. Amen.

Christ's Promise to You

Read 1 John 2:18-27

This is what He promised us – even eternal life. (1 John 2:25)

Many young Christians make premature promises to God. They promise to serve and obey Him to the end. They promise to live pure and righteous lives and to pray every day. From time to time older Christians renew the promises they made to God. But many of us keep our promises for a while and then we neglect them.

Our promises to God are our reaction to the amount of love God has shown us. On God's end of the agreement is the promise of an endless future. He promises us everlasting life. This is the gift of quality of life for us now, but it also points to a future dimension on the other side of human existence. It offers us life after death. The "Jesus quality" of life means that death does not have the final say for any disciple of Jesus Christ.

> *It is not darkness you are going to, for God is light. It is not lonely, for Christ is with you. It is not unknown country, for Christ is there.*
>
> ~ Charles Kingsley

It opens the door not only to a longer life, but also to a more glorious life on the other side of the grave. Eternal life is a life with God in His unquestionable glory and sovereignty. It is unrestrained communion with God and eternal joy and peace in His presence. It is a life of love and beauty, unblemished by human weakness. There will be no more suffering or grief and we will have glorified bodies.

Above all, it is a life in Christ with His truth, glory and love surpassing all. It surely is a future to long for!

Thank You, Lord Jesus, for the promise of eternal life for Your faithful children. Amen.

Is Your Christian Life Losing Its Shine?

Read John 5:30-40

"Yet you refuse to come to Me to have life." (John 5:40)

It is possible for Christians to get caught up in philosophies that seem good on the surface, but that break down the centrality of Christ. Creeds and dogmas are essential in providing intellectual substance to our beliefs, but the moment they overshadow the Person of the Living Christ, they suppress the One they are trying to glorify and explain.

The Christian life involves a set of rules that are based on the teachings of Christ. It is basically a way of life that must be lived in the power of the Holy Spirit. Jesus came to give new life to all who accept Him and His teachings. This new life is a direct outpouring of the Holy Spirit in a person's life as was promised by Jesus to His disciples.

> *Lighthouses don't fire cannons to call attention to their shining – they just shine.*
> ~ Dwight L. Moody

Many Christians are familiar with Jesus' teachings and used to be excited and enthusiastic about their love for Him. Unfortunately their love for Jesus has waned and their faith has become stereotypical; cold and lacking in intimacy with the Master. To keep your spiritual glow you need to continuously strengthen it with prayer and meditation.

To maintain a Christ-centered and Christ-inspired faith, nothing may be allowed to come between you and the Master. Everything you learn about Him must be geared towards this aim. In this regard Paul prays that you might "know this love that surpasses knowledge – that you may be filled to the measure of all the fullness of God" (Eph. 3:19). Your faith can never lose its shine as long as you stay focused on Jesus.

Holy Savior, keep my thoughts focused on You so that my faith will keep shining. Amen.

A Firm Trust

Read John 11:17-32

"I am the resurrection and the life. He who believes in Me will live, even though he dies." (John 11:25)

These words spoken by the Master might seem like a contradiction. Indeed, many of Jesus' teachings seem inexplicable when we try to understand them intellectually.

The Holy Scriptures and the experiences of dedicated Christians, demonstrates that trust, faith and submission to the Almighty God always forms the basis of miraculous events that challenge human logic.

Through the ages, people have had to deal with dangers and testing in a variety of forms. It has always been those with a strong, unshakable faith in Jesus Christ who were able to withstand and overcome the attacks.

> *Life is a mystery to be lived, not a problem to be solved.*
> ~ Søren Kierkegaard

Today our faith is still tested. It might be through persecution, financial difficulties, sickness or some kind of personal setback.

Whatever your situation, always remember that God is with you to support you and to carry you through your time of difficulty. "So do not fear, for I am with you; do not be dismayed, for I am your God. I will strengthen you and help you; I will uphold you with My righteous right hand" (Isa. 41:10).

Cling to the presence of the Living Christ in your life. He will inspire you to a life of trust and firm faith in all circumstances.

My Savior, in You I discover unending joy, love and true life. I thank You for this. Amen.

Using a Crisis as a Turning Point

Read John 9:35-41

Jesus said, "For judgment I have come into this world, so that the blind will see and those who see will become blind." (John 9:39)

We usually perceive a crisis as a time of difficulty. But a crisis can also be a turning point where we move forward in a new and more productive direction. It can create an opportunity that we would never have had if things had stayed the same.

When Jesus said that He came to judge, He meant that His coming would cause a crisis in the lives of the people He met. It placed them in a dilemma where they were forced to choose either for Him or against Him. To react to Him in faith brought insight and light to people, just like it did for the man who was born blind. By refusing to believe in Him they brought upon themselves the darkness of rejection, they were separated from God and placed under judgment.

> *For light I go directly to the Source of light, not to any of the reflections.*
>
> ~ Peace Pilgrim

Whether you live in light or in darkness depends on how you respond to Jesus. When He comes to you it places you in a crisis because a personal experience with Jesus is the most critical moment in your whole life. You must either say "Yes" or "No" to Him. You can believe in Him, entrust yourself to Him, worship and obey Him. If you do this you will walk in the Light and you will begin to see more and more of the Light. Or you can shut out the Light and continue in spiritual blindness for the rest of your life.

Your meeting with Jesus either becomes a golden opportunity or a dire crisis that you will regret for the rest of your life. God says to you today: Choose life!

Jesus, I choose You as the Savior and Light of my life, for now and evermore. Amen.

The Gift of Eternal Life

Read 1 John 5:1-12

This is the testimony: God has given us eternal life, and this life is in His Son. (1 John 5:11)

People's life expectancy is increasing and today the average person is expected to live well into his seventies. Developments in medical science have resulted in people being able to live longer than ever before. In biblical times people didn't live as long and there was a greater consciousness of the brevity of life.

In order to satisfy the human yearning for a long life, many religions offered the promise of eternal life. If you believed, you could live the same kind of life as the idol you worshiped. But only Jesus Christ can truly keep this promise. Eternal life is the life of God, because God alone is eternal. God can give you eternal life because He grants it to all who believe in Him and share in His life.

> *Once a man is united to God, how could he not live forever?*
> ~ C. S. Lewis

Because God is peace, eternal life is tranquil and calm, without stress and pressure. Eternal life grants you victory over frustrations because you receive strength from the life you share with God. God is holy and He transfers His holiness to you and therefore you achieve a higher moral plain and are able to resist temptations and enticements. God is also love and He fills your heart with His love that removes all bitterness, revengeful thoughts and hate. God's life is everlasting, and in Him you have a quality of life that overcomes death. God's life within you is indestructible. Praise God because He is good. There is no end to His love.

Eternal God, fill my life with eternity, that only belongs to You.
Amen.

Do You Have This Life?

Read 1 John 5:1-12

He who has the Son has life; he who does not have the Son of God does not have life. (1 John 5:12)

What is life actually about? For some it is about satisfying their hunger for wealth and possessions: cars, houses and other valuable treasures. For others it's about money: the more you have, the better you live. For some, life is just about pleasure. Others value prestige, power or self-fulfillment.

The Bible has a clear message: Life is about Jesus Christ! If you have Him, you have life, and if you don't have Him, you don't have life.

Knowing Jesus might bring you prosperity – but it might not. Following Jesus brought power to a small group, but for many it led to humble service without any remarkable authority or the slightest reward.

> *Fear not that thy life shall come to an end, but rather fear that it shall never have a beginning.*
>
> ~ John Henry Newman

When Jesus enters your life, He brings wholeness. He gives you healthy and exciting priorities that you never even thought of. Through His forgiveness of your sins, He brings peace into your life – with God, your loved ones and with yourself.

Jesus opens your eyes when you welcome Him into your life. You see your true self, the true God, and the world as it really is. You find perspective on all aspects of life and existence. These things happen to you when Jesus becomes the Savior of your life.

Savior and Redeemer, I have only one short earthly life to live. Help me, through Your grace, to make it the best that I can. Amen.

Become Part of God's Family

Read Galatians 3:21-29

You are all sons of God through faith in Christ Jesus. (Galatians 3:26)

When we read the Bible and see Jesus referred to as the "Son of God" we are overcome by the majesty of Christ – unless we are totally emotionless.

On the level of human relationships as we know them it is difficult to understand how the Son of God could live on this earth as a human being. Sometimes it seems incomprehensible to us. Perhaps that's why some people say that it is impossible for us to follow the example of Jesus, because He wasn't a normal person – He was divine; the Son of God.

> *In His love He clothes us, enfolds and embraces us; that tender love completely surrounds us, never to leave us.*
>
> *~ Julian of Norwich*

Never let this way of thinking keep you from giving yourself to the service of the Master. Remember that through God's limitless grace, you have been called to become His child through your faith in the rulership of Christ in your life. God's family is universal and everyone who accepts Jesus as Redeemer and Savior is welcomed in Jesus' family as a child of God.

Serve God by walking with Christ, and obediently and diligently following His example. As you grow in grace, you will become more and more aware of God's Fathership. You will realize that He watches over you and that through the Holy Spirit, He equips you to fulfill your role in this world as His child.

O Lord my God, I delight in knowing that, through Jesus Christ, I may call You Father. Amen.

So That All Might Believe

Read John 1:1-18

He came as a witness to testify concerning that light, so that through him all men might believe. (John 1:7)

When you come to know Jesus and He enters your life, you become part of a worldwide community. This experience is so intensely personal that we sometimes speak of Jesus as our own private possession. We sometimes hear people say, "My Jesus!"

The New Testament people had passion. They lived to make Jesus known across the whole world. The mindset that God was the God of the Jews alone and that other people had their own gods was totally refuted by the life, teachings, death and resurrection of Jesus Christ.

When the Holy Spirit came at Pentecost, the disciples left Jerusalem. Jesus had said, "You will receive power when the Holy Spirit comes on you; and you will be My witnesses in Jerusalem, and in all Judea and Samaria and to the ends of the earth" (Acts 1:8).

> *God had an only Son, and He was a missionary and a physician.*
>
> ~ David Livingstone

Today there are approximately six billion people on earth. About two billion are Christians. A further one billion have heard about Jesus Christ, but have not made a commitment to Him. That means that half of the world's population has not even heard about Jesus yet. The work that John the Baptist started with His witness about Jesus still has a long way to go.

No matter how challenging the task and the opposition may seem, Christians today have the same mission. This mission will never be completed if we leave it to the professional theologians alone. We each need to be an effective witness for Jesus.

Lord Jesus, grant that Your followers will attempt to bring others to faith in You. Amen.

The Word Became Flesh

Read John 1:1-18

The Word became flesh and made His dwelling among us. (John 1:14)

Actions speak louder than words" is a well-known saying which means that your deeds are more significant than your words. We also refer to people who just talk and don't do anything as "all talk and no action."

The Bible doesn't share this distrust in our words. According to the Scriptures, words contain great power. The Word of God is seen as exceptionally powerful. When God spoke through the prophet, He said, "So is My word that goes out from My mouth. It will not return to Me empty, but will accomplish what I desire and achieve the purpose for which I sent it" (Isa. 55:11). God's words or messages became mighty deeds that spoke louder than human words.

> *Words which do not give the light of Christ increase the darkness.*
>
> ~ Mother Teresa

A word is a sound or thought that comes from deep within a person's being and becomes a reality that we call speech. But God's words are weaved into a life that is far more than just sounds and thoughts. He speaks to us from a heart that beats with love; in actions that heal; in miracles that overrule evil; in parables that us tell what God's kingdom is like; in the building of a community of followers; and in death and triumphant resurrection from the dead.

We must make sure that we don't overflow with words, but lack in deeds. We must strive to follow our words with God-ordained actions. God's words must be visible in our actions. Jesus, our Savior, must be seen and heard in our words.

Let Your Word speak clearly through my life and actions today.

Amen.

Light for a Dark World

"While I am in the world, I am the light of the world." (John 9:5)

To be in the dark without a light is a scary experience. You don't know where you are, you walk into things and you can even injure yourself or damage things that you bump into. Without a light your activities come to a stop. If a power failure caused the darkness, then your activities will cease till the power comes back on. Light is essential for everyday life and we often take it for granted that there will be light.

When Jesus said He was the light of the world, there were few sources of artificial light. People relied on the light of the sun. Just as the sun brought light, so too did Jesus. People who lived in His light saw the world in a completely new way. It was as if they were blind before. A new world opened up for them that enabled them to know, to see and to give and receive guidance.

> *We can easily forgive a child who is afraid of the dark; the real tragedy of life is when men are afraid of the light.*
> ~ Plato

Jesus can bring light to any dark area of your life, whether it be doubt, depression, feelings of guilt or failure. Sometimes people live in darkness because they are confused by false teachings which present themselves as truthful and good.

Allow Jesus to bring light to the darkness in your life. Make Him your Savior and submit to His plan for your life – you will discover a new beam of light shining in your life. It will enlighten your thoughts, guide your footsteps and focus your life on God's love.

Guide to the light, I pray for those who are still walking in darkness. Grant that Your light might be switched on in their hearts and minds. Amen.

Everlasting Light!

Read 1 John 1:1-10

The life appeared; we have seen it and testify to it, and we proclaim to you the eternal life, which was with the Father and has appeared to us. (1 John 1:2)

Have you ever made peace with the fact that life is short and the older you get, the shorter life gets? When people you went to school with begin to pass away, the brevity of life becomes a stark reality. Some people don't even want to think that everything will come to an end for them one day.

But it doesn't have to – not if you believe in Jesus. You are not limited to the length of your earthly life, because the life that Jesus brings and shares with those who believe in Him is eternal. It is eternal because it is a gift from God, and God is eternal. It has been this way from the beginning, and isn't simply a consolation prize for those who have "made it." It is part of God's giving of Himself to us.

> *Where, except in the present, can the Eternal be met?*
> ~ C. S. Lewis

It is also eternal because it has a divine quality to it. The person who lives "in Christ" doesn't just wander around aimlessly, but is transformed into a child of God and is part of the family of Jesus Christ. Eternal life isn't just an extension of our earthly lives, but the beginning of a better, richer life here and now.

Eternal life is eternal because it doesn't end with death. The grave could not keep Jesus and neither can it keep those who have chosen life through faith in Him. They have received the promise, "Because I live, you also will live" (John 14:19). Those who follow our Savior know that this is undeniably true. Do you know this for sure?

Lord Jesus, I kneel in a prayer of thanksgiving to You for making eternal life available to me. Amen.

Fellowship with God and Christ

Read 1 John 1:1-10

We proclaim to you what we have seen and heard, so that you also may have fellowship with us. And our fellowship is with the Father and with His Son, Jesus Christ. (1 John 1:3)

There are many divisions among Christians. The various denominations have different approaches and interpretations. Some are strictly conservative and others are liberal, which results in them seeing things in different ways.

In the early church the greatest difference was between Christians who had been Jews before their conversion, and the Gentiles. The Jews had strict rules about separating themselves from Gentiles and it was extremely difficult for them to accept Gentiles into the fellowship of believers.

At times it seemed that this

> *Friendship between the friends of Jesus of Nazareth is unlike any other friendship.*
> ~ Stephen Neill

problem would divide the church, but wise men saw to it that the church broke new ground and developed instead.

Christ broke down the dividing walls. Christians from different backgrounds were welcomed because they saw Christ as one and that they were one in Him. All were now part of the Church of Christ and united through the Holy Spirit.

The early Christians also supported, taught and instructed one another. In this way both groups grew through the experience of fellowship with the wider group of Christian believers.

Christians today want to have fellowship only with those who share their opinions, but the gospel calls us to greater things. Christians grow and enrich themselves through fellowship with each other. This is what our Savior expects from us.

Lord Jesus, grant that I will accept everyone who accepts You as Savior. Amen.

The Reason for Christ's Coming

Read 1 John 3:1-10

You know that He appeared so that He might take away our sins. And in Him is no sin. (1 John 3:5)

William Barclay, the well-known Scottish New Testament interpreter once said, "Christianity begins with a sense of sin. It begins with the sudden realization that life as we are living it will not do. We awake to ourselves and we awake to our need of God."

In the modern Christian world sin is spoken about very cautiously, yet it is one of the central themes of Scripture. People's lives are destroyed by sin. Sin challenges God and separates us from Him. In today's world God is not obeyed and His commandments are broken at random. Even though we try to minimize our guilt, justify our mistakes and focus on our own empowerment, sin remains a horrible reality.

The consciousness of sin is the straight pathway to heaven.

~ Joseph B. Lightfoot

Jesus came, not to make us happy or successful, or clever or prosperous, but to free us from our sins. He came to establish peace between man and God and to restore harmony and fellowship with Himself. There was only one way to deal with sin and that was to forgive it. Christ was sent by God to remove our sins – to forgive us. Jesus announced to sinners forgiveness through faith in God. A new beginning could be made, but they had to repent and confess their sins to God first.

You can't handle your sinfulness on your own. You need God's help and He knows this, and that's why He sent Jesus. If being a Christian starts with a consciousness of sin, have you already started to be a Christian?

Thank You, Holy Teacher, that You taught me to begin at the beginning: with the realization of my own sinfulness. Amen.

How to Avoid Sin

Read 1 John 3:1-10

No one who lives in Him keeps on sinning. (1 John 3:6)

Life would be very different if there was no sin. We all want to be rid of the desire to sin. If it was in our ability we would resist and overcome every temptation to sin. In our better moments we would wish to overcome the weaknesses and vulnerabilities of our sinful nature, which causes our inability to do good and which tries to force us to do evil.

But the more we love Christ, the more we become convinced of our own sinfulness. Yet the only way to overcome sin is to stay close to Jesus. Only His power and love in our hearts can abate the evil that we are so prone to. This also involves obedience because every time we obey Him,

> *Sin is sovereign till sovereign grace dethrones it.*
> ~ Charles H. Spurgeon

our spiritual strength is built up. Every time we are disobedient to God, we make ourselves a bit more vulnerable to "the sin that so easily entangles" (Heb. 12:1).

Sin in the lives of believers is one of the biggest problems in Christianity. Believers who sin damage the witness of the gospel.

You do not have to carry on living in sin. You can decide to stay close to Jesus. Then you will experience His grace and strength, and the more you get exposed to this influence, the greater your spiritual growth will be.

Master, help those who earnestly fight against sin and as a result feel that they have disappointed You. Give them the grace to overcome and live triumphantly. Amen.

Love Will Triumph

Read Galatians 1:1-10

Grace and peace to you from God our Father and the Lord Jesus Christ, who gave Himself for our sins to rescue us from the present evil age, according to the will of our God and Father. (Galations 1:3-4)

It seems as though evil powers have free reign over the world today. Reports of crime, violence, lawlessness and immorality are delivered daily. People are overwhelmed by these events and many stand by helplessly and wonder what can be done to restore peace and order.

The only way to overcome crime and evil is to follow Jesus' example. In obedience to God's will, Jesus survived the horror of the crucifixion by showering His divine love on this evil world.

> *Love cures people, both the ones who give it, and the ones who receive it.*
>
> ~ Dr. Karl Menninger

Today this seems like an impossibility to many people. It is often thought that violence needs to be fought with violence, but history shows that this is not the solution. Even though we in no way claim that criminals should escape the law, we must still follow the example of Jesus and pray for the offenders and lovingly care for the victims.

In the same way that Almighty God transformed the horror of Good Friday into the glory of Easter, so He will transform the evil of this moment into His goodness. This requires your obedience to Him. It calls you to pray with Jesus' love for the whole world when it is your turn.

Father God, help me to follow the example of my Savior, Jesus, to love all people in Your name. Amen.

God's Indescribable Gift

Read 2 Corinthians 9:6-15

Thanks be to God for His indescribable gift! (2 Corinthians 9:15)

Perhaps you have searched for an exceptional gift for a loved one only to discover that you can't afford it. You feel embarrassed and disappointed. When you eventually find something for the person you feel that it's a weak substitute for what you really wanted to give them. You might even apologize to the person receiving the gift. But the receiver might be overjoyed with the gift – perhaps more than he would have been with the original gift you had in mind.

The Bible says that God's gift was "indescribable." This is how much a human life is worth. It is ironic that Judas and the temple authorities of his day set the price of a human life at thirty pieces of silver. Despite this fact, a poor woman used her savings, an amount equivalent to a year's salary, to buy an alabaster jar of perfume to wash Jesus' feet with.

> *God loves each of us as if there were only one of us.*
> ~ St. Augustine

God's love for you is so indescribably great that He poured the gift of His Son out over you. In human terms it was a priceless gift. God did this, not to buy you, but to save you from sin and Satan.

Some gifts enrich the receivers. A gift can equip them to start a new task, give insight into a certain area of knowledge, or a fresh realization of how valuable they are to you. God's gift to you says that you are the most loved person in the entire universe.

God of love, grant me the grace to regard each gift You give me as valuable. Amen.

A Love That Cannot Be Described by Words

Read 2 Corinthians 9:1-15

Thanks be to God for His indescribable gift! (2 Corinthians 9:15)

Buying birthday, wedding and Christmas presents can be quite demanding. You have to remember to remain within your budget and to make sure that you don't forget anybody important.

In the midst of the hustle and bustle of gift buying it is beneficial to stand still for a moment and consider the gift that stands central to all gifts: Jesus is God's gift to humankind.

Christ is also the Word who became flesh. It was the only form in which God could give Himself to humankind and the only form in which we could receive Him: a human life. Yet this gift of God's Word is indescribable!

God loves us, not because of who we are, but because of who He is.

~ Robert Bolton

It is exciting to receive a gift that is so stunning that it leaves you speechless. We cannot express it in words. This "Gift" – the Gift of Jesus – strikes us inarticulate and speechless with thankfulness, wonder and love.

How can we possibly respond to such a "Gift"? You can accept it by opening your heart in the same way you would open your hand to receive a gift from someone. And then thank God for it by living a dedicated and committed life. The amazing thing about this "Gift" is that it can't be described in words, yet Jesus filled Paul with words: the message of the gospel, its interpretation and a witness to the entire heathen world.

You too can thank God for this indescribable gift. You can thank Him every day you live through words of testimony and deeds of love.

Savior and Lord, show me each day how I can thank You more and more. Amen.

When Mirages become Real

Read Psalm 25:1-22

Show me Your ways, O LORD, teach me Your paths. (Psalm 25:4)

It is easy to get lost while traveling to a new place. The thing you need most during this time is a road map or a trusted friend who can give you directions.

Sometimes you can find yourself on the wrong path in life. Or you have to make an important decision but you are unable to do so because your judgment has become clouded. There could also be external forces and opinions that carry a lot of weight and affect your judgment.

Isaiah offers comforting words for exactly this kind of situation, "Whether you turn to the right or to the left, your ears will hear a voice behind you, saying, 'This is the way; walk in it'" (Is. 30:21). The Christian who constantly follows the path that God shows him will become sensitive to the voice of God.

> The Christian life is not a way "out," but a way "through" life.
> ~ Billy Graham

Subject every decision you make to the approval of God. Wait on Him in silence and in prayer. He will guide you. When you face the world in faith, you will know that you are not doing it alone, because the living Christ is ready to guide you and lead you on the right path.

A personal relationship with Christ is a primary condition for this. It is your road map. It has to apply to all fields of life. Teach yourself to be aware of the Savior's continuous presence in your life. Then the danger of mistaking mirages for something real will disappear and you will be walking in the Light of the world on the right path.

Redeemer and Guide, fill my life to such a degree that I will clearly understand Your will for my life, and that I will walk Your path in obedience. Amen.

The Precious Gift of Freedom

Read Galatians 4:21-5:1

It is for freedom that Christ has set us free. Stand firm, then, and do not let yourselves be burdened again by a yoke of slavery. (Galatians 5:1)

The people of Israel knew what a yoke of slavery meant. Their history shows that many times they were defeated and forced into slavery. At the time of Jesus' birth the Israelites were under the rule of the mighty Roman Empire.

They were also bound by slavery in their spiritual lives through the strict and uncharitable pronouncements of the Law of Moses and the interpretation the temple authorities gave to the Law. They laid more emphasis on demonstrating their piousness and holiness than actually living it out.

We find freedom when we find God; we lose it when we lose Him.

~ Paul E. Scherer

Jesus' coming brought God's love to the hearts and lives of ordinary people, regardless of who they were. His sacrifice and death granted them the certainty of forgiveness and salvation. His resurrection confirmed the promise of eternal life for all who believe. How can we disregard so rich an inheritance?

Joyfully and thankfully accept the promises and sacrifices of Jesus Christ. Believe in His power at all times and resist Satan's attempts to sow the seed of doubt and unbelief in your mind.

Experience the personal and intimate relationship with the living Christ and discover the exultant joy that is a result of salvation from the destructive consequences of fear, sin and death.

Savior, Jesus my Lord, thank You that I may know You as the Truth who sets me free. Amen.

Understanding to Understand

Read 1 John 5:13-21

We know also that the Son of God has come and has given us understanding, so that we may know Him who is true. And we are in Him who is true – even in His Son Jesus Christ. (1 John 5:20)

We often long to understand something better. You might have a hobby that you just can't get enough of. If something is mentioned about it, you listen attentively.

In a world that was flooded with gods and lords, people hungered for a deeper insight into the nature of religion. In biblical times there was little science as we know it today. There was also no secular teaching. In ancient Israel the rabbi was the school teacher and all education and training was the task of the synagogue. As a result, there were few people who had any understanding of the scientific world. Even religious instruction meant learning what other people of that time knew and had learned.

> *A man may be theologically knowing and spiritually ignorant.*
> ~ Stephen Charnock

When people began to convert to Christianity, a great thirst for knowledge existed. Who was Jesus Christ? Where did He come from? Why did He come? Who was the Holy Spirit? What was the relationship between the church and the synagogue? These and other burning questions were repeatedly asked.

The apostle John's answer was, "Because we know who Jesus was, He gives us knowledge about every other aspect of life. We see everything through His eyes and interpret everything in relation to Him." Just as the blind man Jesus healed could see through new eyes, so the Christians of that time began to see and understand God's world in a totally new way. He is still the key that opens the door to deeper insight, truth and life.

Lord, my Savior, continue to lead me to new depths and heights of insight in my life with You. Amen.

Linked to the Source of Power

Read Philippians 4:10-20

I can do everything through Him who gives me strength. (Philippians 4:13)

As a child of God you have infinite spiritual reserves at your disposal. Since these reserves cannot be seen or calculated, they are often not appreciated or valued according to their true worth.

Instead of rejoicing in the power of your faith, you have to struggle against defeat and frustration. You try to keep up the appearance of your devotion to Christ but you are deeply conscious of your inabilities. Admitting your own spiritual needs is the first step on the road to recovery and strength.

Inside the will of God there is no failure. Outside the will of God there is no success.

~ Bernard Edinger

It is only possible to live a Christian life if the strength of the risen Redeemer is present in your life. This knowledge of complete dependence drives you as you search for a power source.

A successful Christian life does not involve a struggle for victory, but rather a claiming of the victory that is ours through Jesus Christ. Your victory has already been secured by Jesus Christ, all you have to do is claim it and accept it in faith.

When this glorious truth becomes part of your thinking and your actions, your attitude towards life will radically change. You will no longer expect defeat and failure, but you will live with the conviction that you can be victorious through the omnipotence of your living Redeemer.

Faith is not what you can do for Christ, but what you allow Christ to do in you through the unlimited power of the Holy Spirit. Only then are there no limits to the possibilities in your life.

Thank You, Lord Jesus, for Your patience with me. I am totally dependent on You. Use me as You wish and to Your glory alone.

Amen.

He Comes in the Name of God

Read Matthew 21:1-11

Hosanna to the Son of David! Blessed is He who comes in the name of the Lord! Hosanna in the highest! (Matthew 21:9)

Jesus' triumphal entry into Jerusalem is celebrated every year by Christians all over the world. Palm branches are waved and hymns are sung to emphasize the magnitude of the occasion.

The shout of the crowds, "Blessed is He who comes in the name of the Lord!" is worthy of us meditating on. God constantly entered into the lives of individuals like Abraham, Moses, Isaiah, the disciples, Paul and those Jesus healed. But He also entered into the world, demonstrating that He isn't limited to the inner consciousness of individuals.

> *Lord, we lift up Your name with hearts full of praise. Be exalted, O Lord my God! Hosanna in the highest!*
> *~ Carl Tuttle*

Through Creation He entered the world and created order out of chaos. With the exodus out of Egypt, the birth of Jesus Christ, the calming of the storm on the sea of Galilee and Jesus' crucifixion and resurrection, He entered the world. And He is still to come into this world on Judgment Day. God comes into this world because it belongs to Him – He creates, brings order, saves, reigns and judges.

Never think that the world is out of bounds for God, not even with the technological advances of our world today. He comes, if only we will see Him, as those crowds did on Palm Sunday. If only we will honor and worship Him. He is not merely a personal God – He is the King who is coming to reign and receive acclamation from His subjects. Start today to give Him the praise and honor that His name deserves.

Holy Jesus, we praise and worship You as the One who came in the name of God. Amen.

February

Faithful Sheep

Thanks be to God, who always leads
us in triumphal procession in Christ.
~ 2 Corinthians 2:14

No man can follow Christ and go astray.
~ William H. P. Faunce

*F*aithful Savior,
We praise and thank You that You came to lead us
in triumphal procession through life and into eternity!
We thank God that You were sent
so that we can love and care for others like You do;
so that our faith can grow and we can persevere till the end;
so that our hope will never die and that
we can experience our tomorrows today;
so that we can learn from Your humility
and be washers of feet for You;
so that we will reveal Your compassion through
the needs and pain of our fellow believers;
so that we will reveal Your obedience at
Gethsemane for the will of the Father.
Carry us in Your love this month
and lead us to where You want us to go.
We pray this in the name above all names,
Jesus, our Savior and Redeemer.

Amen.

A Timeless Reality

Read 1 John 1:1-10

That which was from the beginning, which we have heard, which we have seen with our eyes, which we have looked at and our hands have touched – this we proclaim concerning the Word of life. (1 John 1:1)

Unbelievers sometimes say that to believe in God is simply an illusion. They think it is too good to be true that God answers prayer. They think Christians live in a make-believe world that has no link with the difficult, ruthless and cruel reality.

The early Christians insisted that God came to this world in human form. Unbelievers ridiculed them and said that God was only for angels and old women. But the Bible was written by real people: fishermen, tax-collectors, tent-makers and doctors.

> *Jesus Christ is the beginning, the middle, and the end of all. In the Gospels He walks in human form upon the earth, and accomplishes the work of redemption.*
>
> ~ Philip Schaff

John was not simply a creature in people's dreams; he was a real fisherman. We say that seeing is believing – those early believers *saw* Jesus, the human form of God. They saw Him with their eyes, heard Him with their ears and even touched Him with their hands – that's how real He was! He was made of flesh and blood, just like they were. He wasn't something they invented and tried to present as the truth.

A faith that was based on myth would never have stood the test of two thousand years. It is as real today as it was then. It involves the real world where people touch, see and hear things. People change radically when the Word of Life gets through to them. They no longer seek trivialities which are so acceptable to this world. They become true followers of Jesus, our Savior who leads us to life.

Jesus, Redeemer and Savior, keep my feet firmly anchored in the reality of Your existence. Amen.

It's About Life!

Read 1 John 1:1-10

He is the Word of life. (1 John 1:1 NLT)

The Roman authorities feared the Christians and therefore they cruelly persecuted them. The fortunate ones were thrown to the lions to be torn apart. Others were sent as slaves to the mines in North Africa. They had to row their own galleys over the rough sea and travel through the scorching African heat. They were chained and branded on the forehead with searing hot irons. Then they were whipped and sent underground, never to see the sun again.

> *The world is a tragedy to those who feel, but a comedy to those who think.*
>
> ~ Horace Walpole

Fever spread rapidly among them and many died. The survivors continued to work and on the tunnels where they worked they wrote prayers and messages to their loved ones. Throughout all these feebly scratched messages, one word stood out and was repeated over and over. It was the Latin word *Vita!* which means *Life!* In conditions very similar to concentration camps they knew about "Life" because they knew Jesus. They believed with Paul, "For to me, to live is Christ" (Phil. 1:21).

The Christian witness is the Gospel, the Good News, and the Message, precisely because it is the Word of Life. It brings life, spreads life and lets life grow. It is the golden thread that runs through life which gives it purpose and meaning, even when it hangs on a fine thread. Even in death, Life is there. And Jesus is our Savior who leads us to life!

Lord of Life, You bring us perfect freedom. You are our light in the darkest hour, our comfort in times of trial and our heaven in death.
Amen.

The Mystery of Christ

Read 1 Corinthians 2:6-16

We speak of God's secret wisdom, a wisdom that has been hidden and that God destined for our glory before time began. (1 Corinthians 2:7)

There are many mysteries surrounding Christ that human understanding can't comprehend. Through the ages people have tried to understand His teachings and His person, only to discover uncharted depths that are simply unfathomable to them. Christ is a mystery, but this doesn't mean that we can't know Him.

What is often denied or ignored is that intellectual brilliance doesn't open the door to the heart of the Master. It is those with a humble and positive faith in the living Christ who have the ability to acknowledge Him as the Lord of their lives. To know Christ is

> *At the heart of Christianity there is a mystery, but it is not the mystery of intellectual appreciation; it is the mystery of redemption.*
>
> ~ William Barclay

the highest point of the Christian experience. This is possible when your spirit receives the power of the Holy Spirit and you consciously begin to live in the Presence of the Savior.

All the mental energy used to learn more about the living Christ is worth it, because it brings a sense of balance to what could have been a purely emotional experience. If your Christian experience is not Scripture-based, it will probably become unstable. Knowledge that is inspired by the Holy Spirit brings stability and reality into our spiritual lives.

The great mystery of the living Christ is that He gives Himself to those who humbly seek Him and accept Him as Savior and Lord of their lives. He is willing to share His life with them. He grants all the qualities that are needed to live a full and meaningful life to those who love and serve Him.

I praise Your name, holy Lord Jesus, that I may still know, love and serve You, in spite of my imperfect knowledge of you. Amen .

Beyond Scripture

Read Colossians 3:5-17

Christ is all, and is in all. (Colossians 3:11)

Christianity is divided into different factions. Many claim that they are the only ones who preserve the Christian truth and they regard those who differ from them as backsliders and not part of God's salvation plan.

The majority of churches and sects base their faith on the intellectual interpretation of Scripture. Unfortunately there are as many interpretations as there are organizations, and they all claim to be scripturally inspired. So what should we believe?

> *I may worship in a different building from you, I may worship in a different style, but all we hold dear is God's gift in Christ Jesus, who is our unity. In Him we have all and lack nothing.*
>
> ~ Michael J. Davis

The purpose of the Holy Scriptures is to lead people to a knowledge of the Eternal God and to reveal His will to them. If your studies of the Scripture don't lead you beyond the written Word to an understanding and experience of the living Savior, then your efforts are worthless. Jesus said, "You diligently study the Scriptures because you think that by them you possess eternal life. These are the Scriptures that testify about Me, yet you refuse to come to Me to have life" (John 5:39-40).

Unfortunately many people know the Bible without knowing Jesus. If every Bible student possessed the Spirit of the living Christ, there would still be different doctrines, but the spirit of love and understanding would reign over the intellectual differences, and love for Christ would be the binding force of Christianity.

Holy Spirit of God, lead me beyond the written Word into the Presence of the living Christ, our Savior who leads us to life. Amen.

The Globalization of Our Faith

Read Romans 1:1-7

Through Him and for His name's sake, we received grace and apostleship to call people from among all the Gentiles to the obedience that comes from faith. (Romans 1:5)

How did you, a person in the twenty-first century, come to know Jesus Christ? Simply because faithful witnesses, apostles and teachers received the Good News about Jesus and then passed it on to others. They received grace and undeserved love from Christ. This transformed them from stumbling followers or enemies of Christ into self-confident children of God. They were then called to be apostles, and through Christ's commission, to give themselves to the spreading of the gospel.

> *Evangelism is to present Jesus Christ in the power of the Holy Spirit, that men might come to trust Him as Savior and serve Him as Lord in the fellowship of His church.*
>
> ~ William Temple

The early apostles only preached the message of Jesus to the Jews. Of course, their message was rejected. They then turned to the Gentiles and found a willing audience. Those who were converted passed the message on to others and it carried on like that up until this day.

The majority of Christians today heard about Jesus at Sunday school or catechism. The foundation of their faith was laid by teachers – often untrained – who told them Bible stories. Somewhere along the way they received grace and came to know Jesus as their personal Savior.

The spreading of the Message is as important today as ever before. Billions of people have not heard the gospel message and may never hear it. But they might hear it if we as Christians tell others about our faith in Jesus Christ.

Heavenly Father, bless the spreading of the message of Jesus Christ to the ends of the earth. Amen.

Called to Belong

Read Romans 1:1-7

You also are among those who are called to belong to Jesus Christ.
(Romans 1:6)

The flock mentality runs deep in our human psyche. We gather together as families, we go to school where we are part of a larger community, we participate in team sports, and some nations have different clans. It gives people a feeling of identity and security.

To "belong" doesn't just happen. You are called to belong to Christ. You can choose which sports team you want to belong to, or which university or school you want to attend. But if you belong to Jesus you don't simply choose to "go to church." He calls you to belong to Him. It is a deep relationship and is life-changing. It means that you also belong with others who belong to Him. He didn't call the twelve

> *The Bible knows nothing of solitary religion.*
> ~ John Wesley

apostles to each have an individual relationship with Him, but to belong to each other *in Jesus*. They belonged, not because they chose Him, but because He chose them.

To belong to Christ means that you belong to an extremely large fellowship of believers from the past and the present. You belong to the same group of people as Paul, John, Francis of Assisi, Martin Luther, John Calvin, John Wesley, William Booth, Mother Teresa and Albert Schweitzer.

You derive inspiration and strength from their lives and enjoy solidarity with them. When you are strong they share your joy. When you are weak they encourage you and give you strength. This happens because you were called to belong to Jesus, our Savior.

Thank You, Lord my Savior, that I can belong to You. Amen.

The Path to God

Read 1 Peter 1:17-25

He was chosen before the creation of the world, but was revealed in these last times for your sake. (1 Peter 1:20)

If you ask the vast majority of Christians what their deepest spiritual desire is, they will undoubtedly reply, "To have a more intimate relationship with God." To know Christ and to walk with Him is a precious dream most of us treasure. Many people experience moments of warm fellowship with God, but the feeling quickly vanishes.

Christ came to this world and died to redeem us from the sin that separates us from God. The result is that you have the freedom to move closer to God. He yearns for your attention and love. He loves you so much that He sent His only Son to live and die in order to bring you back to God – the true dwelling place of your heart.

> *Mere change is not growth. Growth is the synthesis of change and continuity and where there is no continuity, there is no growth.*
> ~ C. S. Lewis

God knows that until you respond to Christ's invitation and turn back to Him, you will never experience true peace. He watches over you while you struggle, fight and get frustrated with the inferior things in life.

God yearns to pour His holiness into your heart, to fill you with His love, to use your valuable gifts for His glory and honor, and to see you become a mature Christian, "until we all reach unity in the faith and in the knowledge of the Son of God and become mature, attaining to the whole measure of the fullness of Christ" (Eph. 4:13).

This can only happen if you become aware of your need, realize the uselessness of your own efforts and give yourself totally to Christ. Allow Jesus to guide you there.

Lord Jesus, I pray that through my renewal You will lead me into deeper fellowship with Yourself. Amen.

Where Does Faith Come From?

Read 1 Peter 1:13-25

Through Him you believe in God, who raised Him from the dead and glorified Him, and so your faith and hope are in God. (1 Peter 1:21)

Some people grow up in families where faith in God is a given. Others struggle through intellectual stumbling blocks and eventually find faith. Some people see an unbelievable change in another person's life and are then convinced of a miracle-working God. When a person I know visited Israel and saw "where it all happened" he said, "Now I can believe."

Behind all these different scenarios the Christian faith is built on a historical event: Christ's coming to the world, His life, teachings, deeds, and His death and resurrection. Other religions are based on myths or a collection of ideas. In some religions people use a natural object or carve an idol and that becomes the object of their worship.

> *The essence of faith is being satisfied with all that God is for us in Jesus.*
>
> ~ John Piper

Christians have faith because God became human, and in that one life they saw who God really is: what He looks like and how He works. They know that the God who became flesh still lives and travels with them through life today. He befriends, helps, heals and guides them and finally grants them eternal life.

Don't dare to base your faith on anything other than Jesus Christ. He came specifically to lead you to eternal life. This faith is not simply a faith in faith. It's not the acceptance of the thought that "somewhere out there there's a Higher Power." It's not to try to live a good life. It is to open yourself up to Christ and His Spirit and to become like Him in your being and nature. Christian faith comes from our Savior who guides us to faith: Jesus Christ!

Savior and Lord, lead me daily to a deeper faith in You. Amen.

Your Sin and God

Read 1 Peter 3:13-22

Christ died for sins once for all, the righteous for the unrighteous, to bring you to God. He was put to death in the body but made alive by the Spirit. (1 Peter 3:18)

Human weakness is one of humanity's most troubling characteristics. The Bible calls it sin. We find it easier to do wrong rather than good, and no matter how hard we try, even the best of us fail.

Despite our successes in various areas of life, we always lose our battle against sin. Everyone fails: religious people, good people, bad people, unbelievers – everyone sins and is a sinner in God's sight.

> *Oh, how horrible our sins look when they are committed by someone else.*
>
> ~ Chuck Smith

God's answer to this problem was to provide a Savior. Only His Son, Jesus Christ, is able to save us. With the sacrifice of Himself on the cross, God provided a way to erase the sins of the whole human race. This means that your sins are erased if you have faith in Jesus Christ. Christ knew no sin and yet He died for all of us.

Christ is the only one who can deal with your sin. He can help you to overcome it, and He can place His love in your heart where previously there was only hate. He can free you from the sin that often strangles you.

He not only frees you from past guilt, but directs you forward into a life committed to Him. He calls you to give yourself in love to the salvation and welfare of others.

You can be sure of one thing: resolving not to sin won't get you anywhere. The only successful solution is to give yourself to Jesus Christ in faith.

Savior from sin, please replace the sin in my life with love and joy.
Amen.

Vital Values

Read 2 Corinthians 4:13-18

We fix our eyes not on what is seen, but on what is unseen. For what is seen is temporary, but what is unseen is eternal. (2 Corinthians 4:18)

Developing a false sense of values is easy. You are part of the world and make a living among different types of people. It is inevitable that society's determining norm will have a profound effect on you one way or another.

Before becoming a follower of Christ, you strived for the material things you could see, evaluate and deal with. These things became your aim and goal, even though they brought no satisfaction or peace.

> *"It's not the years in your life that count; it's the life in your years."*
>
> ~ Abraham Lincoln

After surrendering yourself to Christ you underwent a transformation. It became possible for you to see the true meaning of the old values that had carried a false sense of security into your life. Suddenly the world's values are unable to satisfy the soul.

The most important things in life are invisible, intangible and difficult to define. The unconditional love of a happily married couple cannot be explained by cold hard logic. The breathtaking beauty of the sunrise and sunset, which enriches the spirit and soul, cannot be easily described. These things reach past the earthly realm and are elevated into the sphere of the spirit.

These qualities have eternal value. They give new dimension to life and a greater appreciation of the cardinal and intrinsic values of our existence. They reveal to us what can be achieved if we live according to spiritual standards. Then we are living by the grace of God, not in vain or without purpose.

Lord Jesus, grant me an even greater appreciation of You so that I can truly appreciate the invisible things of cardinal value. Amen.

More than Fancy Words

Read Colossians 2:6-15

Just as you have received Christ Jesus as Lord, continue to live in Him, rooted and built up in Him, strengthened in the faith as you were taught, and overflowing with thankfulness. (Colossians 2:6-7)

Many people have honest "scientific" problems regarding Jesus Christ and His gospel. They cannot accept Divinity and they find a virgin birth impossible and therefore treat it as unimportant.

Since the resurrection has never been repeated, they reject and dismiss that too. In fact, anything that they do not understand or cannot explain is written off as impossible. In this way they rob and deny Christ of His uniqueness and divinity.

The truth of the matter is that Christ holds a quality of life and a depth of spirit that the human mind can never fathom. To understand the living Christ completely is to understand God completely – who can presume to have such knowledge?

Jesus was God spelling Himself out in language humanity could understand.

~ S. D. Gordon

The crucial question is whether you have the courage to live according to your own knowledge of Him. It is easier to debate about faith than to subject yourself in childlike faith to the will of God.

If you are committed and obedient, your intellectual doubt will not only disappear but you will be filled with something greater. You'll discover that faith does not adhere to any scientific formula or rules. Then you will live with faith in God and His peace will descend on your soul.

Incomprehensible God, I thank You that through Your Holy Spirit my daily relationship with Christ drives out all doubt and fear.
Amen.

Cultivator of Love

Read Romans 5:1-11

God has poured out His love into our hearts by the Holy Spirit, whom He has given us. (Romans 5:5)

The sure knowledge that Christ lives in you can bring about a powerful spiritual revolution in your life. It inspires your thinking, broadens your perspective, gives you renewed confidence, creates enthusiasm and provides purpose and meaning to your daily existence. This is the work of the Holy Spirit who constantly assures you of your connection with the Source of true love.

This powerful and inspirational connection, which provides mutual love between you and God, must be firmly anchored in the foundation of reality and faith.

Love is a condition in which the happiness of another person is essential to your own.

~ Robert Heinlein

If you truly love Him through the Holy Spirit, it will bring you to the painful awareness of the distress of others, and it will create in you the irrepressible urge to do something about it.

If you lay claim to the love of God in your heart, it will be revealed through your words, your attitude toward others and your willingness to help and serve others through His Spirit and in His strength.

God is revealed through His Spirit's work of love in your life. Then you lovingly accept the full responsibility of your faith by the help of the Holy Spirit.

This love enables us to look at the good in others, despite the insults, hurt and humiliation we might suffer. It is the purposeful will to seek nothing but the best for others with the help of the Holy Spirit. God Himself is the source of this love and this was demonstrated for us through Jesus Christ.

Holy Spirit, love Divine, glow within this heart of mine; kindle every high desire, perish self in Thy pure fire. Amen.

Repentance

Read Mark 1:9-20

"The time has come," He said. "The kingdom of God is near. Repent and believe the good news!" (Mark 1:15)

Jesus taught that repentance and confession are prerequisites to having faith in Him. However, many modern followers of Jesus forget, disregard or reject this. This results in a number of disciples who try hard to build a victorious Christian life on an unstable foundation of unconfessed sin. Their sins have not been forgiven because they've avoided the challenge of asking God's forgiveness.

When you are confronted with God's holiness, you realize the sinfulness of your own life. This realization is a critical point in your spiritual pilgrimage. You can either face your sin, confess it to God and receive His forgiveness; or you can ignore it and try to live in your own strength, but nothing will come of your new life in Christ.

> *Repentance is a grace of God's Spirit whereby a sinner is inwardly humbled and visibly reformed.*
> ~ Thomas J. Watson, Sr.

Until you have confessed your sins to God, you cannot be free from sin, nor have the assurance that is offered by the living Christ to all who believe in Him.

Repentance, confession and conversion presuppose a willingness to abandon the sin that is destroying and alienating you from God. There are people who ask God's forgiveness and then secretly desire the same sins they were guilty of. Repentance requires that you walk away from those sins so that all your spiritual and intellectual powers can be dedicated to God's service. This is where God wants to lead you through His call to repentance.

God and gracious Father, through my repentance and conversion I have entered into a more intimate relationship with You, and have begun to understand Your love. Amen.

Live Like Jesus Did

Read 1 John 2:1-6

Whoever claims to live in Him must walk as Jesus did. (1 John 2:6)

If you have been fortunate enough to visit Israel, you have walked where Jesus walked. This would have been very special to you. However, it is more important to walk *like* Jesus walked rather than *where* He walked. Many people have never visited Israel, but have walked very close to Jesus. How did Jesus walk?

Firstly, He walked conscious of the presence of His heavenly Father. This was the secret to His dignity and calmness. He was continually in touch with the Father and sought His will, which is why He received God's power.

> *You must never doubt that I am traveling with gratitude and cheerfulness along the road where I am being led. My past life is brim-full of God's goodness, and my sins are covered by the forgiving love of Christ crucified.*
>
> ~ Dietrich Bonhoeffer

Secondly, He was sensitive toward other people, especially to those in need. He didn't associate with the high and mighty, but He looked for those who were sick, lonely and rejected. He knew that behind their cry for help was a desperate hunger for God.

Thirdly, He knew and understood the Scriptures perfectly and they were His guide and map.

Fourthly, He had a superordinate goal with everything that He did. He knew where He was going and He was ruled by the presence of God's kingdom.

Lastly, He was never ruled by people or a fear of what people might say. He didn't want to make a name for Himself. His only consideration was, "What is right in God's sight?"

Test yourself against these five requirements and see if you are *living like Jesus.*

Heavenly Savior, each day I marvel in the knowledge that You want to walk with me. Amen.

Walk in the Light of Christ

Read 1 John 2:7-11

Anyone who claims to be in the light but hates his brother is still in darkness. (1 John 2:9)

If you are walking in the light of Christ, it should be real and visible in your life; otherwise it is simply theological talk without any substance. If you truly and intensely love Christ, His glory and beauty will be seen in everything you do. If your commitment is weak, the light of Christ that shines through you will be weak and dim. He can only express Himself through you if you allow Him to. When He becomes the Light of your life, He provides spiritual strength for every situation you find yourself in.

Darkness cannot drive out darkness; only light can do that. Hate cannot drive out hate; only love can do that.
~ Martin Luther King, Jr.

The only way that the world will notice the light of Christ is if they see it through the love and influence of His followers. If your love for Him is just a façade, it will fall short of the true quality that people are yearning for. But if your love for Him is deep and genuine, people will instinctively be influenced by the Spirit that has taken possession of you and they will know that the Source of it is a Power that is greater than you.

Christ needs torch-bearers for Him in this dark world. Dedicated disciples spread light in dark places; they replace misunderstanding with reason and knowledge; they love instead of hate; they are constructive and positive in the midst of destructive thoughts and deeds. The light of Christ shines through them and they experience a greater feeling of joy and fulfillment.

Light of the world, may Your light shine brightly through me, at all times and in all circumstances. Amen.

Faith Restores Sight

Read Matthew 9:27-34

He touched their eyes and said, "According to your faith will it be done to you." (Matthew 9:29)

There is a fundamental difference between true faith and wishful thinking. Unfortunately, many people fail to make this distinction, which leads to spiritual blindness.

There are people who desire certain things with all their hearts, but deep inside they believe that these things are really out of their reach. This creates conflict in their hearts and they become colorless, ineffective people lacking spiritual strength and vision.

If the blind put their hand in God's, they find their way more surely than those who see but have not faith or purpose.
~ Helen Keller

Sincere faith is the conviction that every holy desire is possible and simply waiting to be claimed in the name of Jesus Christ. You do not strive in your own strength for the unattainable, but trust in the deployment of God's omnipotence in your daily existence.

Faith that wants to see results must have its origin and inspiration in God. If we expect great things from God, we will receive great things from Him, and we will perform great deeds in His name. This was the case with the two blind people about whom the Bible tells us today.

If your faith originates from God and is to His honor, you will become an instrument through which His powerful deeds are performed. A new world of active spiritual energy will open to you a multitude of possibilities will arise in your mind's eye.

Remember, you do not restrict His omnipotence through your lack of faith and unbelief. By commitment to Him, your faith becomes a glorious reality.

Almighty God of mercy and love, I thank You for what I am to You and may do for You. Continue to strengthen me through the power of Jesus Christ, my Redeemer and Savior. Amen.

Abundant Love

Read 1 John 3:1-10

How great is the love the Father has lavished on us, that we should be called children of God! And that is what we are! (1 John 3:1)

Most right-minded parents sincerely love their children. They pour out their love on them and sometimes go to great lengths to give them more things than they actually need. They will even go without what they need so that they can provide for their children. Parents don't just give their children material things, but also love, encouragement, support and comfort.

God, our heavenly Father, not only loved us, He poured His love over us in abundance. He did not spare Himself but loved us fully. It was not a sporadic love, as ours sometimes is, but a persevering, constant, stable, warm and understanding love.

> *God proved His love on the Cross. When Christ hung, and bled and died, it was God saying to the world, I love you.*
> ~ Billy Graham

He gives us everything we need – and so much more. He never tires of loving us and never gets irritated with our frequent childishness. He always wants the best for us – spiritually and physically.

In Jesus Christ, God gave us a model, an example, and a guide. Through Christ, God demonstrated how much He really loves us. In Christ, God's love became "human" and went to work under our human circumstances on earth. He loves you as if you are the only person on earth to love.

God of love, we pray today for those who have no experience of love.
Amen.

Follow Christ

Read Acts 10:34-43

You know the message God sent to the people of Israel, telling the good news of peace through Jesus Christ, who is Lord of all. (Acts 10:36)

It is a wonderful privilege to be assured in your heart of the living presence of Christ. To know Him as Lord and Master, and to worship Him as the perfect revelation of God, are the most enriching experiences a person can have.

It is obvious that the method and nature of your meeting with Christ will be something exceptional to you. You must, however, guard against not confusing the path you took to find Christ with Christ Himself. The Christian path is in a certain sense also a very wide path. It is wide enough to contain all the extremes of Christian thinking.

> *May the God who gives endurance and encouragement give you a spirit of unity among yourselves as you follow Christ Jesus.*
>
> ~ Romans 15:5

It is not important whether you follow the sacramental path, the path of the fundamentalists, the orthodox or the charismatic. What truly matters is that these paths should all have one shared purpose, and that is to glorify God through the living and risen Christ.

Jesus Christ is the singular focus and purpose of the Christian path. If you allow yourself to be sidetracked by other ways and theories and you lose sight of Christ, you lose the essential part of your Christianity. Your living faith is founded on a personal relationship with Christ and not on theories relating to Him.

You need not defend Christ. You only need to worship and glorify Him by living and proclaiming His love. Then you will lead a Christian life that is healthy to its core.

Lord Jesus, You are the Center Point of my faith and life. I love You sincerely and want to sing Your praises, always. Amen.

To Truly Know Christ

Read Colossians 2:1-5

In order that they may know the mystery of God, namely, Christ.
(Colossians 2:2)

Many people maintain a faith that they believe is a "genuine" Christianity, but it falls short of the real thing. Some people speak about a "Higher Power" and consider themselves to be believers. Some think that being respectable and polite is all that matters. Others think that "love" is all that is necessary. There are people who think that including a few stereotyped expressions about God in your conversations and thinking "right thoughts" means everything will go well with your Christianity.

Paul, the author of this letter to the Colossians, knew better. Christianity is about an essential knowledge of Christ as your Savior. Christ called, changed and challenged Paul. His true life only began when Jesus entered into it. Jesus did not enter his life as an optional extra, but as the central dominating influence on the apostle's thoughts, deeds and teachings. Nothing and nobody else mattered anymore. Christ was everything! Christ was in him and he was in Christ. His past was erased and Christ became his hope for the future. The entire goal of his life was to bring others to faith in Christ.

> *Not only do we know God by Jesus Christ alone, but we know ourselves only by Jesus Christ.*
>
> ~ Blaise Pascal

We will only come to understand the full meaning of faith when we truly and completely know Christ. It is time that we reject the artificial truths standing between us and a rich experience of fellowship with Christ. It's time to experience the true fellowship with Christ that He desires us to have. Reject all the substitutes and firmly take a grip on the real thing.

Lord Jesus, I humbly pray that I will truly come to know You as my Savior. Amen.

Appreciate Christ's Potential in Others

Read John 1:1-13

The true light that gives light to every man was coming into the world. (John 1:9)

When the Holy Spirit challenges you to live a new life in the power of Christ, you become very aware of your sin and unworthiness. This awareness of your sin should be a passing phase in your spiritual experience, otherwise it causes an unhealthy depression when you dwell on sins that God has already forgiven.

If you can't lift your spiritual vision above your sins, your whole view of life will be influenced by sins you should have forgotten. You will also just see sin and weakness in your fellow believers. You will put them down as sinners instead of potential children of God.

> *Go not only to those who need you, but to those who need you most.*
>
> ~ John Wesley

A Christian disciple often finds it difficult to appreciate the Christ-potential in the people he meets each day. Every evil deed by heartless people emphasizes their sin and overshadows what they can become if they are forgiven and live in the power of Christ. Every person has the ability to respond to the call of the living Christ. In many lives the call of Christ is silenced by the alarming power of sin.

If we accept Christ as Savior and Redeemer, His Spirit enters our lives and the binds of sin are broken in the one who was dead in sin, but who has now miraculously come alive in Christ. The glory of the living Christ enables the receiver to not only rejoice in his salvation, but to also see the potential to be like Christ in others.

Master, I acknowledge the reality of Your indwelling presence which enables me to see the Christ-potential in others. Amen.

Your Attitude toward Jesus

Read 1 Peter 3:13-22

In your hearts set apart Christ as Lord. (1 Peter 3:15)

It seems incredible to talk about an attitude towards Jesus Christ, but because people's attitudes differ it is something that can't be ignored. Some glorify and worship God, others attempt to break Him down, and then there are those who have become so over-familiar that they fall short of worship and respect and try to ignore Him. These and other attitudes belong to those who have formed their opinions about Jesus.

If we had to ask people why they had a certain attitude toward Jesus, they would probably be surprised. Maybe they refuse to accept Jesus' challenge to live committed and holy lives. Maybe they have become disillusioned because of a disciple's failure. It is possible that they have become cynical about Christ's teachings.

> *I am naught, I have naught, and I desire naught but Jesus and His love.*
>
> ~ Walter Hilton

The hypocrisy of some of Jesus' followers might have made them hostile toward everything Christ stands for.

Your original attitude toward Christ was probably formed by your background and traditions, but this doesn't mean you can't form a new attitude. If you have accepted Christ as your Redeemer and Savior, you will love Him sincerely. It is this attitude of love that accompanies worship. If you love and honor God, you will have a receptive attitude that prepares your spirit to receive His Presence and His gifts with thankfulness and appreciation.

I thank You, Savior, that my attitude about You is formed by my awareness of Your indwelling Presence. Amen.

The Privilege of Faith

Read 2 Peter 1:1-15

To those who through the righteousness of our God and Savior Jesus Christ have received a faith as precious as ours. (2 Peter 1:1)

Having faith in Jesus Christ can sometimes be a heavy burden. You might experience intellectual difficulties that unbelievers don't experience. It requires a way of life that seems strange to some people. You could be viewed as narrow-minded or fanatical by the people around you. You can even be rejected by friends and even family members.

To have faith in Christ Jesus is a great privilege and it's good to always remember this. You have the advantage of looking at the world and events with the certainty that there is a holy purpose behind everything. You have the privilege of knowing that your sins are forgiven and that God has adopted you as His child, despite your human weaknesses. Through Jesus Christ you can live with your faults and shortcomings and know that God loves you regardless.

Only he who believes is obedient, and only he who is obedient believes.

~ Dietrich Bonhoeffer

You are in harmony and peace with the Creator of the world. You have the privilege of meeting the future with hope, because you know that the world and you as an individual are in the hands of a kind and loving God. You belong to a worldwide community of believers who know and love the same God. The advantages far outweigh the disadvantages. Enjoy the privilege of faith and follow your Savior.

Lord Jesus, we thank You unceasingly, for the privilege and blessing of being able to believe in You. Amen.

A God of Grace and Peace

Read 2 Peter 1:1-15

Grace and peace be yours in abundance through the knowledge of God and of Jesus our Lord. (2 Peter 1:2)

Not all gods are kind and loving. People in prehistoric times believed in gods who were cruel, warlike and unapproachable. They regarded their worshipers as toys that could be used any way they felt like.

Some people focus so much on God's requirements and judgment, that they lose sight of His grace and compassion. Others distort the concept of an understanding God until He becomes unapproachable, cruel and strict.

The God of the New Testament is a kind God. He doesn't punish us for our offences as we deserve to be punished. He also doesn't look for opportunities to punish us. He isn't a policeman who spies on us. He doesn't single you out for some silly mistake you made. He is kind, loving and gracious.

> *Your worst days are never so bad that you are beyond the reach of God's grace. And your best days are never so good that you are beyond the need of God's grace.*
> ~ Jerry Bridges

God wants you to be successful. He desires that you grow to spiritual maturity in the likeness of His Son. He watches over you like a loving parent; He encourages you when the battle becomes too tough for you; He helps you up when you stumble or fall, and He shows you a better path when you make a mistake. He lovingly watches over you when you are too busy to think about Him. He wipes out the sins of the past and plans a better route for you to follow in the future. He wants to lead you and build you up to be spiritually strong. Since God is gracious and good to you, He expects you to be gracious and good to others.

God of love, help me to spread Your grace and peace to all I meet.
Amen.

What You Are Meant to Be

Read Luke 14:25-35

"Anyone who does not carry his cross and follow Me cannot be My disciple." (Luke 14:27)

There are many Christians who have become tolerant and satisfied with substandard Christianity. Perhaps they gave and committed themselves to God years ago. For some time they experienced a powerful Christian life. Then the experience began to fade until only a faint memory remained. The glory of their faith deteriorated into insignificance.

Even when their faith was ineffective they knew that this was not God's will for them. God's will for His people is only the best. God wants to strengthen us so that we can live triumphantly. In addition, He offers inner peace, which will drive away doubt and make it possible for us to have a balanced and fruitful life.

> *In the cross of Christ I see three things: First, a description of the depth of man's sin. Second, the overwhelming love of God. Third, the only way of salvation.*
>
> ~ Billy Graham

God is willing to give us this and many other spiritual gifts from His treasury, if our commitment to Him is absolute.

God did not remove Himself from you. Your deep desire for spiritual growth is just an inspired restlessness that God gives. He is calling you back to Him, so that you can become what He meant for you to be.

You know what you can be through the power of Christ. God does not call you to an unfulfilled life. That is why He is calling you to renew your commitment today, so that you can regain the fullness of your faith. By doing that you will experience the glory of the power of the living Christ in your spirit and life.

O Master, through my total commitment to You, I rediscover the glory of my faith. Continue to guide me through Your Holy Spirit to a deeper life of complete commitment and obedience. Amen.

A Call to Perfection

Read Ephesians 4:17-24

Throw off your old sinful nature and your former way of life, which is corrupted by lust and deception. Instead, let the Spirit renew your thoughts and attitudes. Put on your new nature, created to be like God – truly righteous and holy. (Ephesians 4:22-24 NLT)

Christ poses a great challenge for His followers. It is the challenge of a new life with changed attitudes, resulting in a righteous and holy life. Unfortunately, to some this appears to be a way of life that is totally removed from the realities of our practical existence. Leading a holy life is unacceptable to many people.

However, the core truth is that we are created to be like God and to strive for perfection. It is the greatest challenge that you will ever face in your life. When this is demanded, you may initially hesitate or shy away. Deeply aware

> *The purpose of revelation is restoration, the renewal in us of that likeness to God which man lost by sin.*
> ~ Stephen Neill

of your inner weakness and sinfulness, you are convinced that Scripture makes a demand that you cannot meet.

Otherwise this calling can be inspiring and challenging. Despite the awareness of your own shortcomings, you know instinctively that you desire to rise up and strive for perfection. Although you are conscious of your sin, you realize that you are meant to walk with God and to live in fellowship with Him. It is your highest goal in life and the source of your purest joy.

When you experience this deep desire and longing to walk with God, do not allow sin or shortcomings to rob you of it. Accept the help of the risen Lord. He offers you forgiveness of sins and the support of His Holy Spirit. With Christ in your life you will be on the right path to a holy life.

Lord Jesus, I praise Your holy name for the serious desire You have placed in my heart for a higher, more noble and more perfect life. Let Your Holy Spirit work in me. Amen.

Christ: Our Hope in Glory

Read Colossians 1:23-29

To them God has chosen to make known among the Gentiles the glorious riches of this mystery, which is Christ in you, the hope of glory. (Colossians 1:27)

Some people strive to achieve distinction by performing heroic deeds on the sports field. Others try to achieve it through accumulating loads of money. People want acknowledgement and power – they want to come out on top. Some people use all their energy to achieve success, but when they eventually get it, they find that it is empty and meaningless.

> *You are called not so much to do great things, as to be a great person – and that person is Jesus Christ in you.*
>
> ~ Jerry Cook

In terms of faith, there are also people who think that they can impress God with their dutiful obedience to the moral laws and religious customs of the church. If they behave themselves and live good lives, God will pat them on the back and open the gates of heaven to them when they die. In this way they will succeed in reaching the glory of God.

But God has a totally different idea. He sent Jesus to be your Savior and to help you overcome sin, to fill your life with love, joy and peace, and to be a dynamic, living part of your whole being. He came to take possession of you. If you have given your life to Him and allowed Him to enter, then He lives in you!

This is the key to being accepted by God, and not your religious duties or moral uprightness. If you reach heaven because Christ is in you, it won't be just your own little sparkle of glory that you will enjoy. You will glow in the resplendent glory of Jesus Christ who is *in* you.

Savior, give me grace to gather my few small victories, but to depend on You alone. Amen.

God-given Authority

Read Matthew 28:11-20

Then Jesus came to them and said, "All authority in heaven and on earth has been given to Me." (Matthew 28:18)

If you think that Jesus Christ was a "Great Teacher," then you are right. If you regard Him as a "Great Physician," then you would also be right. Certain people saw Him as a notorious rebel because He challenged the authorities in His day.

The secret of Jesus' authority did not lie in His achievements. It was granted to Him as a gift from God the Father. He was appointed by the Father to be God on earth, in the form of a human being. But He wasn't inferior to God's authority. God gave Him "all authority." When God raised Jesus from the dead, He confirmed and declared that Jesus' authority came from heaven.

> *There is not one square centimeter of this universe over which King Jesus does not proclaim – This too is Mine!*
>
> ~ Abraham Kuyper

The authority that God gave Jesus is directly related to our everyday lives. Jesus has the authority to teach, heal, guide and give direction. As a result, you can give yourself to Him in full confidence. In your uncertainty and confusion, He leads you to clear thinking. In your attempts to discern between good and evil, He guides you in the right direction.

Jesus discerns between truth and falsity when people compete for your loyalty. When you must decide what God wants from you in your service to Him, Jesus shows you where you can most effectively serve Him. Jesus has God-given authority – obey Him and live!

Lord Jesus, I acknowledge You as the greatest authority in my life and in the world. Amen.

Guarded by the Peace of God

Read Philippians 4:1-9

The peace of God, which transcends all understanding, will guard your hearts and your minds in Christ Jesus. (Philippians 4:7)

We live in evil times where criminals lurk behind every corner. It's not unusual to see security guards at shopping malls, businesses, banks and even at private homes.

It's not only your physical well-being and property that are at stake, though. Your inner thoughts and feelings are threatened by fear, temptation and feelings of guilt. This leads to stress and anxiety. If you haven't yet given your life to Christ, you will also experience spiritual anxiety in your deepest soul. Even if you are unaware of it, it is there.

There may be those on earth who dress better or eat better, but those who enjoy the peace of God sleep better.

~ L. Thomas Holdcroft

Open your heart to Jesus and instead of fear and anxiety you will find peace in God. He will place a guard at the door to your heart who will keep out fear, as well as feelings of insecurity, doubt, self-reproach and despair.

No one can explain or understand this peace. It is above human capacity to analyze this peace. But it is real, deep, quiet, invisible and strong. For some people this is God's greatest gift, because it gives them stability, worthiness and an inner feeling of safety by the most powerful and tender force in the universe. It keeps you safe in Christ Jesus.

Gracious Father, so many people don't have the peace that comes from You. Grant that they might give themselves to You so that they can share in this peace. Amen.

Grace and Peace

Read Ephesians 1:1-14

Grace and peace to you from God our Father and the Lord Jesus Christ. (Ephesians 1:2)

Someone once responded to the question, "How are you?" with the words, "How much time do you have to listen?" Such an answer reveals that our greetings are often just habits – an attempt to get a conversation going.

In today's reading, Paul also addresses his Christian friends with a common greeting of those days. But at the same time he was saying something deep, rich and meaningful. It was through God's grace alone that they were Christians and that the gospel message came to them. They were "under grace" and this is why words of grace were spoken to the people of Ephesus.

Grace is the free, undeserved goodness and favor of God.
~ Matthew Henry

Grace is the undeserved love of God in action in people's lives – in Ephesus and across the whole world. Since you received God's grace as a believer, you are at peace with Him. But the peace you experience is far more than the absence of war with God. It is the wonderful awareness that you are accepted by Him and that you can rest safely in Him. It is borne from the knowledge that He is at work in you to make you spiritually functional.

You live in peace with Jesus because you are not at war with yourself anymore. Since you have received these great gifts from God, are you a source of grace and peace to the people around you? May Jesus lead you to this.

God, how can we thank You for Your grace and peace? Fill our hearts with grace and peace and let us send it out to the world. Amen.

March

His Name

She will give birth to a Son, and you
are to give Him the name Jesus, because
He will save His people from their sins.
~ Matthew 1:21

The name of Jesus is the one lever
that lifts the world.
~ Anonymous

*J*esus, You are our Savior and Redeemer –
the sweetest name in the angels' song.
Christ, You are the Anointed One of God,
who brought the message of redemption to us.
We glorify Your name and bring You honor:
With our mouths we confess and with
our hearts we confirm that we belong to You.
You are our Wonderful Counselor, Mighty God,
Everlasting Father and Prince of Peace (Isa. 9:6).
God gave You the name above all names;
A name that is praised in heaven,
on earth, and under the earth.
We bow before You and confess,
"Jesus Christ is Lord, to the glory of God the Father" (Phil. 2:11)
"Salvation belongs to our God,
who sits on the throne, and to the Lamb" (Rev. 7:10).
We thank and praise You that You will return
to this world and bring Your reward with You.
We worship and glorify Your name as "the Alpha and Omega,
the First and the Last, the Beginning and the End" (Rev. 22:12).
"Amen. Come, Lord Jesus" (Rev. 22:20).

A Dynamic Christian Experience

Read Hebrews 12:1-12

Let us run with perseverance the race marked out for us. Let us fix our eyes on Jesus, the author and perfecter of our faith. (Hebrews 12:1-2)

The Christian experience seldom progresses without tension and trauma and sometimes it can be weakened by disinterest and lethargy. The true Christian experience doesn't develop easily, but is the direct result of a deepening prayer life and an increasing awareness of the presence of the living Christ.

Spiritual growth requires time, commitment and the realization that there can't be a slacking off of the pace of our pilgrimage. There must also be a greater awareness of God's Presence in our lives.

Some people's religion reminds me of a rocking horse, which has motion without progress.

~ Rowland Hill

If your Christian experience is not as real and dynamic as it was with your conversion, or when you pledged your everlasting faithfulness to Jesus Christ, then the fault lies with you and not the Master. His love for you is eternally strong and secure. Your weakened faith is the result of other interests in your life taking precedence over Him. You still respect Christ, but you don't place your trust fully in Him.

If you desire a dynamic Christian experience that will form a powerful and meaningful part of your life, you have to be willing to meet the high requirements that the living Christ sets for all His followers. A spiritual experience is not possible without obedience to the Master. The responsibility to acquire it lies with you alone. Christ honored His promises and now it depends solely on you to make it a workable proposition in your life.

Faithful Savior, grant me the inspiration of the Holy Spirit so that I can have a living and dynamic faith. Amen.

Living Faith

Read Galatians 2:15-21

And I no longer live, but Christ lives in me. (Galatians 2:20)

Too many Christians do not experience the power and joy that the living Christ has promised them in their daily lives. They accept the viewpoints of the church, but lack the essential and dynamic personal experience with Christ.

God has many treasures available for those who trust Him. If you walk with Him through Christ every day and accept the gift of the Holy Spirit, you will be spiritually strengthened in your faith and can face daily demands with confidence.

To be in Christ is the source of the Christian's life; to be like Christ is the sum of His excellence; to be with Christ is the fullness of His joy.

~ Charles Hodge

He gives you the discriminative ability to expose temptations and the strength to live victoriously. God is there to provide in every human need if only we live in dependence on His will.

God's greatest and most precious gift to humankind is Jesus Christ. If you have a hunger in your soul, and long for a spiritual experience that will renew your tired spirit and give you the courage to move forward confidently, you need God.

You then have the assurance that you will never be alone. God has met your need by giving you Jesus Christ. Only once you have accepted Him as your personal Redeemer and Savior, can He work effectively in your life.

You must accept Christ in faith and love by serving Him with your entire being. Then you will experience the total satisfaction that only He can give you.

Living Christ, by accepting You and living in harmony with Your will, I will experience complete peace and happiness. Amen.

The Command to Believe

Read 1 John 3:18-24

This is His command: to believe in the name of His Son, Jesus Christ, and to love one another as He commanded us. (1 John 3:23)

There are people who say that it doesn't matter what you believe "as long as you are sincere and try your best." Others say, "We all worship the same God and in the end it all depends on love." They are hopelessly wrong! What you believe definitely matters because it determines how you live and who you serve.

It is very important to identify the God you believe in. He commands you to believe in Jesus and to believe that Jesus Christ is the Son of God; that He is the Savior of the world who rose from the dead and sits at the right hand of God. If you reduce faith to an insipid, general faith that believes vaguely in "a Supreme Being and everything that is good," something as special, dynamic, powerful and world-conquering as faith will become meaningless.

> *A little faith will bring your soul to heaven, but a lot of faith will bring heaven to your soul.*
>
> ~ Dwight L. Moody

Faith has made bad people good. It is a faith for which some people were burnt at the stake or thrown to the lions. You don't do this for a Supreme Being, but for a Savior who carried your sins on the cross and who triumphantly rose from the dead.

Make sure that you know and understand what you believe. If you aren't sure, then find out. Don't listen to people who say, "You don't have to worry about all that dogma." You *must* worry about it. It is necessary for you to know. You should live by it and die by it. It is the most glorious truth that human thought has ever captured. Whatever you do, don't miss this faith in the Son of God!

Lord Jesus, thank You for the faith that the Holy Spirit put in my heart. Amen.

In the Name of Jesus

Read Colossians 3:5-17

Whatever you do, whether in word or deed, do it all in the name of the Lord Jesus, giving thanks to God the Father through Him.
(Colossians 3:17)

Many people become fanatical in their support of a particular cause. Sport fanatics get carried away by the team they support: they eat, sleep and live for their team. They don't talk about anything else. They spend a lot of money to see their team in action and buy clothes and accessories in the team color. An excited commentator at a derby between two school teams in the same town said, "This isn't just a sports occasion. It is a spiritual experience."

> *It is of no use to walk anywhere to preach unless our walking is our preaching.*
> ~ Francis of Assisi

Paul encouraged the Christian believers to be fanatical about Jesus Christ, just like sports fans are fanatical about their sports heroes. Jesus – a true spiritual experience – was to be the focus point of all they said and did. In effect Paul was saying, "Eat, sleep and live Jesus!" But "in the name of" means much more. It means "in the character or style of Jesus."

As Jesus' disciple, you should speak the same kind of words Jesus would speak. Everything you do should be done in the manner Jesus would do it. If you do everything in the name of Jesus, it should be in accordance with the will and love of our Savior. Christ must speak through everything you do. When people hear you speak or see what you do, they should be reminded of Christ.

Loving Savior, through the Holy Spirit please make me fanatical about You. Amen.

The Christian's Responsibility

Read John 1:1-18

There came a man who was sent from God; his name was John. He came as a witness to testify concerning that light, so that through him all men might believe. (John 1:6-7)

As a Christian you have the important responsibility of leading others to an intimate relationship with God through Jesus Christ. It might seem like a super-human and terrifying task, but it is your duty if you want to wear the name of Christian in a worthy manner. Many break under the weight of this responsibility. If you try to escape this responsibility even once, your faith will weaken and the flame of your spiritual involvement will flicker and eventually die.

To fulfill Jesus Christ's requirement of leading others to an intimate relationship with God, you have to have an intimate relationship with God yourself. You must open your heart and thoughts to the influence of the Holy Spirit. Allow Him to control your life: every word, thought and deed. Submit yourself completely to Him so that Jesus can lead you and dictate the quality and character of your life.

> *The hero is one who kindles a great light in the world, who sets up blazing torches in the dark streets of life for men to see by. The saint is the man who walks through the dark paths of the world, himself a light.*
>
> ~ Felix Adler

Through the Spirit of the living Christ within you, your life will be one of love, compassion, humility and forgiveness, and Jesus' glow will shine through your life. If you live such a Christ-like life, you will win souls for His kingdom. People will see an inexplicable quality of life in you that they desire. It can only be acquired if Jesus is your light and Savior.

Be gracious to me, Lord Jesus, so that I can be an example and lead others to Your light. Amen.

Overcome Spiritual Lethargy

Read 1 John 5:1-12

Who is it that overcomes the world? Only he who believes that Jesus is the Son of God. (1 John 5:5)

Every disciple of Jesus Christ knows that there is both sunshine and shadows on the path of life. There are times when your spirit is filled with the glory of God and an indescribable joy fills your life. God is an unfathomable reality and you face the future with certainty, inspired by the Holy Spirit. At times this uplifting spirit wanes, a dark cloud descends on your life and you experience a time of indescribable depression.

We must always change, renew, rejuvenate ourselves; otherwise we harden.

~ Johann Wolfgang von Goethe

Many of our Savior's disciples stay in this state of depression for too long. They get to a point where their faith is kept alive by memories alone. When the memories fade, they long for the love, enthusiasm and trust they possessed in the past. And then the greatest tragedy occurs – their faith rests on their memories of the past and doesn't live in the reality of the present. Every Christian counselor has heard the words, "I was once a committed Christian and I enjoyed going to church, but ... " Spiritual deterioration caused by spiritual lethargy and laziness is common.

To experience the joy and fullness of a living and dynamic faith, it is essential to break the chains of lethargy and to stop thinking that the glory of the Lord has forever left you. Your Savior hasn't changed and He is waiting patiently for you to return to Him so that you can experience His full, joyous, never-ending and forgiving love once again.

Every time I return to You, heavenly Father, I marvel in the knowledge that You are waiting to receive me back. Amen.

To Behold His Greatness!

Read 2 Peter 1:1-21

We did not follow cleverly invented stories when we told you about the power and coming of our Lord Jesus Christ, but we were eyewitnesses of His majesty. (2 Peter 1:16)

To experience true greatness is unforgettable. You might hear a timeless piece of music performed by a master or attend a sports event where new records are set. You might observe an incredible deed of endurance or service performed.

Jesus' disciples were present at His transfiguration on the mount, when His clothes became dazzling white and He spoke to Elijah and Moses (see Mark 9:2-12). It is this strange, yet unforgettable experience that Peter refers to here. Undoubtedly the other disciples remembered other events which they regarded as occasions when they experienced Jesus' true greatness.

> *He became what we are that He might make us what He is.*
> ~ Athanasius of Alexandria

We will never be privileged enough to experience *those* moments. But you can receive a part of it in your spirit when you read about it and allow the Holy Spirit to make it real to you. But you will see more of His greatness when somebody you know is transformed from sinfulness to holiness. You will see His greatness when an earnest prayer is miraculously answered.

You will see Jesus' true greatness when an unbeliever comes to faith and looks at God and the world through new eyes. You will see it when you experience the miracle of healing – or when you discover that you yourself are filled with His Holy Spirit. It's not something you only hear or read about. You can see it with your own eyes and then spontaneously say, "Our Savior is truly great!"

Holy Spirit of God, open my eyes so that I can see the glory and greatness of Jesus. Amen.

The Source of Life (1)

Read Colossians 2:16-23

Christ holds the whole body together with its joints and ligaments, and it grows as God nourishes it. (Colossians 2:19 NLT)

There are many theories and ideas about the origin of life. Some people think that life is simply about physical existence and lean toward the tendencies of evolutionism. Others search for a higher source in wisdom, idolatry or ancient mythology. The Greek philosophers tried to discover the origin of all things and simplified it to one element: earth, air, water or fire. Other people regard the sun as the center and soul of all life.

> *Out of God we have all come, in Him we are all enfolded and toward Him we are all journeying.*
> ~ Julian of Norwich

For the Christian, an understanding of human life centers on Christ. Since He was with God before Creation, was present at Creation, and because He was God in human form, we regard Him as the source of true life. He is more than Christ "in us." He is the Source and the Giver of life. He is the Author of eternal life. He saves your life from destruction and grants you Redemption and Salvation. He gives you life on a totally different and higher level than merely a physical existence.

Don't look to your ancestors, your own resources – especially if you consider yourself "a self-made man" – the human race, or idolatry. Christ is the Source of Life, not only in the context of the origin of life, but as the guarantee of a true, deep and meaningful life. You don't have to think up something mysterious or be highly intelligent. It's simple – Christ is the Source of Life! Look to Him as your Savior and draw your life from Him. Live your life for Him – you don't need anything else!

Lord Jesus, You are my origin and my ultimate destination, and therefore I unceasingly praise and thank You. Amen.

The Source of Life (2)

Read Colossians 2:16-23

Christ holds the whole body together with its joints and ligaments, and it grows as God nourishes it. (Colossians 2:19 NLT)

There are many different and diverging forms of strength. A balanced diet will give you the energy to work and play and strengthen your body. You also need intellectual strength concerning a positive self-image, motivation to excel, and persistence to see things through to the end. Courage is another form of strength.

When Paul wrote this letter to the Colossians he knew how necessary it was to have spiritual strength. In his personal life he discovered that only Christ can give that strength. He tried to please God in his own way and fell far short. But Christ provided where Paul and the church – the body of Christ – were lacking.

> *The LORD is the stronghold of my life.*
>
> ~ Psalm 27:1

We also need spiritual strength, regardless of how physically and mentally strong we are. Christ is the only One who can give you that strength. First acknowledge your own weakness, and then accept the offer of strength that He has promised you.

Exercise your faith and prove Him to yourself. Constantly acknowledge that the strength you have is not your own, but His, and realize your deep dependence on Jesus. Feed your faith by pondering on God's greatness and the incomparable sovereignty of Christ. Go to Jesus, the Source of spiritual strength, daily and renew your strength through Him. He will lead you to true and everlasting life.

Powerful Jesus, I come to You daily in my weakness to receive my strength from You. Amen.

Powerful in Word and Deed

Read Luke 24:13-30

"About Jesus of Nazareth," they replied. "He was a prophet, powerful in word and deed before God and all the people." (Luke 24:19)

Not many people can be considered as truly powerful. Some people are in leadership positions because of the office they hold, even though they might not be strong people. Others have authority, but are only powerful in a limited way – like heavyweight boxers. Others are powerful business wise because of their skills or fortune, but reveal shocking weaknesses towards those they live with each day.

The disciples on the road to Emmaus described Jesus as a man and a prophet – someone who was considered "powerful in word and deed" by both God and man. He demonstrated His power in His teachings and His omnipotence in the healing of the sick.

> *Don't fear change, embrace it.*
> *~ Anthony d'Angelo*

He drew people to Himself like a magnet draws iron filings. He challenged the leaders of His time. He exposed transgressions in the temple. Then His power suddenly disappeared and He was crucified. But according to the disciples on the way to Emmaus, there were reports that He had risen from the dead. Was He, or was He not as powerful as they thought? They would soon know the truth.

His omnipotence is the mightiness of love and the power of God. It is the power to lift ordinary people from the depths to the heights; to give hope rather than despair; joy instead of sadness, and love instead of hate. His omnipotence is the power to build up rather than to break down, and to create rather than to destroy. Has this omnipotence started to work in your life yet?

Almighty Spirit of God, fill me with power from on high. Amen.

When Your Hope Is Shattered

Read Luke 24:13-30

We hoped that He was the one who was going to redeem Israel.
(Luke 24:21)

You build your life around the hopes you have for the future. You hope for a successful business and risk your life-savings to attain it. You hope for a stable and enriching family life. You hope for political changes that will make your life safer. Sometimes your hopes are realized – but sometimes they are shattered.

The disciples on the road to Emmaus placed their hope in Jesus. Like many other people in Israel at that time, they hoped that the Roman authorities would be defeated and they would be set free. But then the church leaders crucified Jesus and that was the end of their dream. Had God betrayed them? Was Jesus a fraud who had misled them? Did

> *To live without hope is to cease to live.*
>
> ~ Fyodor Dostoyevsky

He really rise from the dead? They were disappointed and disillusioned as they traveled to Emmaus.

We also face disappointment from time to time. When your hopes are shattered and you have to start over with new goals; when you have to ask what went wrong; when you have to investigate your faith on a deeper level than ever before. Whatever might have happened in your life, you are always under God's sovereignty. Although we live in a cruel world, He promised to give meaning and purpose to your life.

Eventually you will be forced to create new hope and not allow disappointment to make your life bitter. Jesus gave the men on their way to Emmaus a new perspective – and He will do the same for you.

Holy Savior, help me to put the disappointments of the past behind me, to pick up the pieces of my dreams and to move forward with the new hope that You have placed in my heart. Amen.

Never Belittle Yourself

Read 1 John 5:13-21

We know also that the Son of God has come and has given us understanding, so that we may know Him who is true. And we are in Him who is true – even in His Son Jesus Christ. He is the true God and eternal life. (1 John 5:20)

There are Christians who suffer from an inferiority complex and who confuse this with humility. They struggle through life and give others credit for doing things better than they can. They think that this attitude honors God.

Despite what your limitations might be, God expects you to walk tall and proud as a masterpiece of His creation. Get to know your strengths and emphasize those gifts that can glorify God and enrich others.

> *If you think you can do a thing, or if you think you can't do a thing, you are right.*
> ~ Henry Ford

It is very easy to focus on your failures and weaknesses and to ignore your hidden potential. Figure out what you can do well and develop it to the maximum. If you accomplish something worthwhile and a feeling of contentment fills your entire being, offer it to the Master and thank Him for what you have achieved. Thanksgiving awakens the power of creative energy.

When you think of yourself as sadly lacking, form a new opinion about yourself. God has granted you intelligent and creative power. Remember that you were created in God's image – when you belittle yourself, you also belittle God. When you allow God to express Himself through you, you will no longer struggle through life and apologize for your presence. Meet every challenge with joy, certainty, positive thinking and the right attitude toward yourself. Only Jesus, our Savior, can lead us to this.

Lord Jesus, through Your indwelling presence I have a positive attitude towards life. Amen.

The Requirements of Discipleship

Read John 1:1-18

To all who received Him, to those who believed in His name, He gave the right to become children of God. (John 1:12)

The disciple's role is demanding. It requires absolute faithfulness, obedience and commitment to Jesus Christ. There is no room for compromise.

This is clearly stated in Scripture – especially those parts that not only declare the teachings of Christ, but also in the way He explains the cost of discipleship to those who indicated that they wanted to be His followers.

The requirements are still the same today. Some people tend to present a watered down Christian faith that emphasizes love, ecstatic emotions, peace and joy, with little respect for the demanding requirements of the cross of Golgotha.

> *To endure the cross is not tragedy; it is the suffering which is the fruit of an exclusive allegiance to Jesus Christ.*
> ~ Dietrich Bonhoeffer

If you want to become a member of a social club you have to obey all the rules. Why then should membership to the Christian faith be less demanding? If a group presents itself as a branch of the church of Christ, yet have teachings that contradict unconditional submission to God, it must be rejected.

Remember what Paul said, "If we are children, then we are heirs – heirs of God and co-heirs with Christ, if indeed we share in His sufferings in order that we may also share in His glory" (Rom. 8:17).

Take my life and let it be consecrated, Lord, to Thee. Amen.

To Receive Jesus; to Believe

Read John 1:1-18

To all who received Him, to those who believed in His name, He gave the right to become children of God. (John 1:12)

You have probably asked, or at least wondered, "What must I do to become and remain a Christian believer?" If you asked this question, you were probably advised to read your Bible, pray, attend church, and get involved in a Christian fellowship.

To start *doing* things is necessary for becoming a disciple of Jesus Christ. But before you can become active, you first have to be passive – you have to receive and accept. You don't become a believer through something you do, but through what God does. Firstly, He does it *for* you by sending Jesus Christ to this world as Savior and Redeemer. You can't do anything about that – God has already done it.

When you receive Christ, God's work in you has just begun.

~ Anonymous

Secondly, He does it *to* you by entering your life and saying, "Here I am! I stand at the door and knock. If anyone hears My voice and opens the door, I will come in and eat with him, and he with Me" (Rev. 3:20).

To "receive Him" is the way you react to the initiative that God takes in and through Jesus Christ who comes to you. That is where you start. But you continue to receive Him because He repeatedly comes to you. If you have not yet received Him, is now not the perfect time to do so?

Son of the living God, thank You that You came to me and that I opened the door of my heart to You and welcomed You in. Remain in me, Lord Jesus. Amen.

The Right to Become

Read John 1:1-18

To all who received Him, to those who believed in His name, He gave the right to become children of God. (John 1:12)

We often wonder, "What is going to happen to me?" Most of us hope that something good will happen. Others think that the conditions in the world will disrupt the peace and destroy the structures that support us. You can never be sure about the future – especially not in human terms.

As a child people probably asked you, "What do you want to be when you grow up?" You might have answered, "A doctor!" or "A movie star!" The choices were endless. But as you grew up you became more realistic and accepted your limitations. Yet, you still dreamed about what the future might have in store for you.

> *Never be afraid to trust an unknown future to a known God.*
>
> ~ Corrie ten Boom

When you become a child of God and place your faith in Christ Jesus, He gives you the power to become something you presently are not. He grants you the gift of an open future – the right to become something!

Whether you are nineteen and life lies before you, or whether you are ninety and most of your life has passed, you can always look forward to what God can make you become. Whether you are spiritually young or spiritually mature, God always maintains your right "to become." Don't sadden God by letting this opportunity pass you by.

Father God, give me grace to reach out to the future possibilities that You have for me and to believe in Your purpose for my life. Amen.

Beyond the Clouds

Read Acts 1:1-11

He was taken up before their very eyes, and a cloud hid Him from their sight. (Acts 1:9)

Sometimes the clouds of despair, doubt, disappointment and worry cause our Master to be hidden from our eyes. When this happens, prayer is essential.

When, for some reason or another, you feel that you have lost contact with Jesus and it appears as though He is far removed from you, it is important to remember that He is the living Christ. He is Immanuel; the Lord who is present in every situation and who makes Himself known in every facet of life and in every person. It does not matter where you are or what your circumstances are, you can be sure that Jesus Christ is present there.

Even if it's a little thing, do something for those who have need of help, something for which you get no pay but the privilege of doing it.

~ Albert Schweitzer

To break through the clouds that are obstructing your view and making Christ seem far away, you should persevere in prayer for strength and guidance. Then look around you. Wherever you see distress, do what you can to alleviate it. Help those who are less privileged than you. Show others your loving compassion and involvement. Support them as far as possible.

Do as your perfect example, Jesus Christ, did and be good to others. While you serve others in His name, the clouds will vanish and you will find yourself face to face with your Guide and Perfecter. Then you can bathe yourself in the bright sunshine of His presence.

Holy Spirit, give me the ability to look past my own worries and concerns so that I may see the distress of others and help to alleviate their pain. Amen.

Abundant Life

Read John 10:1-21

"I have come that they may have life, and have it to the full." (John 10:10)

Relatively few people really think of religion as a force with life-giving power. They rather think that it will restrict the way they want to live. They look at the lives of Christians and are not at all impressed with what they see.

Secretly they fear the surrender of their lives to a Power that requires wholehearted loyalty and commitment. Why, they ask, should they get involved in a way of life that is restrictive, unattractive and demanding?

If you consider Christianity with an open mind, you will discover that its apparent failure cannot be ascribed to faith, but to the presentation of it.

It is absurd that the Creator

> *The law of God and also the way to life is written in our hearts; it lies in no man's supposing, nor in any historical opinion, but in a good will and well doing.*
>
> ~ Jacob Böhme

of life will keep people from enjoying life. That He, who is the reflection of perfection and beauty, will make it unattractive to follow Him, that He will demand your love and commitment and not give you life in abundance.

Christianity is a way of life that includes the abundance of God through Jesus Christ. Because Christ promised to live in you and you accepted this promise, it is your privilege to allow the living Christ to live to the full through you.

If the revelation of Christ becomes the main objective of your life, you will experience the Holy Spirit working through you. The more your life reflects the glory of Christ, the more abundant will be your joy and peace.

My sincere prayer is, O Lord, that my life will reflect Your glory more and more through the work of the Holy Spirit in me. Amen.

Work, for Night Is Coming

Read John 9:1-12

"As long as it is day, we must do the work of Him who sent Me. Night is coming, when no one can work." (John 9:4)

Time, and how you use it, is of the utmost importance. However rich or poor, intelligent or average you are, you have the same amount of time as everyone else. Kings, presidents and farm workers all have twenty-four hours in their day – and so do you. You can either use these hours productively or you can waste them.

Jesus, our Savior, only lived on this earth for thirty-three years and He had only three years of ministry. He knew that the cross lay before Him and that His time was limited. He had to use all the time He had available to make God's glory a reality. He came from eternity and would return to eternity, but His days on earth were numbered.

> *Dost thou love life? Then do not squander time, for that is the stuff life is made of.*
>
> ~ Benjamin Franklin

When a deadline is looming, you are busy with things you have to do, instead of with things you have all the time in the world for. Unlike Jesus, you don't know how soon you will have to give an account of your time on earth; whether it will be years, months, weeks, days, or hours. Tomorrow there might not be enough time to do the things that God wants you to do. "Night" is always approaching: today's night, the world's night, and God's night.

Therefore, never allow yourself the luxury of wasting time. Time is one of the most valuable things that God grants you. If God has given you something to do, do it now, before the night comes and it will forever be too late.

*Lord, I thank You for the opportunity I have of doing something for You **now**. Amen.*

Light of the World

Read John 9:1-12

"While I am in the world, I am the light of the world." (John 9:5)

The world desperately needs light – but not the light you can switch on and off with the flick of a button. It needs light because the forces of darkness are hard at work. They are trying to cause war and increase the possibility of terrorist attacks. They flood the market with drugs, gather nuclear weapons, drive the slave trade, distribute pornography, increase corruption and spread plagues.

It has always been this way, although darkness changes shape from one generation to the next. Jesus Christ is God's light in a dark world because He opens our eyes and enables us to see and recognize the darkness. He is also the light because He drives out the darkness in which people live.

> *An age is called Dark, not because the light fails to shine, but because people refuse to see it.*
>
> ~ James A. Michener

By giving sight to the blind, hearing to the deaf, speech to the mute, healing to the sick; He has lead everyone to a new and better life.

Jesus brings the most light when He fills hearts with His love, where before there was no love. He also brings light when He awakens faith where before there was unbelief, and enables people to see themselves, God and other people in a completely new way.

We have the choice either to see the light in Jesus, or to refuse to see it. If His light has shone into your darkness, you become a source through which others can see His light. You can also work against the forces of evil that are wreaking such havoc in the world. Our Savior invites you to follow Him in this.

Lord and Savior, make me a shining light that reflects Your glory in this world. Amen.

The Mystery of Christ

Read Colossians 4:2-9

And pray for us, too, that God may open a door for our message, so that we may proclaim the mystery of Christ, for which I am in chains. (Colossians 4:3)

At first glance you would never think that there was anything mysterious about Christ. All four Gospel writers give a detailed account of His life and teachings. These books have been studied, analyzed and preached for over two thousand years. Is there anything left to think or say about Him or something we don't know?

When Paul wrote this letter, he was trying to establish the Christian faith in a community that had many "mystic" religions. They all involved learning certain secrets which would result in identification with the so-called god – the final secret.

> *A religion without mystery must be a religion without God.*
>
> ~ Jeremy Taylor

Christ is a mystery because He comes from God the Father. Through His coming He revealed the mystery of God to us. Since His coming, we are able to know God like we know our own fathers – and even more so.

Christ is also a mystery because we will never know all there is to know about Him. Our human understanding is too limited to absorb the full truth about Jesus and to know all His deeds. We know enough to believe and we can continue to explore and discover, but there will always be unanswered questions and problems that we can't understand.

Despite all the scientific knowledge that came to light over the last two centuries, the ultimate mystery in this world is God Himself. He invites you to discover Him through Jesus Christ, but it will take you a lifetime and eternity to do so.

Holy God, who inhabits the inaccessible heavens, reveal more and more of Yourself to me. Amen.

The Choice is Yours

Read Matthew 27:21-26

What shall I do then, with Jesus who is called Christ? (Matthew 27:22)

If I should ask you what the most important questions of today are I would receive a wide variety of responses. Some people might say environmental conservation is the greatest question of the day. What are we doing about the pollution and destruction of our planet?

Others might say that inflation and recession is the burning problem of our time. How will we deal with the rising costs and unstable economy?

Some people feel the orphaned and sick are the most pressing problem. How are we going to cope with the increasing number of orphans and diseases?

Nature gives man corn but he must grind it; God gives man a will but he must make the right choices.

~ Fulton J. Sheen

Others see the youth as the greatest problem. With almost half our population under the age of 25, we wonder if they will ever be able to focus and channel their energy in the right direction.

These issues are important, but there is one question that is much more important: "What am I to do with Jesus Christ?" This is not a new problem. Pilate had already asked the same question more than 2,000 years ago. So much depends on the answer. The wrong answer could mean that you lose everything of any worth. To keep quiet and not answer is to reject Christ.

Some people ignore Christ. Like Pilate, they wash their hands in innocence and announce that they do not want anything to do with the matter. Some people oppose Christ. With their voices they shout, "Away with Him!" Others praise the Lord and choose Him as their King. By accepting Christ, they find redemption from sin and death and gain peace, joy and eternal life.

Yes, Lord Jesus, my heart chooses You as King for eternity! Amen.

The Savior

Read John 14:1-14

Jesus answered, "I am the way and the truth and the life. No one comes to the Father except through Me." (John 14:6)

It very sad when people claim that they can't find God, or that they have lost their faith to such an extent that they even question His existence. In many cases these people once had an intimate relationship with God, but something happened that hurt or disillusioned them. As a result the flame of their faith threatens to flicker or die out completely.

One of the greatest joys of the Christian faith is the certainty from the Master that He will never leave you nor forsake you, and that He is always ready to take you back if you will just return to Him. His love is unconditional; to such an extent that His arms are always open to pick you up and carry you back to the flock.

> *There is no more urgent and critical question in life than that of your personal relationship with God and your eternal salvation through Christ.*
> ~ Billy Graham

If you turn to Jesus and allow Him to control your life, you will experience the indwelling of the Holy Spirit that will lead you to paths of service in His name. It is in these situations – especially if you serve people – that you will become aware of the Presence of God. Jesus leads us there!

Lord Jesus, I praise You for leading me to God's loving heart.
Amen.

Faith in Action

Read Colossians 2:1-5

Though I am absent from you in body, I am present with you in spirit and delight to see how orderly you are and how firm your faith in Christ is. (Colossians 2:5)

Some people make the mistake of thinking that everything will go well as long as their faith is strong and they believe the right things. According to this viewpoint you can get away with any behavior, no matter how dubious it might be. Others think that it doesn't matter what you believe as long as you do your best. Both of these viewpoints are wrong.

Faith and action always go hand in hand. Both are necessary to live in harmony with Christ. In most of his writings, Paul went to great lengths to explain how faith in Christ stands in relation to problems people experience, or to correct wrong teachings that the congregations have heard.

> *The whole being of any Christian is faith and love. Faith brings the man to God, love brings Him to men.*
>
> ~ Martin Luther

Paul said that on account of the truth, avoid it (false teaching) and live worthy of a disciple of Jesus Christ.

For Paul it was important to know and declare the truth, and in this way to live out the example of Christ. It was just as important to live uprightly so that God could be obeyed and Christ could be made known. These two things could not be separated.

It's the same today. You must behave like a follower of Jesus. To do this under all circumstances requires a strong faith in Christ. You have to know why you should behave in the right way and you need the faith to know that Christ alone, through His Spirit, can empower you to live uprightly.

Holy Jesus, strengthen my faith and fill my deeds with love. Amen.

Acceptance of Christ

Read Colossians 2:6-15

Just as you accepted Christ Jesus as your Lord, you must continue to follow Him. Let your roots grow down into Him, and let your lives be built on Him. Then your faith will grow strong in the truth you were taught, and you will overflow with thankfulness. (Colossians 2:6-7 NLT)

You might think that the "acceptance of Christ" means that Jesus *is* the Lord. It is like accepting that your eyes are getting weaker. It is more than agreement or the acknowledgement of an issue.

It means to invite Christ into your life and to accept and allow Him to take control. In the Bible idols were also lords. If you worshiped the Egyptian god, you did more than mumble a few words – you gave yourself to his control. In the Old Testament of certain Bible versions the name of the Lord is written in capital letters: LORD.

> *Our satisfaction lies in submission to the Divine Embrace.*
>
> ~ John of Ruysbroeck

The New Testament writers used the same title for Jesus Christ. This meant that Jesus was more than an understanding friend, and not only a forgiving Savior or a faith healer. He is your LORD; the One you submit yourself to as a slave submits to his master.

In so far as you have been the master of your own destiny, you must give yourself to Him and acknowledge that He is your personal Lord and Master, your Savior and Redeemer. Ask Him how you can adjust your life to fit into His holy purpose. Let Him steer your life's boat, choose your course and plan your journey until He brings you safely to where He wants you to be. You will never regret it.

Jesus, my Redeemer, I give myself to You anew – both now and for eternity. Amen.

Simple Faith

Read John 6:60-71

We believe and know that You are the Holy One of God. (John 6:69)

The way in which people believe is often determined by their personalities. An exceptionally gifted person might reason intellectually about problems a less gifted person wouldn't care about.

Thomas was known as the "doubter" among the disciples. Peter was at the other end of the scale – his faith was strong, firm and simple, "We believe and know" (John 6:69). He was willing to take a risk or make a mistake in order to confirm His trust in Christ. He had already seen the work that Christ was busy doing and he had listened to His teachings. Deep in his heart he realized that Jesus was the One sent by God and he was willing to risk his life for this conviction.

> *The man who insists on seeing with perfect clearness before he decides, never decides.*
> ~ Henri-Frederic Amiel

You should also have a strong and simple faith. Let others reason about trivialities and argue about religion. Place your faith in Jesus, the living Christ. Make it a simple, strong faith that is sure and convinced. Don't doubt or look for certain parts to believe or to reject.

When it comes to trusting Jesus as your Redeemer, you must give it your all. A half-hearted attempt will lead to confusion, doubt and indecisiveness. There might be things that bother you or that you can't understand, but take a leap of faith and place your trust in Jesus, your Savior.

Holy Jesus, with all that I am and possess, I believe that You are Christ, the Son of God. Amen.

Christ Is All!

Read Colossians 3:11-17

Here there is no Greek or Jew, circumcised or uncircumcised, barbarian, Scythian, slave or free, but Christ is all, and is in all.
(Colossians 3:11)

The awareness of the Presence of the living Christ in one's life can take place in different ways with different people. For many it occurs at the moment of their conversion. When they accept Jesus as Savior it is as if they come out of the darkness into the light. For others, their conversion was mainly an act of the will without any emotional involvement. They never experienced a burst of spiritual zeal, but persevered in modeling their lives on the Master's life and gradually they became aware of His love and power at work in their lives.

Within you, just waiting to blossom, is the wonderful promise of all that you can be in Christ.

~ Anonymous

Those with a gradually developing faith often envy those who had an instant experience of God's Presence. The latter look so joyful and full of faith from the moment they accepted Christ, while those who develop gradually seem as if they lack the excitement that is so desirable.

In both these cases the Christian is exposed to unique temptations. Those mentioned first can fall prey to pride and feelings of superiority and criticize those who didn't have the same experience as they did. The latter can become bitter and disappointed because of depression and feelings of inferiority.

There is room for a variety of spiritual experiences in the Christian life, but the final test of discipleship is not your emotions or intellect, but the complete surrender of your body, soul and spirit to the Master. You must love Him wholeheartedly and allow the Holy Spirit to lead you.

Holy Spirit of God, lead me on the path that Christ has chosen for me without criticizing or envying others. Amen.

Spell It Out!

Read John 10:22-33

How long will You keep us in suspense? If You are the Christ, tell us plainly. (John 10:24)

History has seen many great figures come and go. Some of them presented great teachings which formed the foundation of religions and worship. Some of these included Moses, Plato, Confucius, Buddha and Mohammed – among many others. In some religions the teachers were so adored that they achieved a godlike status and were worshiped by their followers.

In Jesus' time the people were confused about who He was. They had been promised a Messiah – a human leader from God with supernatural powers. They thought that He would free them from domination by other nations, heal the sick, put an end to poverty and lead Israel into a golden age. Jesus taught, healed, fed the hungry, but He wasn't busy training an army to overthrow the Roman authorities. Was He, or was He not, the Messiah?

> *Christ is the greatest influence in the world today. There is, as has well been said, a fifth Gospel being written – the work of Jesus Christ in the hearts and lives of men and nations.*
>
> ~ W. H. Griffith Thomas

The problem was that Jesus was God's Messiah, but He was not the people's Messiah. He brought God's greatest gift – eternal life – but they wanted something different. And their leaders deceived them by not acknowledging Jesus as the Promised One.

We can still make the mistake of not understanding who Jesus is. But this is unnecessary, because the Bible spells it out for us – Jesus is God's one and only Son. Millions have discovered that He is true to His promises and have placed their trust and faith in Him. He alone is our Savior and God's way to you. Make Him your Messiah.

Lord Jesus Christ, Son of God; You are my Lord and my God, You are my Messiah. Amen.

The Power of Deeds

Read John 10:22-33

Jesus answered, "I did tell you, but you do not believe. The miracles I do in My Father's name speak for Me." (John 10:25)

In the early years of the Salvation Army, a man in London witnessed something that he would never forget. He was walking down the street when he saw an elderly man with a wheelbarrow. The man was busy loading bags of scrap metal onto the wheelbarrow, but one bag was too heavy for him. Suddenly a tall, well-dressed man appeared and approached the old man and lifted the heavy bag onto the wheelbarrow. The man who witnessed this event asked the helpful man's name. It was William Booth, the founder of the Salvation Army. The eye-witness was so impressed by this spontaneous deed of kindness that he became a life-long supporter of the Salvation Army. He never heard Booth preach, but his deeds spoke volumes.

> *The first great gift we can bestow on others is a good example.*
>
> ~ Thomas Morell

Although Jesus performed the kind of miracles that the prophets said the Messiah would do, the people's leaders refused to believe in Him. This wasn't because they couldn't believe, but because they didn't want to. Jesus' deeds were there for all to see but only some people got the message that He was so clearly conveying to them.

Remember that your words and deeds must complement each other and not oppose each other. Then you will deliver a powerful message. You might not convince those who do not want to believe, but you will reach those who want to hear. You might find it difficult to witness verbally, but if your deeds speak of Jesus, others will hear you loud and clear.

Lord Jesus, lead me so that my words and deeds will complement each other. Amen.

Persevere in Hope

Read 1 Thessalonians 1:1-10

We continually remember before our God and Father your work produced by faith, your labor prompted by love, and your endurance inspired by hope in our Lord Jesus Christ. (1 Thessalonians 1:3)

Nowadays there is much despair and it is difficult for Christians to continue placing their hope in Jesus. So many things discourage us. The population explosion worldwide is accompanied by starvation, rising poverty, the spread of AIDS, an increase in crime and the threat of terrorism.

How do you live with your feet on the ground while still placing your hope in Christ? For many it is impossible. Their hope for a better future under God's rule fluctuates with current circumstances. Because Jesus promised that He would come again, we must look forward, knowing

> *In all things it is better to hope than to despair.*
> ~ Johann Wolfgang von Goethe

that this could happen at any time. We believe that He will come in glory and power and that He will establish His kingdom in all its glory.

But sometimes evil looks so threatening and powerful that it is difficult for us to persevere in hope. However, our hope is not determined by the events around us, but by the promises of God and His final victory over evil. This will be the decisive factor, however long it will take to happen.

Great achievements are possible for those who persevere in hope. They look past daily problems and see the magnificence of a triumphant God. Persevere in hope.

God, give Your children the ability to spread hope in this despondent world. Amen.

Fix Your Eyes on Jesus

Read Hebrews 12:1-12

Let us run with perseverance the race marked out for us. Let us fix our eyes on Jesus, the author and perfecter of our faith. (Hebrews 12:1-2)

In the Christian life there is power in simplicity. With the passing centuries many opposing dogmas and strange theories about the living Christ have appeared.

Today there are literally thousands of interpretations of who He was and what He taught. Many people want to know Him, but don't know what to believe about Him. This confusion has a strong presence in theological circles.

Every man would agree that man's spiritual health is exactly in proportion to his love for God.

~ C. S. Lewis

This confusion is not as great as it appears, though, because the majority of Christians acknowledge Christ's divinity and His work of salvation. If they don't want to declare this simple statement of faith, they are not worthy to be called Christians. The living Christ is the unifying factor among His followers. People with different theological viewpoints all declare their love for Him and faith in Him. The tragedy is that many good people can't acknowledge that their love for Him must rise above their dogmatic theories about Him.

To love Jesus Christ implies that you will also love your fellow disciples, even those you differ with intellectually. It is possible to love, despite differences. If the Holy Spirit is at work in your life, there is an urgent desire to obey God as well as His basic command to love others. All dogmatic and theological discussions are worthless without love.

Holy Master, please grant that my love for You will be the focal point of my life. Amen.

Grace Alone!

Read Colossians 4:10-18

Grace be with you. (Colossians 4:18)

We have many ways of saying goodbye. We end our letters and e-mails with formal greetings, such as "Kind regards" or "Yours sincerely." Or we may say "Love to all" or "God bless you." Most of these greetings are simply conventional ways of concluding a letter.

Paul ends his letter to the Christians in Colosse with the words, "Grace be with you." Christians today think that *love* is the greatest word in the Christian faith. But, Paul uses *grace*. It speaks of an attitude and an action of God regarding Himself and the entire human race.

In the blessing that ends another of Paul's letters we read, "The grace of our Lord Jesus Christ be with you" (1 Thess. 5:28). Christ always acted with grace. But grace was not just a characteristic of God and Jesus Christ, but also that which God promised Paul in response to his prayer for the removal of the thorn in his flesh, "My grace is sufficient for you" (2 Cor. 12:9).

> *Like any other gift, the gift of grace can be yours only if you'll reach out and take it. Being able to reach out and take it is a gift too.*
>
> ~ Anonymous

God's grace is also sufficient for you and me. If you are being tested by a serious illness – as was the case with Paul – or if you are depressed by loneliness or loss, hold fast to God's grace. His grace is enough when you face financial difficulties, when you have to handle conflict or family problems, or when you experience pressure at work – every time you feel hopeless or at your wits' end! God's grace is sufficient for you in death – then it is the only thing you need.

God of grace, how can I ever thank You enough for all the grace You have showered upon me and the whole of humankind? Amen.

April

God and Man

As they talked and discussed these things with each other,
Jesus Himself came up and walked along with them.
~ Luke 24:15

As the centuries pass the evidence is accumulating that,
measured by His effect on history, Jesus is the most
influential life ever lived on this planet.
~ Kenneth Scott Latourette

*L*ord Jesus, our Savior:
You became what we are, so that we can become what You are.
In our pain and suffering, You are the Great Physician;
in our confusion and darkness, You are the Light;
when we wander and get lost, You are the Way;
in this world of corruption and lies, You are the Truth;
when we are dead in sin, You are Life;
in our spiritual hunger, You are the Bread of Life;
in our thirst for God, You are the Water of Life;
in our brokenness and sorrow, You are the Balm of Gilead;
in You, Lord Jesus, heaven and earth come together
so that You can create a heaven on earth for us.
You fulfill our every spiritual desire.
We worship You as our Incarnate God
and praise Your name for eternity.

Amen.

As Predicted by the Prophets (1)

Read Luke 24:25-35

Beginning with Moses and all the Prophets, He explained to them what was said in all the Scriptures concerning Himself. (Luke 24:27)

Pastor James Hayes presents this Scripture verse as follows:

In Genesis He is the Seed of the woman; in Exodus the Lamb for sinners slain; in Deuteronomy He is the Great Rock; in Ruth our Redeemer; in 1 Samuel He is seen as the Great Judge; in 2 Samuel He is the Princely King; in 2 Kings as the Holiest of all; in 1 Chronicles as the King by birth.

In 2 Chronicles as King by judgment; in Ezra He is seen as Lord of Heaven and Earth; in Nehemiah as the Builder; in Job our Risen Returning Redeemer.

> *The name of Jesus is in my mind as a joyful song, in my ear a heavenly music, and in my mouth sweet honey.*
>
> ~ Richard Rolle

In Psalms the Son of God and the Good Shepherd; in Proverbs our Wisdom; in Ecclesiastes as the One Above the Sun; in Isaiah He is the Suffering and Glorified Servant; in Jeremiah the Lord Our Righteousness; in Ezekiel the Glorious God.

In Daniel the Smithing Stone and the Messiah; in Hosea He is the Risen Son of God; in Joel the Out-Pourer of the Spirit; in Amos the Eternal Christ; in Nahum He is the one who brings the Good Tidings; in Zephaniah the Merciful Christ.

Lord Jesus, we thank and praise You that in all things You are for all people. Amen.

As Predicted by the Prophets (2)

Read Luke 24:25-35

Beginning with Moses and all the Prophets, He explained to them what was said in all the Scriptures concerning Himself. (Luke 24:27)

In Matthew He is the King of the Jews; in Mark He is the Servant; in Luke He is the Son of Man, in John He is the Son of God; in Acts He is the Risen Savior; in Romans He is our Righteousness; in 1 Corinthians He is the Resurrection; in 2 Corinthians He is our Comforter.

In Galatians He is the End of the Law; in Ephesians He is the Head of the Church; in Philippians He meets our every need; in Colossians He is the Fullness of the Deity.

> *To the educator He is the master Teacher. To the philosopher He is the wisdom of God. To the lonely He is a brother; to the sorrowful, a Comforter; to the bereaved, the Resurrection and the Life. And to the sinner He is the Lamb of God who takes away the sin of the world.*
>
> *~ John H. Gerstner*

In 1 Thessalonians He comes for His Church; in 2 Thessalonians He comes with His Church; in 1 Timothy He is the Mediator, in 2 Timothy He hands out crowns; in Titus He is our Great God and Savior; in Philemon He is our Intercessor.

In Hebrews He is the Rest of Believers and the Defender of Persons; in James He is the Coming Christ; in 1 Peter He is the Substitutionary Savior; in 2 Peter He is the Lord of Glory; in 1 John He is the Way, in 2 John He is the Truth; in 3 John He is the Life; in Jude He is our Security.

In Revelation He is the Lion of Judah; the Lamb of God, the Bright Morning Star, the King of kings and the Lord of lords.

Thank You, mighty Lord, for all that You encompass. You are truly everything. Amen.

Jesus' Miracles in People's Lives

Read John 9:1-12

"Neither this man nor his parents sinned," said Jesus, "but this happened so that the work of God might be displayed in his life."

(John 9:3)

There's an old saying that goes, "Man's disappointment is God's appointment." Although it is difficult for us to deal with vulnerability, weakness and adversity, God can perform miracles in such circumstances.

Jesus' disciples met a man who was born blind and they wanted to know whether this man or his parents had sinned. The disciples had grown up with the belief that any form of hardship was the punishment for sin. Jesus answered that it isn't always so simple. Instead of blaming someone, rather look at how God can demonstrate His greatness and omnipotence through the man's problem.

> *The miracles of Jesus are the works of His Father wrought small and swift that we might take them in.*
>
> ~ George MacDonald

When we are insufficient, God is All-Sufficient. If you are going through a crisis, don't panic or lose hope; ask God to work through it and to glorify Himself. Stand aside and allow God to demonstrate His omnipotence. It is more likely that God will perform a miracle when you are at your weakest than when you are riding the crest of a wave.

In your disappointment and time of trouble, turn to the Savior and allow Him to turn your darkness into light, your blindness into sight, and your defeat into victory. He will carry you through. In the darkness of your loss He might perform a miracle that not only demonstrates His omnipotence, but that will also be beneficial to your faith.

Jesus, Almighty Savior, let the world see Your omnipotence at work in my life. Amen.

God of No Limitations

Read John 9:1-12

Having said this, He spit on the ground, made some mud with the saliva, and put it on the man's eyes. "Go," He told him, "wash in the Pool of Siloam." (John 9:6-7)

There seems to be no limitations to the ways in which God can work. Sometimes He uses known and typical methods, at other times He uses unknown methods. Jesus used a well-known method of healing with the man who was born blind: the combination of saliva and mud to form a mixture. In those days it was believed that saliva had certain healing qualities. There are also other documented cases where this method was used.

Conversion is not implanting eyes, for they exist already; but giving them a right direction, which the have not.

~ Plato

Jesus can open your spiritual eyes by using known methods. Although dramatic conversions do take place and God is glorified through them, most people come to know Christ in ordinary ways like attending worship services, reading the Bible, and attending Bible studies or catechism classes. Because our God is almighty and loving, He can come to you at any time, on any day and in any way He chooses.

He may come to a family member or friend in a remarkable and unique way, but may not open your eyes in the same way. Trust Him – He knows best which method to use at the right time in your life. Don't look for dramatic events or astonishing signs just because this is the way He came to other Christians.

It's unnecessary to envy those who have more exciting stories to tell. Just be sincerely thankful that He has opened your spiritual eyes and that you can now see Him in all His glory. That is a miracle in itself.

Light of the world, thank You for touching my eyes and making me see. Amen.

Sent by God

Read John 9:1-12

"Go," He told him, "wash in the Pool of Siloam" (this word means Sent). (John 9:7)

We always try to provide obvious solutions for extraordinary events. If we can't find any solution, then we think that someone is holding back a part of the story.

There are people who try to find common solutions to Jesus' miracles. "Saliva *does* have healing qualities," they claim. This explains how Jesus could make the blind man see.

John suggests another way of interpreting and understanding this story. Jesus told the man to wash himself in the Pool of Siloam. This bath was built to provide Jerusalem with an external supply of water when they were under siege. The water was "sent" from the outside and therefore the bath was called "Sent!"

> *Our power in drawing others after the Lord mainly rests in our joy and communion with Him ourselves.*
>
> ~ J. G. Bellett

For John it was clear that Jesus was "sent" to heal the blind man. His healing came from God. It is pointless to try to explain how Jesus healed people. All Jesus' healings were "sent by God" – just as Jesus Himself was sent by God. The man wasn't really healed by the mud that was mixed with saliva, or by the water in the pool, but by Almighty God!

Expect God to work in your life in the same way. Seek your own growth, progress in skill, wisdom and maturity. But open yourself and your life completely to the healing of Jesus Christ – the One sent by God! Be prepared to be sent to open the eyes of others.

Here I am, Lord. Send me. Amen.

Get Your Priorities Straight

Read John 9:13-23

They brought to the Pharisees the man who had been blind. Now the day on which Jesus had made the mud and opened the man's eyes was a Sabbath. (John 9:13-14)

Religions tend to develop strange ideas about faith and behavior. Different groups choose different lifestyles which they think is the essential choice for true faith.

The Jewish religion in Jesus' day made a great deal about keeping the Sabbath day holy, which was of course on a Saturday. Healing was considered work and should not be performed on the Sabbath. Because Jesus healed the blind man on the Sabbath, He received the disapproval of those who strictly conformed to the keeping of the Sabbath.

In faith and hope the world will disagree, but all mankind's concern is charity.
~ Alexander Pope

But Jesus had His priorities straight. God's compassion and omnipotence were available on the Sabbath, just as on every other day of the week. Jesus knew that He would probably not meet the blind man again because He was continually on the move. He considered the law about healing on the Sabbath a trifling matter that stood in the way of God's Kingdom acts.

We must try our best to get our priorities straight. What is it about? Compassion, love, acts of grace and faith, healing, the work of the Holy Spirit, evangelism and reaching areas where Christ is unknown – this is what Christ focused on. To maintain traditions and keep to the letter of the law as prescribed by denominations and academic debates, is not unimportant, but it is *less* important. Follow the example of our Savior and hold on to the basic things.

Lord Jesus, help me to see and do the greater and more important things. Amen.

How Can You Tell?

Read John 9:13-23

Others asked, "How can a sinner do such miraculous signs?" (John 9:16)

It is often difficult to know whether someone is a true servant of Christ or a deceiver. If a person is pleasant he is usually accepted as being sincere. But it is more difficult to identify a false person from a sincere one.

The Pharisees didn't want to accept that Jesus was sent from God. Their criterion was whether He obeyed the letter of the Law. God's laws were multiplied and made much more difficult by adding human interpretations to them. Only a few – of which the Pharisees' were most important – could be kept fully. Jesus regarded love for God and people as more important than keeping laws. Therefore, He was a sinner in the Pharisees' eyes and He could not have come from God.

> *People may doubt what you say, but they will believe what you do.*
>
> ~ Lewis Cass

Jesus taught that you should be able to tell whether a person has been sent by God by what he *does* rather than by what he *says*. He performed the kind of deeds that was said the Messiah would do, the kind of deeds people in trouble needed to live strong and healthy lives. The people could see that His actions supported His teachings. They could gather that He was sent by God from what He *did*.

To be an effective witness for Christ, you need to do things that a person sent by God would do. Simple, honest godliness speaks louder than many sermons. Acts of compassion, support in times of crisis, love and care all speak of Jesus. Pray that it will happen in your life that people will know you have been sent by God.

Good Master, grant that my actions will support my words.

Amen.

Making the Blind See

Read John 9:13-23

Finally they turned again to the blind man, "What have you to say about Him? It was your eyes He opened." (John 9:17)

We don't change our opinions easily. To discover the truth is a step-by-step process that often takes years.

The man who was born blind was healed in two quick steps. Firstly Jesus put mud on his eyes, then he had to wash it off and he could see again. As John's story unfolds we see how God gradually restores the man's inner vision.

At first the man referred to Jesus simply as "the man they call Jesus" (John 9:11). At this stage Jesus was only a man to him. Later on the unbelieving leaders questioned the man and we see that he has reached a new level of insight about Jesus as he declares, "He is a prophet!" (John 9:17)

> Our knowledge of God must lead to a more intimate relationship with Him or we run the risk of becoming Pharisees.
>
> ~ Douglas Rumford

A prophet is a servant or messenger from God. Later the man also declares that Jesus has been sent from God (see John 9:33). As his spiritual eyes gradually opened, the man came to full faith in Jesus and also worshiped Him.

You might also be traveling the difficult road from unbelief to true faith. God is leading you gradually to the next step of faith, as you become ready to take it. Your spiritual eyes are continually opening. On this side of eternity you will always be able to move toward greater faith and deeper devotion. When you eventually grow into His full Presence, you will find yourself lost in praise and worship for Him as your Savior and Redeemer.

Savior and Redeemer, lead me daily into deeper insights of faith and love. Amen.

Undeniable Facts!

Read John 9:24-34

He replied, "Whether He is a sinner or not, I don't know. One thing I do know. I was blind but now I see!" (John 9:25)

Some people like to argue about religion. They grab hold of any incident in Scripture and question whether it really could have happened. It can become an interesting and pleasant pastime and people use it to escape from the requirements that come from believing in God and following Jesus.

The religious leaders questioned the man who was born blind for the second time. They tried to force him to say that he wasn't healed and that Jesus didn't heal him because He was not a prophet. The man replied that he couldn't judge the situation, but that there was one all-important undeniable fact that could not be argued away, "I was blind but now I see."

> *God alone satisfies.*
> ~ Thomas Aquinas

All believers who have come to know Christ's power and love in their lives and who have been irrevocably changed, base their understanding on their own experiences. Some can't understand how Jesus calmed the storm on the Sea of Galilee, yet they experienced that He has calmed the passions, desires, hurt and hate in their own hearts. They might not understand how He changed water into wine, but they know that He filled the emptiness in their own lives with purpose, love and hope.

They know that He has forgiven their sins, healed their sinful and hurting hearts, restored their broken marriages and reunited them with people they had become estranged from. They have hard, undeniable facts on which they firmly base their faith. I trust that this is also true in your own life – or that God, through Jesus, will make it true to you.

Holy Lord Jesus, please guard against my faith ever wavering through the unbelief of others. Amen.

Testify Again and Again!

Read John 9:24-34

He answered, "I have told you already and you did not listen. Why do you want to hear it again? Do you want to become His disciples, too?" (John 9:27)

Many people resist the message of Jesus. They hear Him, but they don't listen carefully to the message. Some people develop a resistant layer that makes them incapable of reacting. Their hearts have been hardened to the gospel message.

The religious leaders in Jesus' time didn't want to know anything about Him. They stubbornly refused to listen to anything that had to do with Jesus. They asked the man who was born blind to repeat his story in the hope of trapping him and making him say something negative about Jesus. The man refused to repeat his story and quite sarcastically asked them whether they wanted to become disciples of Jesus too.

> *It is the duty of every Christian to be Christ to his neighbor.*
>
> ~ Martin Luther

What was once said in sarcasm actually contains more than just a bit of truth. People need the story of Jesus to be told to them again and again. Those who resist the message need to hear it repeatedly until it touches them. Disciples of Jesus also need to hear it often because it strengthens us and causes us to grow in faith.

We need to hear it again and again – when you are consumed with doubt or despair, and even when you are strong and confident in your faith. You benefit from good times, but also from bad ones. You need to hear the Good News because the impact it makes grows stronger the more you hear it.

Heavenly Teacher, grant that I may still discover new truths in the Gospel message. Amen.

The First Time

Read John 9:32-34

Nobody has ever heard of opening the eyes of a man born blind.
(*John 9:32*)

When something unique happens or we do something we have never done before, someone usually says, "There's always a first time for everything!" It's exciting when a new invention is tried out for the first time. "Firsts" are important milestones that emphasize humankind's progress – whether it is climbing Mount Everest, setting a sports record or the discovery of a cure for a deadly disease.

Jesus was the first to heal a man born blind. This was because Jesus performed a new act from God that had never been done before. God is always original. He breaks into our circumstances with surprises, miracles, new creations, and new words of direction. He works with His people in a new way and leads them to the final destination of the world according to His sovereign will in a way that people have never expected. We often don't recognize these acts, like His deeds in those days. Only when we look back can we identify that they were acts of Almighty God.

> *The greatest distinguishing feature of the omnipotence of God is that our imagination gets lost in thinking about it.*
> ~ Blaise Pascal

Always look for the new things that God is busy doing. He still has surprises in His treasure chamber that He wants to reveal. There are glorious possibilities ahead. He might lead scientists to a cure for cancer, reveal ways for communities to overcome poverty and starvation, or even lead nations to live together in peace. He might also do new things for you personally – there is always a first time for everything.

Holy Spirit of God, help me not to limit God's innovative powers through unbelief. Amen.

God Can Do Anything through You Too!

Read John 9:24-34

If this Man were not from God, He could do nothing. (John 9:33)

Despite the tremendous progress that has taken place over the last two hundred years, there are still things that seem impossible to us. We can't live in peace with each other; we can't share natural resources in such a way that everyone gets the opportunity to live a good life; we can't prevent millions around the world from dying of AIDS, malaria and tuberculosis; and we can't provide each child the security that he will grow up in love and trust.

God doesn't call the equipped, He equips the called.
~ Anonymous

The man who was born blind and who Jesus healed had more insight into God and Jesus than all the learned leaders, even though he was just a beggar. He could not only see Jesus, but could see *into* Him. The awesome power that Jesus revealed proved to the blind man that God was at work in Jesus. It was just as obvious that God was not at work in the religious leaders.

Is God at work in you? He performs mighty deeds through some people and is surely waiting to do it through you. He might be waiting for you to humble yourself and acknowledge your emptiness and failures, because you have probably tried to perform deeds in your own limited strength and power. Likewise, He might expect you to discover your strengths, gifts, and potential and grant them willingly to His service. He expects you to be obedient and to envision what you can do for Him and for others. You probably have abilities you have never even dreamed of – and Jesus wants to work through you.

Lord Jesus, guide me to discover my full potential in Your service.
Amen.

Spiritual Blindness

Read John 9: 35-41

Jesus heard that they had thrown him out, and when He found him, He said, "Do you believe in the Son of Man?" (John 9:35)

There are many well-meaning people, Christians included, who are not sure what they believe. They know that one should have faith in God and that Jesus and the Holy Spirit are involved somehow – but they aren't exactly sure about it. As far as they are concerned this is the responsibility of the teachers, theologians and pastors.

Jesus is the Object of our faith. He healed the blind man, and the man became an active partner in the miracle. When the man could see and become part of the community with all its demands and differences, Jesus invited and challenged the man to believe in

> *Faith is extending an empty hand to God to receive His gift of grace.*
>
> ~ A. W. Pink

Him as the Son of God. There is no doubt that the man believed in God before, but believing in Jesus as God was a totally new step of faith that the man had to take.

Jesus also stands before us. He will find you, wherever you are in your wanderings and battle to believe, or how far you have wandered off. He finds you, not only to help you, comfort you and make it easier for you – He challenges you to move beyond the vague notion of "God that is up there somewhere" and to focus on Him as the object of your faith!

Regardless of your past problems with faith, focus on Jesus, the Man from Nazareth, the Son of God, and the crucified and resurrected Lord who ascended to heaven. He is the only Redeemer, Savior, and hope for humankind. Make Him your God and your King!

Savior, broaden my faith and deepen my love for You and my fellow man. Amen.

Who Is He?

Read John 9:35-41

"Who is He, sir?" the man asked. "Tell me so that I may believe in Him." (John 9:36)

Even though two thousand years have passed since Jesus walked the streets of Jerusalem, people still find it difficult to determine who He really is.

For some He is a "prophet from long ago." For others He is "a good man who performed acts of love." Some see Him as a teacher who spoke beautiful words. Others see Him as the rebel leader of His time and even call Him a revolutionary.

The miracle that happened in the blind man's life plunged him unexpectedly into a series of amazing experiences and discussions that must have confused him. Suddenly he was not blind anymore – he could see! Then the religious leaders tried to argue that his experience never happened. They cast him out of the synagogue where Jesus found him and spoke to him about faith. No wonder the poor man wanted to know, "The Son of Man, who is He, Sir?"

> *Jesus was God spelling Himself out in language humanity could understand.*
>
> ~ S. D. Gordon

However strong, weak, confused or full of self-confidence your faith might be, you will benefit from knowing exactly who Jesus Christ is. He is the God who became Man to open your spiritual eyes, to expose you to God's light, and to become your Friend and Savior. Through the ages He comes to find you anew, to lead and accompany you through life and death, and to show you the future that He has prepared for you. No matter how confusing life might be, learn to know Jesus more and more every day. For the first time your eyes will open and your life will make sense.

Teacher and Savior, teach me more about You every day. Amen.

Please Tell Me!

Read John 9:35-41

"Who is He, sir?" the man asked. "Tell me so that I may believe in Him." (John 9:36)

Some people believe everything they hear, no matter how far-fetched it sounds. Other people will only believe something if it is told by a person they trust or who has authority. And some don't believe anything and they go through life suspicious and distrusting.

Jesus healed a man who had been born blind. Undoubtedly the man would have great respect for the person who performed this miracle. But when Jesus challenged him to believe, he was still trying to figure out who Jesus really was, even though he accepted that Jesus came from God. "Who is He, Sir?" he asks. He had to be told. His faith alone was not

> *I seek not to understand in order that I may believe; but I believe in order that I may understand, for I believe for this reason: that unless I believe, I cannot understand.*
>
> ~ Anselm of Canterbury

enough. He needed help to get to the point where he could place his faith in Jesus.

We are normally slow to understand. We have to be told, shown, guided, helped and sometimes spurred on to surrender ourselves. Faith is seldom our own accomplishment. We need to be coached by someone with greater faith than our own. We have to hear it from others because the small flame of faith in our hearts is often ignited by the fire of faith in another person's heart. We are constantly busy receiving from external resources. It is made alive in us through the power of the Holy Spirit. Maybe someone will ask you today, "Tell me so that I may believe in Him."

Lord my God, thank You for those who told me about You and who irrevocably changed my life. Amen.

Now You See Him

Read John 9:35-41

Jesus said, "You have now seen Him; in fact, He is the one speaking with you." (John 9:37)

We sometimes look at people and things without really seeing them. We watch football, rugby or cricket matches on TV, but it's only when there is an action replay, or when the commentator explains the details, that we really see and understand what happened.

Countless people met Jesus, but few really saw Him. When Jesus found the man who had been born blind and healed him, the man had not had much time to see many people. But even so, he saw Jesus better than many who regularly kept an eye on Him.

In answer to the man's question, Jesus revealed Himself as the Son of God, "You have now seen Him." This was the culminating point in Jesus' self-revelation and became the greatest moment in the man's life.

> The difficulty in life is the choice.
>
> ~ George Moore

Jesus, the Savior, seeks to guide you to the point where you can see Him as He really is. He wants to be your Friend and Master. You have possibly read about Him, heard about Him and discussed Him for years already, but He stands before you now, as you read this page, and He says to you, "I am the Light of the world, the strength you need for your specific task and your Guide for your journey through life. Open your eyes and see Me in a new light, then you will see things around you differently." He challenges you with a decision: to see Him spiritually or to live in spiritual darkness forever. The choice is yours.

Savior and Light of my life, grant that I may never miss an opportunity to see You. Amen.

"I Stand at the Door and Knock!"

Read Luke 19:1-10

When Jesus reached the spot, He looked up and said to him, "Zacchaeus, come down immediately. I must stay at your house today." (Luke 19:5)

We all enjoy receiving guests – at least most of the time! Jesus Christ enjoyed visiting people. The Bible is full of incidents where God unexpectedly paid people a visit. He visited Abraham, Jacob, Moses, Samuel, Amos, Isaiah and Jeremiah in this way. Most of the New Testament instances where Jesus met people tell how He came to them first.

Jesus' visit to Jericho was not just a casual or random visit. He went straight to Zacchaeus's house, into his heart and into those things that were closest to Zacchaeus – his possessions! This was very important because Zacchaeus's possessions owned him.

> *To be in Christ is to be saved, but to have Christ in you is a sanctuary.*
>
> ~ Alexander Grosse

That is exactly where Jesus touched him – in the sanctuary of Zacchaeus's true self. As a tax collector for the Roman authorities, Zacchaeus was a social outcast.

Zacchaeus opened his home and heart to Jesus. Jesus entered and took possession of the rich man's possessions. Christ is only truly in you when He takes possession of those things that own you. It might be your house, business, career, sport, abilities, or even your failures. You might be addicted to your sins, your fears, or your problems. Let Jesus come in. He made a difference in Zacchaeus's life and He can make a difference in your life too.

Redeemer, come into my life and take full possession of my inner being. Amen.

How Big Is Your Heart?

Read Luke 19:1-10

But Zacchaeus stood up and said to the Lord, "Look, Lord! Here and now I give half of my possessions to the poor, and if I have cheated anybody out of anything, I will pay back four times the amount."
(Luke 19:8)

When Jesus enters your life and your heart, your hands reach out to a world in need. Mother Teresa knew Jesus and she reached out to the poor on the streets of Calcutta. When Jesus broke down the stumbling blocks in Paul's thinking, his heart went out to the heathens with the gospel message. When Jesus entered Zacchaeus's heart, he compassionately reached out to the poor. In the past he didn't care about the poor because he was too busy making money.

> One can give without loving but one cannot love without giving.
> ~ Amy Carmichael

When the love of Jesus reached him deep inside, the smallest man in Jericho obtained the biggest heart on earth. This stingy little man reached out to others with grace that could only come from Jesus.

When Jesus Christ comes into Christians' hearts, they reach out to others. Some reach out with money, like Zacchaeus did. Others reach out with prayer; the gospel message; good deeds of compassion; the gift of healing; the joy of music or by simply caring for and encouraging others. You can almost determine the depth to which Jesus has entered a person's life by the extent to which they reach out to others.

If your faith focuses exclusively on yourself and what you can get out of God and religion, then it's time to seriously consider what it's all about. Faith in Jesus is primarily about the giving of yourself – time and time again.

Spirit of God, show me the place where Jesus expects me to reach out to others in love. Amen.

A Bubbling Spring

Read John 4:11-26

"Those who drink the water I give will never be thirsty again. It becomes a fresh, bubbling spring within them, giving them eternal life." (John 4:14 NLT)

Water is a source of life. Some streams and rivers are permanently full while others fill up with rain and then eventually dry up again. People often depend on this temporary water supply and collect it in dams or containers to keep their animals alive or to water their crops.

The Israelites knew about temporary and disrupted water supply. But they also knew about the much greater value of a permanent water supply. Flowing water was also much better than stagnant water. They spoke of flowing water as "living water." Jesus used this image to describe the spiritual life that was possible through His Spirit and love. This water not only flowed, it bubbled up. Jesus spoke about a vibrant flow of water and the spiritual dynamic it brings, which leads to eternal life – just like a living spring supports plant and animal life on a continuous basis.

> *Life is like a play – it is not the length, but the quality of the acting that counts.*
>
> *~ Seneca*

The spring freely shares its valuable, life-giving water with the surrounding landscape all the way down to the sea. Therefore, the eternal life that you receive from Jesus is not something you can keep to yourself. It gives you life as you give hope, joy and love to the people around you. It can never remain static. It must always bubble up and flow over to others to really be living water.

Lord and Master, make my life a fountain of living water that bubbles up and gives eternal life. Amen.

Give Me This Water!

Read John 4:11-26

The woman said to Him, "Sir, give me this water so that I won't get thirsty and have to keep coming here to draw water." (John 4:15)

Most of us know how to ask for things that we want. When we were children we nagged for sweets. As we grew older we asked for love and success. In a way these things are selfish, but a normal part of being human.

The woman at the well came to fetch her daily supply of water, just like many others in rural areas do. This woman came with a basic need of life. Even when Jesus spoke of the "living water" she thought of what she could get out of it. She would "never thirst again," in a region that was very hot and dry. She would never have to carry the water can all the way to the well and back home again. She was only aware of the short-term benefits she would get.

> *If we don't change, we don't grow. If we don't grow, we are not really living.*
> ~ Gale Sheehy

It is okay to come to Jesus to ask for something. You might be yearning for security; peace of mind, or healing from a serious illness. You might be battling with bitterness, depression or loneliness. You might feel that it is dishonorable to come to the Master with an apparently selfish need. No, come as you are in your weakness and need. Jesus will accept you, help you and make you whole. Then you can spend the rest of your life in praise to and worship of the Savior.

Holy Lord Jesus, transform my demands and needs into joy and thanksgiving. Amen.

Our Steadfast Rock

Read Hebrews 13:7-19

Jesus Christ is the same yesterday and today and forever. (Hebrews 13:8)

It is only natural that our image of Jesus Christ would be of someone with a Palestinian background from the Roman golden age. It was at that time that God chose to reveal Himself to the world and ever since people have thought of Christ in terms of the idiom, costume and customs of that time. Because we imagine Him in that time, we easily lose sight of the eternal and unchanging Christ.

He can only enter your life effectively if you experience Him in the context of modern times and within the frame of reference of your own existence. Because He is eternal He lives today! He is forcefully present in your life and waiting to guide you.

We have within ourselves enough to fill the present day with joy, and overspread the future with years of hope.

~ William Wordsworth

As He taught, guided and blessed His first disciples, He wants to do the same for you. Unfortunately our perspective on His ability to help and bless us is clouded by the problems and confusion of our modern society.

You may think that you are living in a unique period of time, and in a certain sense this is true. But the basic problems of the world today are still the same as when Jesus was on earth. Greed, lust, self-centeredness, pettiness, hatred and bitterness are still powerful influences in man's existence.

The living Christ can deal with these deviations and illness of man's spirit and intellect, just as He could centuries ago, because He is eternal and unchanging. On this steadfast Rock we can build our lives.

Holy Master, I gain peace of mind from knowing that You are eternal and steadfast in this ever-changing world. Amen.

Our Example of Love

Read John 13:1-17

"Now that I, your Lord and Teacher, have washed your feet, you also should wash one another's feet. I have set you an example that you should do as I have done for you." (John 13:14-15)

Throughout Christ's earthly ministry He demonstrated through word and deed the kind of life God wanted people to live. Every lesson was based on love in the truest sense of the word – love that was willing to make sacrifices to prove its truth and trustworthiness.

Christian humility is based on the sight of self, the vision of Christ, and the realization of God.

~ William Barclay

One of the most moving and striking examples of this was on the evening before the crucifixion and glorification of Christ, when the Son of God took on the form of a servant and performed the humble task of washing His disciples' feet – including Judas Iscariot who would soon betray Him.

Some consider this act of Christ as menial and inappropriate. On the contrary, this humble act revealed the gracious charitableness that characterizes the Christian faith which every Christian should strive toward.

Let us learn from this and follow Jesus' example. In this way we will become true and trustworthy ambassadors for Christ in a world that desperately cries out for Christian love.

Gracious Lord, make us worthy to follow Your guidance and become servants and ambassadors for Your kingdom. Amen.

Another Lesson in Humility

Read Mark 14:3-9

He was in Bethany, reclining at the table of a man known as Simon the Leper. (Mark 14:3)

Jesus knew exactly what was going to happen to Him. With divine knowledge and insight He was fully aware of the plot to kill Him, the methods His enemies would use, and the cruel way in which He would die through the crucifixion.

But at the same time He knew, in the fulfillment of God's plan of redemption, that He would gloriously triumph over death, rise from the dead and rule with God for all eternity.

When we know that we are going to be honored at a particular occasion, most of us bask in expectancy about the coming exaltation. We enjoy the attention we get before and after the event. It is human nature for us to seek this kind of attention.

> *Humility is not a grace that can be acquired in a few months: it is the work of a lifetime.*
>
> ~ François Fénelon

Jesus, however, sought the quiet loneliness of Simon the Leper – away from the crowds and out of the spotlight. Because lepers were banned and rejected from society, Jesus was sure that He would not be accompanied by a cheering crowd. This indicates the humility of the Son of God and is the example He sets for all Christians. Let us follow in His footsteps and humbly walk with Him.

Lord Jesus, teach me each day to follow Your example and walk the road of humility. Amen.

A Good Deed

Read Mark 14:3-9

"Leave her alone," said Jesus. "Why are you bothering her? She has done a beautiful thing to Me." (Mark 14:6)

After Malcolm Muggeridge visited Mother Teresa to find out more about her work, he wrote a book entitled, *Something Beautiful for God*. She cared for the sick, fed the hungry, and prayed for the people on the streets of Calcutta. She knew that Christ was present in those people and she wanted to do it out of love for the Lord and out of compassion for them.

People often do beautiful things for God for different reasons. In his testament one affluent believer bequeathed an amount to a Bible school. In a colorless city a church is surrounded by a garden with the most beautiful flowers. Passersby stop just to admire the beautiful flowers. An elderly member of the congregation who lives in an apartment building took over the care of the garden and used his "green fingers" to demonstrate his love for God. One person might demonstrate it through music or singing; another through encouraging words and another through serving the community with dedication and love.

> *In the evening of life, we will be judged on love alone.*
> ~ St. John of the Cross

As a Christian you may think that you do your duty when you have your quiet time, attend church and tithe. The woman in today's reading went further than mere duty. Jesus approved of what she did because He understood the nature of love. He saw that her expression of overflowing love far exceeded duty. May this inspire us to do something beautiful for God and for people.

Faithful Savior, help me to perform my duties and to look for opportunities to perform beautiful deeds of love. Amen.

Help for the Poor

Read Mark 14:3-9

"The poor you will always have with you, and you can help them any time you want. But you will not always have Me." (Mark 14:7)

Poverty is a huge problem all over the world and this global crisis is worsening. Half of the six billion people on earth survive on less than $2 a day. While most Christians feel powerless in the face of this overwhelming challenge, we can't simply turn a blind eye.

Jesus was very serious when He said that we would always have the poor with us. But He didn't say that we should not do anything about it. In fact, He said that we should *always* do something to help them. Jesus moved among the poor, the outcasts of society and the mentally ill. He said that God was present in them and in their need.

> *No society can surely be flourishing and happy, of which the far greater part of the members are poor and miserable.*
>
> ~ Adam Smith

One way in which we can help the poor is through personal gifts. Some of them live in such dire conditions that an item of clothing or a proper meal would be of great help. You could also offer them a job, even if it is temporary or for a small wage. To reward their work also allows them to feel worthy and have self-respect.

Another way of helping is to support organizations that specialize in assisting the poor. You can also encourage movements that attempt to better conditions and social economic practices. In any of these ways we can follow Jesus' example and act in love.

Master, deepen my empathy and understanding of poverty.

Amen.

Jesus at an Ordinary Meal

Read Luke 24:28-35

When He was at the table with them, He took bread, gave thanks, broke it and began to give it to them. Then their eyes were opened and they recognized Him. (Luke 24:30-31)

It's true that God visits us on special occasions. He comes to numerous people during a worship service or a Christian gathering. He has appeared at countless youth camps where He called many to love and serve Him. Some people met Him during Baptism and Communion services.

The two disciples Jesus met on the road to Emmaus asked Him to stay the night at their home. It was an unforgettable day and a strenuous walk to their house. The Stranger had led them to truths they had never known before. They were starving after their long walk. Then Jesus gave thanks for the meal and broke the bread – and suddenly they knew it was Him! It was an ordinary meal and the food was nothing exceptional because they had been away from home for days. But it didn't matter because Jesus made Himself at home in their house. He revealed Himself to them while they ate that ordinary meal.

> *When Christ reveals Himself there is satisfaction in the slenderest portion, and without Christ there is emptiness in the greatest fullness.*
>
> ~ Alexander Grosse

Jesus can come to you at any time and on any occasion. It doesn't have to be a special, religious or spiritual occasion. He comes to touch the ordinary moments and days in your life with His special Presence, love and acceptance. He comes to share food, joy and fellowship. He comes to bless the commonness of your ordinary life. Do you have a place for Him at your life-table?

Jesus, my Lord, touch my everyday life with Your Presence and love. Amen.

Is Your Heart Burning within You?

Read Luke 24:28-35

They asked each other, "Were not our hearts burning within us while He talked with us on the road and opened the Scriptures to us?" (Luke 24:32)

There are various and diverse forms of touch. The doctor touches you on the spot where the pain is and you say, "Yes, there!" The parent touches the crying child and kisses the pain away. If your spouse falls asleep during the Sunday service you nudge him with your elbow to wake him up.

When God touches people, He awakens hidden and, until then, unknown senses. When Jesus touched the two friends on the road to Emmaus, He ignited a flame within them. They were sad, disillusioned and felt that they had been let down. Their thoughts were clouded by confusion, but Christ enlightened their thinking. His questions directed them to what really mattered and His love set their hearts on fire. When they recognized Him and He disappeared from before them, they were wide awake and speedily traveled back to Jerusalem to share the good news with the others.

> *Christ is my Redeemer. He is my life. He is everything to me in heaven and earth.*
> ~ Sadhu Sundar Singh

When the risen Christ touches your heart it fills you with passion, warmth and conviction. He gives energy to your soul and motivates you like you have never been motivated before. When you understand Christ, then you will love Him and be filled with His love, which will reach others through you. May Christ our Savior ignite that flame in your life today.

Lord Jesus, may You ignite the holy fire in my life and purge away all wayward and evil desires. Amen.

Get Up and Walk!

Read John 5:1-17

Jesus said to him, "Get up! Pick up your mat and walk." (John 5:8)

It's easy to fall into a rut. Some people dig ruts for themselves that are so deep they can't see anything else. Someone once said that the only difference between a rut and a grave is the depth. The routine of everyday life and the necessity of reliability can easily turn into monotony and a resistance to change. Sometimes it takes a kick-start or a disaster to get us out of the comfortable rut in which we live.

Jesus summed up the sick man who lay beside the pool at Bethesda for thirty-eight years, waiting for someone to help him. He thought that he needed a helping hand. Jesus must have surprised him when He said, "Come on, don't just sit there – get up and walk! Start to really live for a change!" Jesus said it with love, but also forcefully. It challenged the man to leave his comfort zone of weakness and dependence. It created the possibility of walking instead of just waiting; of moving instead of keeping still; of reaching out instead of being closed within himself.

> *We turn to God for help when our foundations are shaking, only to learn that it is God who is shaking them.*
> ~ Charles C. West

Jesus commands you and me to also get out of our rut. A better and greater life awaits us. There are no limits to the possibilities that stretch out before us. You can explore, "How wide and long and high and deep is the love of Christ" (Eph. 3:18). Our spiritual journey doesn't begin when we die. It begins now – the minute you stand up and walk! With Jesus as your Savior.

Savior and Redeemer, help me to move towards the place You are sending me. Amen.

Immediate Action

Read John 5:1-17

At once the man was cured; he picked up his mat and walked. (John 5:9)

Many things in this life can lead to our downfall. Custom and habit ensure that we get stuck in a rut. Fear prevents us from moving in a new direction. Doubt continually gnaws away at our faith and trust, both in God and ourselves. Failures of the past haunt us. Many things in the world around us, as well as within us, threaten to destroy us.

But it doesn't have to be like this. The man at the pool of Bethesda was a failure for thirty-eight years. He was ruled by sickness and self-pity. Then a word from Jesus transformed him from failure to faith, from sickness to health, from self-pity to radiant self-confidence.

> *Regret for time wasted can become a power for good in the time that remains, if we will only stop the waste and the idle, useless regretting.*
> ~ Arthur Brisbane

Two things happened to lift this man out of his depressing condition. The one was a command from Jesus, and the other was his own immediate move away from failure. At Jesus' word, and apparently also His gaze, the man believed that he could be healed – and it happened.

Jesus does not want you to wallow in the mud of self-pity for one day longer. No matter how long you have battled with your doubt, defeat or failures, you don't need to stay trapped there. You can stand up today and leave your negative past behind you. Your Savior will give you strength. He will inspire you with hope and fill you with trust; He will accompany you on the path with new energy and a new beginning. All that is required of you is immediate action – NOW!

Lord my God, forgive me for allowing negative things to rule my life. Help me to make a new start now. Amen.

The Great Physician

Read Mark 1:32-39

The whole town gathered at the door, and Jesus healed many who had various diseases. He also drove out many demons. (Mark 1:33-34)

In a radio interview a pastor was asked what percentage of people who went for healing was really healed and he replied, "About one out of three." The advert for the campaign marketed the gathering as an opportunity for "miraculous healing." The pastor admitted that no follow-ups were done to see whether the healings lasted permanently.

In Jesus' time, before technology and science, sickness was a far greater threat than it is today. There were many false healers on the scene. Many healers claimed that they could perform miracles. The lack of adequate medicine increased the popularity of faith healers.

> *We are all healers who can reach out and offer health, and we are all patients in constant need of help.*
>
> ~ Henri Nouwen

When the Israelites dreamed of God's coming Messianic generation, it included healing (see Isa. 35:3-6). They knew that it had to come from God. Through Jesus Christ it did happen. Health and wholeness is God's desire for us, and Christians thank God for the many ways in which healing takes place.

One form of healing is by spiritual means, which is known as divine healing. Jesus might use a great gathering, like previously mentioned, to bring healing. He might also use the quiet road of prayer, or even the laying on of hands by an exceptionally gifted person. God also uses the medical profession and its advancements to aid healing. Death is sometimes God's final act of healing when He allows the frail person to enter heaven's glory. Jesus, our Great Physician, is in this also our Savior.

Lord Jesus, we pray for all who are involved in medical research and for those who make healing their calling. Amen.

May

Listen to His Voice

"The sheep listen to his [shepherd's] voice.
He calls his own sheep by name
and leads them out."
~ John 10:3

Happy the soul which by a sincere self-renunciation,
holds itself ceaselessly in the hands of its Creator,
ready to do everything which He wishes.
~ Francois Fénelon

*L*ord Jesus, our Savior,
We worship You as the Good Shepherd who
knows each of us by name;
Grant that I will hear Your voice
clearly when You call my name.
That I will willingly and
obediently follow Your leading.
Lead me to the green pastures of Your grace
and to the quiet streams of Your love.
Thank You for being concerned about me – a sinner.
Thank You for calling me out of
my sinful state to redemption.
Thank You for dying in order to reconcile me to God.
Thank You, faithful Savior, for coming to fetch me
each time I wander off and for lovingly
including me in Your flock again.
Give thanks to the Lord, for He is good;
His love endures forever.

Amen.

Let His Love Strengthen You

Read John 13:1-10

Having loved His own who were in the world, He now showed them the full extent of His love. (John 13:1)

It is very easy to lose faith in yourself. For a while things go well and you feel a surge of self-confidence over what you can achieve. At such times life is good. But then your self-confidence begins to wane for no specific reason, and you experience a shattering feeling of incompetence. You become convinced that you will never be successful in anything you attempt to do. To add to your depressed state, you begin to think that God doesn't care about you anymore and that He even no longer has faith in you.

The Scriptures reveal the amazing truth that even though Jesus knew that His disciples would let Him down, deny, and betray Him, He persisted in His love for them and confidence in them. He looked past their failures and defeat, and observed what they could become in the power of His living Spirit. He continued to love them, despite their weakness and untrustworthiness.

Love takes off masks that we fear we cannot live without and know we cannot live within.

~ James Baldwin

The principle demonstrated by the Master so long ago remains true and effective today. He knows you for what you are. Nothing remains hidden from Him, but He continues to love you and lead you to a richer and more purposeful life. You might have lost confidence in yourself, but the living Christ believes that you can still become a channel through which His love and grace can be spread to the world in which you live and work.

Through Your love for me and my love for You, Lord Jesus, let my self-confidence grow daily. Amen.

Our Purpose Is to Worship

Read John 9:35-41

Then the man said, "Lord, I believe," and he worshiped Him. (John 9:38)

What do you think is the purpose of human life? Is it to be successful, rich or famous? To be popular? Some Christians regard "being good" or "being deeply religious" as the purpose and objective of life. Others think that knowing God is the highest purpose of life. Many centuries ago there were a group of students in London who said, "Man's primary purpose is to glorify God and enjoy Him forever."

The climax of the story of the man who was born blind is not when Jesus cures His blindness, but when he gives himself to Jesus in faith and falls at His feet to worship Him. He meets Jesus in the depths of his need and eventually not only gains sight, but sees who Jesus is and worships Him. In this instant he performs the greatest activity a person is capable of – to see God and to worship Him in Jesus Christ.

> *It is in the process of being worshiped that God communicates His presence to men.*
> ~ C. S. Lewis

The primary purpose of your life is to worship and glorify God. You might be successful, rich, popular, and happy in the eyes of those around you. You might experience health problems, business or family difficulties. Indeed, life might be one long struggle. But you will reach the greatest heights that you are capable of when you worship Jesus and "enjoy Him forever". Then your high and low points will be seen for what they really are – only milestones along the road. You touch eternity when you worship Jesus – and eternity touches you.

Holy Master, I fall before You in reverence and worship You as my Savior. Amen.

The Divinity and Humanity of Christ

Read John 11:33-44

Jesus wept. Then the Jews said, "See how He loved him!" (John 11:35-36)

Many people erroneously believe that to demonstrate grief, anxiety, fear or any other feeling that influences our emotions, is to contradict or deny our faith. Such people reason that a Christian should overcome setbacks and that their faith should be strong enough to help them handle all adversities.

While it is true that Christians can fight the storms of life in Christ's strength, an important characteristic of our faith that makes this possible is that we have the living Christ as our example. He offers His companionship on the path of life and He has experienced all these emotions Himself. This is because He lived with people and understands feelings and emotions very well. Emotions can take us from the heights of ecstasy one moment to the depths of hopelessness the next.

> *If ever man was God or God was man, Jesus Christ was both.*
>
> ~ Lord Byron

While you travel the winding road of life, the only way to be sure that you will be able to handle all that comes your way is to have a personal relationship with the Master. Keep close to Him through prayer, meditation and Bible study. Then you will be able to handle whatever happens because the Author of life is at your side.

By sharing my life with You, Lord Jesus, I know that I will be able to handle any situation through Your grace and strength. Amen.

The Unpredictable Christ

Read Luke 6:6-11

Jesus knew what they were thinking. (Luke 6:8)

Christ's way of doing things differs from ours. We often formulate our plans in a way we think will be acceptable to the Master. But what appears to us as simple common sense might seem like foolishness to the living Christ.

When the rich man came to Jesus to ask for personal spiritual guidance, the Master loved him. He was a person with great potential. Riches, personality and a desire to serve made it look as if he had all the qualities for discipleship. But instead of inviting him into the group of disciples, Jesus challenged him to hand over all his possessions – and he simply could not do this.

> *The strength and happiness of a man consists in finding out the way God is going, and going that way too.*
> ~ Henry Ward Beecher

A respected leader of the Jewish Council came to Jesus one night with the hope of having a reasonable theological debate with the great Teacher. His opening remark was courteous and revealed his willingness to learn. He was willing to discuss difficult spiritual issues. The Master's direct answer cut through all Nicodemus's generalizations and left no room for doubt.

Christ met people at the point of their deepest needs in His own unique way, and not in the way expected of Him by popular opinion. With some He was gentle and tender, while with others He was painfully direct. With some He acted with dramatic suddenness, while with others He took His time to win their love and trust. He knows what goes on in people's thoughts, and adjusts His challenge to fit each one's personal need.

Thank You, loving Master, for all You do to draw people to Yourself. Amen.

To First Find Your Brother

Read John 1:35-42

The first thing Andrew did was to find his brother Simon and tell him, "We have found the Messiah" (that is, the Christ). (John 1:41)

There is much more to Christianity than having a friendly smile and being kind-hearted. Friendliness and kind-heartedness are wonderful and allow the daily interaction between people to flow freely. However, true Christianity is about Jesus – about meeting Him, recognizing Him, accepting Him, and allowing yourself to be lead to true life through Him. It is also about reaching out to others and doing good because of Him and for Him.

There is much more to Andrew's comment than it seems at first. To find his brother wasn't just the first thing he did, but the most important thing. God was looking for Peter, and so was Jesus. They used Andrew to find Peter. After Jesus, Peter became the first leader and missionary in Christianity. It was on Peter's testimony that the Church of Christ would be built. Andrew found him for Jesus and introduced him to Jesus.

> *We cannot hesitate to believe that the great mission of Christianity was in reality accomplished by means of informal missionaries.*
>
> ~ Adolf von Harnack

Around you are people who wait and hope to be found for Jesus. Some of them have empty lives, worried hearts, or confused thoughts. Others are in financial difficulties so bad that they think of committing suicide. Others are dying and urgently need Jesus. Then there are those who don't know what to do. Tell them about Jesus. Do it quietly, confidently, and simply. It might be the most important thing they will ever hear.

Savior and Master, give me the words, courage, and commitment to tell others about You. Amen.

"Follow Me!"

Read John 1:43-53̶51

The next day Jesus decided to leave for Galilee. Finding Philip, He said to him, "Follow Me." (John 1:43)

To be Jesus Christ's disciple is a one-on-one issue. It is also an issue of one-for-one. Despite all that is said about following Jesus and being included in a fellowship of believers, the truth remains that Jesus comes to you as an individual and invites you to follow Him. He invites you with your own unique identity, strengths, gifts, abilities, mistakes, failures, and your own small one-person history. All of this is important to Him.

> *If our common life is not a common course of humility, self-denial, renunciation of the world, poverty of spirit and heavenly affection, we do not live the lives of Christians.*
>
> ~ William Law

It was a critical meeting when Jesus came to Philip in this manner. Out of the millions of people Jesus could have chose, He chose Philip. We don't know why, because Philip was just an ordinary person. Between all the disciples it seems as if he was a background worker. We only hear about him twice in the Gospels. He allowed others to stand in the spotlight. Even so, Jesus wanted him because He knew what Philip could become. That day in Galilee, history stood still while Jesus spoke to Philip. Christ's decision to call Philip, and Philip's reaction, meant that he changed from an observer to a participant in Jesus' service.

Jesus is not only looking for important people like leaders and celebrities. He also wants ordinary people, those whose names never reach the headlines. He wants to fill their ordinary days with unknown depth, hope, and glory. Does it sound like Jesus is calling you?

Lord Jesus, bless all Your ordinary followers. Let the fact that they are following Your lead be the most fulfilling experience in their lives. Amen.

To Love and To Believe

Read 1 Peter 1:1-9

Though you have not seen Him, you love Him; and even though you do not see Him now, you believe in Him and are filled with an inexpressible and glorious joy, for you are receiving the goal of your faith, the salvation of your souls. (1 Peter 1:8-9)

There are people who disregard the gospel message as a fairy tale. Others believe it, live by it, and are even willing to die for it.

After the outpouring of the Holy Spirit in Jerusalem at Pentecost, Christianity spread to the surrounding areas and eventually to faraway countries. Since then it has been accepted by many countries and cultures. Almost one third of the earth's population are confessing Christians. Yet only a small group of people saw Jesus two thousand years ago. The rest believe because of what they have heard from other people or from experiencing His love and power in their own lives. The people to whom Peter wrote this letter lived in the northern part of what is today known as Turkey. They had never met Jesus, and yet Peter was calling them to die for Jesus.

> *As we let our own light shine, we unconsciously give other people permission to do the same.*
> ~ Marianne Williamson

Today he calls us to believe in Jesus, to love Him, and if required, to die for Him. If you are willing to do this, you will know Him better than many of those who saw Him in human form. You will live closer to Him, absorb more of His nature and model your life on His. You might become someone in whom Jesus finds form again, and through seeing Him in you, someone else will come to know and believe in Him.

May You be present in my life, Savior Jesus, so that others might come to know You and believe in You. Amen.

Joy Beyond Words

Read 1 Peter 1:1-9

You are filled with an inexpressible and glorious joy. (1 Peter 1:8)

What makes a person really happy? Economic conditions might improve, but this doesn't necessarily bring more happiness. Some rich people are happy, and some aren't. Some poor people are happy, while others aren't.

The Christians Paul addressed in this letter lived under the threat of the death penalty. Some of their fellow believers had already been killed. Yet Peter says that they were, "Filled with an inexpressible and glorious joy." In the shadow of death they were not only happy, but inexpressibly happy. Faith in Jesus Christ had changed things. In the place of despair they were filled with hope, both for this life and the next. Instead of feeling guilty about their sins, they experienced true freedom and forgiveness. Instead of confusion they had peace of mind.

> *Joy is the experience of knowing that you are unconditionally loved and that nothing – sickness, failure, emotional distress, oppression, war, or even death – can take that love away.*
>
> *~ Henri Nouwen*

They knew who God was and that they were His children. And above all, they knew that God accepted them and loved them. No words could describe the joy and thankfulness that this new way of life had brought them. In the face of death they lived more powerfully than ever before.

You can also experience this inexpressible joy. Sometimes it will be as gentle as a bubbling brook, while at other times it will be like a river in flood. It is born from faith in Jesus Christ and cannot be acquired in any other way.

Savior, please fill my life with inexpressible joy. Amen.

Searching for Jesus

Read Mark 1:2-39

Simon and his companions went to look for Him, and when they found Him, they exclaimed: "Everyone is looking for You!" (Mark 1:36-37)

If asked what they are searching for most in life, most people would answer, "Happiness!" Others might say, "Peace of mind," "Truth," "Fun," or "Money!"

Sometimes people search for God because they have a feeling that He has all the answers to their questions and problems. The people in Galilee who saw Christ's miracles, heard Him teach, or had just heard about Him, began to search for Him. But like the people in Capernaum, they searched for Him in the wrong places.

> *To pursue joy is to lose it. The only way to get it is to follow steadily the path of duty, without thinking of joy.*
> ~ Alexander Maclaren

People who search for wealth often feel unprotected and unsure. They think that money will bring the security they desire. Others who are unhappy live with deep personal conflicts and waste a lot of energy looking after themselves. The true driving force behind everything is often feelings of guilt, fear, bitterness, or hurt. All these people urgently need Jesus.

If they would only face the truth, see their problems for what they really are and get to know Jesus, then they could find the meaning of life in Him. He would offer them better security than money can; inner peace instead of conflict; and healing from their memories, instead of bitterness.

Most of Jesus' disciples testify that He has given them joy, peace, and truth. Those who have found Him have discovered the uselessness of earthly things and that through His love they no longer experience fear.

Thank You, heavenly Father, that in You I have discovered true life.

Amen.

Always Be Humble

Read 1 Peter 3:1-12

Finally, all of you, be humble. (1 Peter 3:8)

A priest in a small French village lived close to God. He wasn't as learned as the other priests and his mistakes often revealed his lack of education. Other priests in the congregation were angry and set up a petition for him to be removed. The last priest to receive the petition had an objection based on principle and instead of sending the petition straight to the bishop, he sent it to the priest in question. The priest read it and sent it on to the bishop. The bishop read the list and couldn't believe his eyes when he saw the last signature. The priest concerned had added his own signature to the list that demanded his dismissal.

> *Humility is a grace in the soul. It is indescribable wealth, a name and a gift from God.*
> ~ St. John Climacus

Christians have two reasons to be humble. Firstly, they know that they are human and are totally dependent on God. They know that anything they do or accomplish is God working in their lives. Secondly, they know that Christ is their example and standard. They don't compare themselves with others, but look to Jesus and know that they fall short of perfection.

If you think you are important, think again. Remind yourself that even acts of kindness are often motivated by desires other than true love. Your best is polluted by baser desires. Your greatest glory must always be found in your service to Jesus, whichever path He may send you on. When you receive praise, give the glory to God. If you receive criticism, ask God to help you improve.

Lord Jesus, help me to forget about myself and to seek only Your honor and glory. Amen.

Jesus Can Be Strict

Read Matthew 21:2-17

Jesus entered the temple area and drove out all who were buying and selling there. He overturned the tables of the money changers and the benches of those selling doves. (Matthew 21:12)

The image that many people have of Jesus was etched in their youth, when as children they sang, "Gentle Jesus, meek and mild, look upon this little child." If this is your opinion, you will have to make a mind shift.

One event that happened the week before the crucifixion is known as the "Clearing of the Temple." Jesus saw the blatant evil that was taking place in the temple and stormed in. The use of animals in sacrificial offerings resulted in the priests using the temple to buy and sell animals. The people's faith was misused to generate wealth for the religious

> *The deadliest sin were the consciousness of no sin.*
> ~ Thomas Carlyle

leaders. Jesus was furious about this. He knew that this was wrong, that God was dishonored through it, that the people were misled, and that the temple was desecrated. Jesus took on the role of Judge and drove out the sellers. He could be very strict when the situation required it.

Jesus doesn't condone the wrong things we do. He judges and hates everything that is wrong. He will not allow you to get away with it. Take a stroll through the temple of your own life and be honest about times when you have misled and cheated other people. Do not make a mockery out of God because He is always holy. Clean your temple before the strict Jesus calls you to order.

Holy Jesus, help me, through Your Holy Spirit, to get rid of everything that is wrong in my life. Amen.

Pure Love

Read Matthew 26:6-13

While Jesus was in Bethany in the home of a man known as Simon the Leper, a woman came to Him with an alabaster jar of very expensive perfume, which she poured on His head as He was reclining at the table. (Matthew 26:6-7)

Outside of the family circle it's very difficult to practice pure love. Often people's motives for showing love are very selfish. A few days before the crucifixion a woman anointed Jesus with expensive perfume. She loved Jesus so much that she went to great lengths to buy the expensive perfume.

If Jesus Christ be God and died for me, then no sacrifice can be too great for me to make for Him.

~ C. T. Studd

By anointing Jesus in this way the woman performed a beautiful deed that cost her a lot of money. She threw caution to the wind and recklessly spent her money. This caused her to receive harsh criticism from the disciples. Jesus, however, set them straight and expressed His appreciation for her act of pure love. While others were planning His death, the woman poured out her love and commitment to Him.

When last did you show your love for Jesus by performing an act or giving a gift that required extra time or cost from you? Think about the sacrifices that Jesus has made on your behalf and ask yourself what you can do for Him out of love and gratitude. What can you give, not to get something in return, but to show your love and thankfulness to Jesus for what He has done for you?

Spirit of God, please show me how to love as selflessly and sacrificially as Jesus did. Amen.

To Truly See

Read John 9:1-12

His neighbors and those who had formerly seen him begging asked, "Isn't this the man who used to sit and beg?" Some claimed that he was. Others said, "No, he only looks like him." But he himself insisted, "I am the man." (John 9:8-9)

A common saying goes, "There is none so blind as those who will not see." We usually choose to see only what we want to see. Sometimes we refuse to believe what we do see if it doesn't fit in with our own ideas or viewpoints.

The people who knew the blind man that Jesus healed were confused. He was the man who had sat and begged for years and now he was walking around and saw things like they were. They couldn't believe that he had been healed, and yet there he was for all to see the miracle. They had perfect sight, yet they couldn't recognize this changed man. He was healed for two reasons: Firstly, God touched his life through Jesus and he was whole again – he was different. Secondly, they couldn't recognize the almighty power of God because they were personally blind to His glory and grace. It was necessary for their inner sight to be restored so that they could recognize Jesus.

> *I never have any difficulty believing in miracles, since I experienced the miracle of a change in my own heart.*
> ~ St. Augustine

It is the same with you and me. It is possible to become cynical and skeptical about God and His omnipotence. Even some Christians can't see Him at work around them. Even so, He is still doing mighty things in the lives of ordinary people. You need eyes that have been opened by God in order to recognize the Presence of Jesus and to see His glory.

Thank You, Heavenly Father, for opening my eyes so that I can truly see Jesus. Amen.

"How Then Were Your Eyes Opened?"

Read John 9:1-12

"How then were your eyes opened?" they demanded. (John 9:10)

If someone suddenly changes, we always wonder why. A politician goes over to the opposition; a sportsman changes teams; a friend emigrates; a businessman moves from one business to another, and we wonder what has caused these changes.

Some of the bystanders were probably shocked by the sudden change in the man who had been blind until Jesus healed him. The man who could not see caused the bystanders to see, but not perceive. Many of them didn't want to believe that Jesus could bring about such a transformation. They had no power and therefore they refused to acknowledge that all true power comes from God and that God was busy working through Jesus.

> *A miracle is an event beyond the power of any known physical law to produce; it is a spiritual occurrence produced by the power of God, a marvel, a wonder.*
>
> ~ Billy Graham

If you give your life to Jesus, people will always want to know what has happened to you. It is of utmost importance to know how God has been at work in your life. You might recall a single incident where you met Christ and He changed your life forever. Or you might be aware that God has been gradually leading you from childhood to accept Christ as your Savior.

What is of cardinal importance is that you will know that Christ has given you your spiritual sight – regardless of the circumstances. You didn't receive it as a result of your own search for it. You will then always gratefully attribute this miracle to Jesus Christ.

Lord, grant that I may see You more clearly and distinctly. Amen.

The Man They Call Jesus

Read John 9:1-12

He replied, "The man they call Jesus made some mud and put it on my eyes. He told me to go to Siloam and wash. So I went and washed, and then I could see." (John 9:11)

In order to operate a machine we fortunately don't need to know everything about it. Many people who drive cars don't have a clue about how they work. The same applies to telephones, radios, televisions, and many other things.

The man who was born blind didn't really understand exactly how Jesus went about restoring his sight. But he did know that a man by the name of Jesus performed the whole miracle. About that he was sure, and nobody could convince him not to speak about Jesus. He knew nothing about Jesus' lofty titles such as "Son of God," "Son of Man," or "Son of David". But he did know that the man who performed the miracle was called Jesus, and that was enough for him.

> *I have a great need for Christ, I have a great Christ for my need.*
>
> ~ Charles H. Spurgeon

We might know all the theories and dogmas and all the debates about religion and Jesus Christ. You need not know the Bible from cover to cover – from Genesis to Revelation. But you must know the man they call Jesus! It's all about Him: His love, grace, compassion and His life-changing, saving omnipotence. Don't believe that you are a second-grade believer just because you can't remember the names of all the disciples or those of the minor prophets. Just know the man they call Jesus and stand firm in Him.

Thank You, Savior, for coming into my life and that I can know You as Jesus. Amen.

Where Is He Now?

Read John 9:1-12

"Where is He now?" they asked. "I don't know," he replied. (John 9:12 NLT)

Some people struggle to find God. They go to great lengths to discover Him. Some read the Bible and become lost in the regulations. Others visit holy places like great cathedrals or places in Israel where Jesus lived and walked. There are those who read widely, while others go to church.

> *Salt, when dissolved in water, may disappear, but it does not cease to exist. We can be sure of its presence by tasting the water. Likewise, the indwelling Christ, though unseen, will be made evident to others from the love which He imparts to us.*
> ~ Sundar Singh

Those who didn't see how Jesus healed the man who was born blind were suspicious. It seemed too good to be true. Their question, "Where is He now?" has more meaning than the simple and obvious issue of geographical knowledge. This is the question everyone who wants to be a disciple of Jesus must both ask and try to answer.

On the surface, the modern world looks stripped of spiritual values and is often seen as antagonistic toward Jesus Christ. This means that Jesus' disciples must make a purposeful attempt to be Christians in this world so that if anyone asks, "Where is He now?" the correct answer can be given. Christian disciples must also know where Jesus acts through the caring and compassion of His followers and servants. We can find Jesus every time the naked are clothed and the hungry are fed. When Christians come together in worship, Jesus is there. If one believer turns to God in prayer, Jesus is present. He listens, He acts, He shows love and He cares. Jesus is in the church and in the hearts of individuals – He is everywhere!

Light of the world, penetrate all the dark places of this world.
Amen.

Thrown Out!

Read John 9:24-34

To this they replied, "You were steeped in sin at birth; how dare you lecture us!" And they threw him out. (John 9:34)

Many people spend a lot of time and energy trying to be "in." At school there is always the "in group" that kids want to be part of. There are students who try hard to be "in" with the teachers. And so it continues throughout life. If you want to get ahead, you must be "in." As a result, you get people who think that they must be "in" at church and with God.

The man who was born blind gave the religious authorities a hard time. The deepening of the man's faith could not be stopped by any of their threats. Then they threw him out of the synagogue. He was rejected by his people, removed from their traditions and the teachings about God that could have led him on the right path.

> *The awareness of a need, and the capacity to meet that need: This constitutes a call.*
>
> ~ John R. Mott

But what they didn't realize, was that by throwing him out he could tell of his experience with Jesus. He sowed doubt about their respect for God. He was thrown "out" of the synagogue and directly "in" to the Bible. He was "out" of the flock, but "in" to the gospel. His story would be told through the ages and would open the eyes of many unbelievers and lead them "into the Light".

At Pentecost the Holy Spirit sent the church into the world. When persecution came, He sent His disciples to faraway lands. For Christians, "out" simply means forward in missions, hope, and new life.

Lord Jesus, send me out to where it will really matter. Amen.

Sought and Found

Read John 9: 35-41

Jesus heard that they had thrown him out, and when He found him,
He said, "Do you believe in the Son of Man?" (John 9:35)

It's very frustrating to lose an every-day item and then not be able to find it. Spectacles and keys are inclined to disappear. You search and search and think yourself dizzy trying to remember where you put them last. It's a great relief when you find them again. If a child gets lost, the search is much more serious and the relief much greater when the child is safely back with his parents.

Jesus heard that the man who was born blind had been thrown out of the synagogue and He went to look for him. This man was very important to Jesus, but for everyone else he was just a beggar. For the religious leaders, he was an embarrassment. For his parents, he was a grown man who should look after himself. For Jesus, he was a person in whose thoughts and body God was at work. For this reason Jesus searched for him until He found him. The man didn't find Jesus; Jesus found him.

> *That is the deepest truth of Christian faith; Jesus found me. Our fellowship with Him is rooted in His compassion.*
> ~ William Temple

Jesus is searching for you too. If society has rejected you, if you are estranged from your family, or banned from your church, Jesus hasn't given up on you yet. And He never will. If your name has been blackened or if you have drifted away from God in any way, Jesus is searching for you. He wants to find you and speak to you and rebuild your broken world. If you are lost, let Jesus find you today and lead you back to God.

I thank You, gracious Redeemer, for finding me where I am. Amen.

Not Everybody Can Be Satisfied

Read Matthew 11:2-19

To what can I compare this generation? They are like children sitting in the marketplaces and calling out to others: "'we played the flute for you, and you did not dance; we sang a dirge and you did not mourn.'" (Matthew 11:16-17)

If you try to satisfy everyone, you will ultimately satisfy no one. There comes a time when you should take a stand on account of principle and disagree with others.

To small-minded and immature people, a difference of opinion means conflict and estrangement and they cannot be in the company of someone who holds an opposing view without becoming angry. If you don't agree with them and disagree with their opinion they won't be friends with you.

> *The most satisfying thing in life is to have been able to give a large part of one's self to others.*
> ~ Teilhard de Chardin

You will experience clashes of opinion with others if you are true to your principles, this is inevitable. A wise person regards two things of primary importance: the principles that are supported through study, meditation and prayer; and the right for other people to have a differing point of view.

You do not have the right to force anyone to accept your viewpoint purely for the sake of friendship. Trying to do this only creates a spirit of hostility where there would otherwise be love and understanding.

The fact that you cannot agree with everyone should not influence your relationship with others negatively. As a disciple of Christ, with His love in your heart and mind, you should love even where there is a difference of opinion. It is impossible to agree with everyone, but it should not keep you from loving them.

Help me, Lord, to show respect and love to those from whom I differ.
Amen.

Jesus Stands Watch

Read John 6:16-21

A strong wind was blowing and the waters grew rough. (John 6:18)

We all go through stormy times. Family conflicts threaten to sink our ship; financial crises make you feel lost; it is difficult to find a job and you wonder if you are going to crash into the rocks. In the midst of it all, someone close to you gets seriously ill and all you can foresee is disaster.

The disciples wanted to cross the Sea of Galilee but a storm suddenly arose. Jesus was walking along the beach and reached their destination first. He saw the storm come up and the disciples' desperate attempts to get the boat to shore. He wasn't with them in the storm at this time, but He knew the dangers and watched what happened with concern.

> *Courage consists not in blindly overlooking danger, but in seeing it and conquering it.*
>
> ~ Jean Paul Richter

There might be times when you feel alone on a stormy sea and feel that no matter how you plead, Jesus doesn't turn up. You might not feel as if He is there, but He still watches over you. He knows the power of the storm winds that harass you. He sees the height of the threatening waves. He sees the darkness of the night which surrounds you.

Until Jesus comes (and He will come), do what the disciples did – carry on. Continue with the task you are busy with and don't lose courage. Keep on course – He is nearer than you can ever imagine.

Lord Jesus, thank You for keeping watch over me through the roughest storms and darkest nights of my life. Amen.

Jesus Will Come!

Read John 6:16-21

When they had rowed three or three and a half miles, they saw Jesus approaching the boat, walking on the water; and they were terrified. (John 6:19)

To row a fishing boat is a strenuous task. You have to pull with your arms, heave with your body, push with your legs and turn the oar with your hands. All these actions must be co-ordinated and all the rowers must do them together and at the same time. When the wind is strong and the sea is rough, it then becomes a task not only for the strongest bodies, but for the most courageous hearts.

The disciples were exhausted after their hard battle and then Jesus suddenly appeared. It is useless to speculate how He could have walked on water. It is far better to get to the heart of the story: Jesus came to be with the disciples and to help them in their moment of need.

> *Courage is grace under pressure.*
>
> ~ Ernest Hemingway

Throughout the Bible God "comes" time and time again. The Bible is a story of His many "comings": to Moses, David, Isaiah, Jeremiah, the disciples and Paul, just to name a few. He also "comes" to you and me. However seriously His "coming" is hindered, He always comes. When storms threaten your life's boat, He comes. When your own strength is exhausted, He comes. When your hope is shattered and your faith begins to dwindle; when your thoughts are threatened and your self-esteem is destroyed and your grip on life is beginning to loosen; He comes. He comes to calm, restore and renew you – to make you whole again. Today might be the day He "comes" into your life.

Lord Jesus, come across the water and help me to get through this difficult day. Amen.

Don't Be Afraid!

Read John 6:16-21

He said to them, "It is I; don't be afraid." (John 6:20)

Human beings are incurable worry warts. We worry about our health, old age, our deteriorating lives, and financial affairs. We worry that terrible things will happen to our children and that they will get into trouble. We worry about change and convince ourselves that the world is falling apart. Some people are so conditioned to worry that they aren't happy if there isn't something to worry about.

Time and again Jesus says in the New Testament, "Do not be afraid! I am here!" This isn't just good advice, it is a divine command. If it was possible for strong fishermen to be afraid, even with Jesus close by, then it's no wonder that we also get scared. Jesus encouraged them, and He encourages us too. You don't stop fearing because Jesus is nearby. You leave fear behind when you realize that besides the forces that seem to control your daily life, there is Someone far more powerful – Almighty God!

> *Jesus came treading the waves; and so He puts all the swelling tumults of life under His feet. Christians – why afraid?*
>
> ~ St. Augustine

Behind the human rulers who try to capsize your boat, there is a heavenly Ruler that commands you, "Be strong and courageous. Do not be terrified; do not be discouraged, for the Lord your God will be with you wherever you go" (Josh. 1:9). God is as powerful today as He was in Joshua's time – believe Him, trust Him and obey Him.

Gracious and Almighty God, strengthen those who are worried today and heal them from their fears. Amen.

Appreciating Others

Read Galatians 6:1-10

As we have the opportunity, let us do good to all people, especially to those who belong to the family of believers. (Galatians 6:10)

Never hesitate to express sincere appreciation. It is so easy to take for granted the work someone did with great effort and sacrifice, or to undervalue the sacrifices made for us.

Appreciation does not only delight the hearts of those who receive it, but it also brings you joy.

Guard against being self-centered and taking more from life than you are prepared to put into it. If you make a conscious effort to be aware of things to be grateful for, you will realize that there are a number of blessings that you have taken for granted.

> *The finest test of character is seen in the amount and the power of gratitude we have.*
> ~ Milo H. Gates

Love, loyalty, and generosity of spirit are beautiful gifts people give to you every day. Recapture the God-given insight to see the glory of these daily acts of love that people continuously perform for you. Respond to these with your own acts of grateful love.

Never forget the acts of mercy God has shown you. It is impossible to stand in the glory of our gracious God and still feel depressed. Allow your gratitude for God to spread out into acts of unselfish love for your fellow man. This will become a rich source of blessing to you and others.

If you have the urge to express your appreciation or do a kind deed, don't delay or postpone it. Act as soon as possible to show your appreciation.

Help me, heavenly Father, always to be full of appreciation for the love and help I receive from so many people, and especially from You. I thank You humbly for all Your blessings in Jesus Christ which I undeservingly receive. Amen.

Human Need and Divine Grace

Read Mark 3:1-6

Another time He went to the synagogue, and a man with a shriveled hand was there. (Mark 3:1)

Estate agents believe that for every house on the market there is someone out there who will be perfectly satisfied with it. Their task is to find the buyer, show them the house and settle on the price. One person offers exactly what another person needs.

This is precisely what happened at the synagogue Jesus visited. Jesus brought the grace, mercy and healing love of God. The man He met had a shriveled hand and desperately needed healing. They met, but not by coincidence. They came together to worship God and to hear His word. A Higher hand led them to each other. Jesus offered precisely what the man needed.

No one is safe in his own strength, but he is safe by the grace and mercy of God.

~ Saint Cyprian

For the deepest need in every person's life, God has an abundant supply of grace, strength, and healing. Whatever your need is, He has the power, the word, and the act of compassion that will fit your situation perfectly.

If you are overwhelmed by sorrow, He offers to hold you in the darkness until the light shines again. If you are overwhelmed by stress, He will renew your strength like that of an eagle. If you stare a bleak future in the face, He promises to guide you. Whatever your need might be, God grants you His abundant grace through Jesus.

Lord and Master, please meet me, here and now, with all my need. Amen.

Will He ... or Won't He?

Read Mark 3:1-6

Some of them were looking for a reason to accuse Jesus, so they watched Him closely to see if He would heal him on the Sabbath .

(Mark 3:2)

One of Satan's most clever tricks is to make your thoughts get stuck on one or other difficult theological question. It can be quite pleasurable to speculate over an intellectual question with "ifs", "whys" and "wherefores". A popular topic is the Trinity. How on earth can three be one, or one be three? You can reason, debate and argue about this for hours. It is intellectually stimulating and historically interesting. The real danger of this type of seemingly laudable exercise is that it can easily lead you away from the simple faith that you need to live as a Christian disciple.

Let us learn more about the power of temptation in order to avoid it.

~ John Owen

The Pharisees played a similar game with Jesus. They never doubted that Jesus could heal the man; the question was rather whether He would! For them, to heal a man on the Sabbath was equivalent to work and therefore unlawful, unless the patient was in danger of dying. They overlooked the core issue. The law was originally given to protect life. But instead, it had become an obstacle to life. Jesus was willing and able to give a quality life. For Jesus it was primarily about what God wanted to do with the disabled man. It was not about the trivialities of rules and regulations.

Don't get sidelined by less important issues, arguments or debates. Focus on the main issues: Put your trust in Jesus and refuse to be taken in by clever arguments. Look up to Jesus and be healed, strengthened, and empowered.

Savior and Master, keep my thoughts focused on You so that I can experience Your healing power. Amen.

"Stretch Out Your Hand!"

Read Mark 3:1-6

He said to the man, "Stretch out your hand." He stretched out his hand and his hand was completely restored. (Mark 3:5)

You can decide whether to work with God or against Him. There are people who ridicule the Christian faith; they work against God. Sometimes people who profess to be followers of Jesus do things that reveal that their faith is not very deep or sincere. They put other people off and thereby oppose God.

In the account of Jesus and the man with the shriveled hand, the Pharisees worked against Jesus. They even began to look for ways to kill Him. In contrast, the man with the shriveled hand did exactly what Jesus commanded him to do. He worked with Jesus and didn't try to argue or prove a point. He came in his weakness and need; this is the way we should also come to Jesus.

We are all healers that can reach out and offer health, and we are all patients in constant need of help.

~ Henri Nouwen

However strong you think you are, come to Jesus in your weakness and need. Forget about clever arguments and debates. Meet Jesus face to face and bring only your problems with you – your shortcomings, your weaknesses, your emptiness, and your need. Let Jesus touch you at the point of your greatest weakness. Present Him with anything that is broken in your life – whether it be your body, your spiritual life, your conscience, or your relationships. He makes bad things good again – He wants to do this for you too.

Lord, I come to You with my broken life. Please touch me and heal me. Amen.

Life or Death

Read John 4:43-54

Jesus replied, "You may go, your son will live." Then the father realized that this was the exact time at which Jesus had said to him, "Your son will live." (John 4:50, 53)

Death is the greatest of all mysteries. A healthy fear of death determines many things that we believe. After administering a lethal injection to a suffering animal, a vet remarked, "It's strange: we don't think twice about putting an animal to sleep, but we can't convince ourselves to do it to people." When death looms threateningly we keep saying, "Where there is life, there is hope!"

The Bible tells us that life is threatened by death. This is the thing we fear most, for ourselves and for our loved ones. Paul viewed death as "the last enemy to be destroyed" (1 Cor. 15:26). Jesus establishes life, because in Him life has triumphed over death. This is why so many incidents in His earthly ministry involve healing. Every miracle of healing is preparation for, and an indication of, the final miracle – the resurrection.

> *Our old history ends with the cross; our new history begins with the resurrection.*
>
> ~ Watchman Nee

In this story of the healing of the royal official's son, three times it is repeated that the boy lives. This is to emphasize Jesus' triumphant power over death, because Jesus is the Source of life.

Life and death battle endlessly in every human being, young or old, sick or healthy. It is happening in your body at this very moment. If you have let Jesus into your life through faith, then you have the Source of life within you – and this is the kind of life that Jesus wants to lead you to.

Thank You, resurrected Lord Jesus, that You triumph in me now and forevermore. Amen.

Privileges and Responsibilities

Read Ephesians 3:14-21

Christ will make His home in your hearts as you trust in Him. (Ephesians 3:17 NLT)

There is no substitute whatsoever for a personal relationship with the living Christ. Doctrines and creeds are essential to clarify the Christian faith.

Unfortunately, many people place the main emphasis on the peripheral issues and forget that they are only guidelines that help direct us to a true meaning with the risen Savior.

The indwelling Christ is one of the greatest themes of the gospel of Jesus. The committed disciple of Christ should not use knowing Christ as an excuse to withdraw from the world. To isolate yourself from your fellow man because they do not share the same spiritual experiences as you is merely spiritual arrogance. It leads to fruitless isolation and cries out against the example Jesus Christ set when He lived and worked on earth.

> *We don't follow Him in order to be loved; we are loved, so we follow Him.*
> ~ Neil Anderson

Because Christ lives in you, you have specific responsibilities. You are responsible for reflecting the glory of Christ. To think that non-Christians form their opinion of Christ through the way you live should be an eye-opener. After all, they see the way you handle certain situations that they have to face themselves.

The great privilege in giving yourself to Christ is in the fact that He knows everything about you. He supplements your imperfection with His complete perfection; your weaknesses He strengthens with His power; your lack of love He transforms through His perfect love. Nothing can surpass the peace and love that He offers to those who are rooted and grounded in His love.

I praise You, Lord Jesus, for the privilege of belonging to You, and in Your Name I accept my responsibilities. Amen.

The Essence of Christianity

Read Philippians 3:7-16

God is working in you, giving you the desire to obey Him and the power to do what pleases Him. (Philippians 2:13 NLT)

There are many worthy organizations that use the name of Christ to emphasize their achievements and credibility. Even political parties and social groups use the Master's name to make these groups acceptable to the public.

By using His name to further their ideals or products, they dishonor Him. They make promises they can't keep; they make decisions that oppose His Word and His will; and they disregard the interests of those who are dependent on them.

True Christianity is a life changing power that starts to work when you give yourself completely to the living Christ and accept His discipline and way of living. From whichever side you approach dynamic Christianity, at the end of the day it is about a Man-to-man relationship. To try and improve society and make it Christian without personal contact with the living Christ, will only lead to frustration and failure.

> *A revival is nothing else than a new beginning of obedience to God.*
> ~ Charles H. Finney

A new society doesn't depend on new laws, but on new people. The fact that Jesus changes the character and personality of those who accept Him in faith is one of the miracles of the Christian message. If you want to see a new world, start with yourself and make Him Lord of your life.

Holy Master, through the work of the Holy Spirit, give me character and a personality that are acceptable to You. Amen.

Perseverance until the End

Read Philippians 3:7-16

I press on toward the goal to win the prize for which God has called me heavenward in Christ Jesus. (Philippians 3:14)

It's fascinating to watch a weaver build his nest. One is amazed by the stubborn determination and perseverance this bird shows and the exceptional attention he gives to make the nest perfect. When the task is then rejected by the mate, or destroyed by strong wind, the brave bird starts building the nest from scratch.

The Christian can learn much from this because his path is seldom smooth and easy. Jesus warned His followers about the stumbling blocks and pot holes that would lie ahead if they proclaimed the gospel in His name. In your own spiritual journey there comes a time when your most honest attempts are rejected by others. You may also face a crumbling faith when hit by disaster or grief. In your Christian witness you will undoubtedly know that dark moment when you will want to ask the unanswerable question, "Why?"

Victory goes to the player who makes the next-to-last mistake.
~ Savielly Grigorievitch Tartakower

Now is the time, illogical as it might seem for many people, to turn to Jesus for strength and determination to walk the path He has chosen for you to the end. Hold fast to the Rock of Ages in the face of obstacles and persevere for Him. He will never let you down and in Christ, victory is assured!

Savior, lead me step by step so that I will persevere in following Your leading until the end. Amen.

To Be Effective and Productive

Read 2 Peter 1:3-15

For if you possess these qualities in increasing measure, they will keep you from being ineffective and unproductive in your knowledge of our Lord Jesus Christ. (2 Peter 1:8)

On one occasion a dedicated child of God prayed, "Lord, let me not live to be useless." This is surely one of the most productive prayers that has ever been said.

Unfortunately, some people lead empty and pointless lives. They fill their days with frivolous and foolish entertainment. Christian believers are called to live effective and productive lives, because only then will your life have meaning. You can do this in two ways: Firstly, you acquire as much knowledge about Jesus as you can. You read His Word, meditate on His deeds and seek to bring your own thoughts and deeds in line with His example.

Secondly, you continuously grow in these things. You grow in Christ by conforming to His image more and more. You expand your circle of love. You become friendlier. You sharpen your understanding of truth as you discover it in Jesus. You learn to pray more. Daily, you become more submitted to Him. He becomes the One who fills your life with purpose and meaning. In this way you become more useful to Him and you strive to do His will and work. It requires increasing love. The miracle is that in this Jesus is also your Savior.

> *Jesus Christ did not come to this world primarily to say something or even to be something. He did not only come to lead people to a greater and better life through His example; through His life, death and resurrection, He came to give life to everyone who was dead in their sins and transgressions.*
>
> ~ Michel de Montaigne

Lord and Savior, teach me to work in such a way that my life is not useless. Amen.

June

His Eternal Friendship

"Greater love has no one than this,
that he lay down his life for his friends.
You are My friends if you do what I command."
~ John 15:13-14

Friendship consists in forgetting what one gives,
and remembering what one receives.
~ Alexandre Dumas

*S*avior and Teacher,
You sacrificed Your life on the cross
to prove that there is no greater love
than to lay down one's life for one's friends.
This is how I know that You are my Friend!
Help me to remember that You have
promised to always be with me,
until the end of the world.
Thank You for leading me and
giving me direction in times of confusion;
for comforting and encouraging me in times of sorrow;
for strengthening and inspiring me in times of temptation;
and for consoling me in times of loneliness.
Thank You that there is nothing
that can separate me from Your love.
Help me, through Your example,
to be a true and faithful friend to others;
to always be willing to share my possessions with them;
and to pray for them without ceasing.
Help me to be a living embodiment of Your love
so that my friends will see You through
the compassion in my eyes;
experience Your love through my smile
and sense Your support in the touch of my hands.
I pray this in the ever-present name,
Jesus, my Savior.

Amen.

Family

Read Luke 8:19-25

He replied, "My mother and brothers are those who hear God's word and put it into practice." (Luke 8:21)

It is good and proper to cherish our family relationships. When disaster strikes and family members gather around, other people are amazed at the support family members can offer each other. Then it's usually said, "That's what family is for after all."

For Jesus, family meant more than only blood relations. Throughout His entire life He obeyed His "other Father" in heaven, and that Father's will and desires were His commands. He dedicated Himself fully to achieve that Father's purpose. Jesus was so totally committed to hearing God's Word and applying it in practice that He could say, "I and the Father are One" (John 10:30)

> *God is the first object of our love. Its next office is to bear the defects of others. And we should begin the practice of this amidst our own household.*
> ~ John Wesley

and, "The world must learn that I love the Father and that I do exactly what My Father has commanded Me" (John 14:31).

Obedience to God bound Jesus inseparably to anyone and everyone who was committed to the same goal. When Jesus said, "My mother and brothers are those who hear God's Word and put it into practice," He did not disrespect His own family. He simply extended His family circle to include His spiritual family who were one with Him in their faithfulness and loyalty to the heavenly Father.

This means that you are one of Christ's brothers or sisters when you hear God's Word, submit yourself to it and obey it. You grow in grace within His family. It is a network of people who belong together because they are *in* Christ. What a privilege this is for every Christian believer!

Thank You, Lord Jesus, that I have the privilege of being part of Your family. Amen.

Our Christian Lives Must Grow Spiritually

Read Ephesians 4:9-16

Until we all reach unity in the faith and in the knowledge of the Son of God and become mature, attaining to the whole measure of the fullness of Christ. (Ephesians 4:13)

The quality of your spiritual life must be determined by high standards. Remember that it is impossible to exceed the standard that you have set for yourself.

Many people who don't go to church claim that they are as good as those who attend church regularly. The average church member won't argue, because he knows that churchgoers aren't saints, but redeemed sinners who, despite their shortcomings, sincerely love their Lord.

> *The mark of a saint is not perfection, but consecration. A saint is not a man without faults, but a man who has given himself without reservation to God.*
>
> ~ W. T. Richardson

Therefore, the standard of holiness that is set by Scripture is not attained by comparing non-Christians with Christians. The comparison is always with the life of our Savior, Jesus Christ. It is a disturbing prospect for anyone who desires to attain such spiritual heights.

Christ is the perfect and final standard for all Christians, and to grow in likeliness to Him must be every Christian's goal. No matter how insignificant and uneventful the beginning might be, let us begin to grow in likeliness to Him.

After you have set yourself a spiritually-inspired standard, don't become discouraged by your imperfection or past failures, but make time to intimately spend with the Master each day.

Lord Jesus, I place You in the center of my thoughts and pray that I will become more aware of Your Presence in my life. Amen.

Calm in the Eye of the Storm

Read Luke 24:36-49

Jesus stood among them and said to them, "Peace be with you." (Luke 24:36)

At times life is full of frightening and horrifying experiences for all of us. These experiences can come at you from many different directions. Before you realize it, they cause you to feel stressed.

Since you are continuously under pressure, it is imperative that you develop inner reserves from which you can draw strength in situations fraught with stress. Only in this way will you be able to withstand storms.

The most important source of power in such a time is the peace that Jesus Christ offers to everyone who loves Him, lives close to Him and serves Him in obedience. To possess His particular peace and to live according to it every day is liberating and fulfilling, it is available to everyone who is willing to maintain being a Christian disciple in spirit and thought.

> *The world can create trouble in peace, but God can create peace in trouble.*
> ~ Thomas Watson

When stress occurs and things start falling to pieces, refuse to be swept along – purposefully guard against bad temper and irritability.

Do not get caught up in the breakneck pace of the masses surrounding you. Stop, calm down and spend a few minutes alone with Christ. Once again, just confirm your dependence on Him and believe that His peace is available to you.

Very soon your tired and rushed spirit will become calm and His peace will revive your life like refreshing rain. Nothing and no one can take this peace from because it is God Himself who whispers to you, "Peace be with you!"

Eternal God, who gives me peace in Jesus Christ, lead me to quiet waters where there is peace in the midst of the hustle and bustle of life. Amen.

On the Other Side of the Cheering

Read John 2:13-25

While He was in Jerusalem at the Passover Feast, many people saw the miraculous signs He was doing and believed in His name. (John 2:23)

There come times when we fervently wish for a miracle. Many people pray to God to heal a loved one who is seriously ill; or to eliminate someone who they despise. Some people even dare to bargain with God for a miracle: Heal my mother and I will believe in You and serve You!

Miracles do happen. Creation was a miracle, so was the exodus out of Egypt. The birth of Christ was a miracle and the Resurrection was the greatest miracle of all. Some people followed Jesus to see a real miracle take place in front of their eyes and to join in the cheering. Others discovered that the miracles were far more than just entertainment.

> *At strategic moments God again and again manifested Himself to man by miracles so they had outward, confirming evidence that the words they heard from God's servants were true.*
>
> *~ Billy Graham*

The truth that they discovered was that in Jesus, God came to earth in the flesh. They knew that He could do wonderful things in and through them. Through the miracles they heard God calling them to believe in Him and serve Him, and they gave themselves unconditionally to Him. On the other side of the applause there was a totally new life – a life of discipleship, surrender and commitment.

It is just as big a miracle when an unbeliever accepts the faith, when a sinner repents before God, or when a believer grows in the faith and takes responsibility for spiritual leadership. Jesus wants to perform a miracle *within* each of us which will be just as wonderful as the miracle you want Him to perform *for* you.

Miracle-working Jesus, thank You for the miracle that You have performed in my life. Amen.

He Knows Us through and Through

Read John 2:13-25

He did not need man's testimony about man, for He knew what was in a man. (John 2:25)

Every person has his own peculiarities: some people look funny; others speak funny and others act in strange ways. Some people are good, others are not so good and some are even wicked. Most of us are a peculiar mix of good and bad.

You probably see yourself as normal and others as abnormal. Other people think the same way you do. Some people develop amazing insight into the behavior of others. But even then, some things still surprise them. Jesus "knew what was in a man."

Christ knows who, what and how you are. He knows your peculiarities and personal way of thinking. He knows about your stubborn conservatism and your blind spots. He knows your mistakes, your failures, and your weaknesses. He knows the hidden motives behind every good deed you do. He notices the way you twist the truth to place yourself in a good light. He knows the person behind the mask you sometimes wear.

Above all the grace and the gifts that Christ gives to His beloved is that of overcoming self.

~ St. Francis of Assisi

He also knows about the problems you have to overcome, the difficulties you are struggling with, the battles you must fight and the criticism you must endure. He knows about the good things you have done that have passed by unnoticed. He knows about the love you have shared that was never returned. He believes in you and has hope for you and everything that He wants to accomplish through you. Don't disappoint Him.

Gracious Jesus, You know me better than anyone else and You still love me. That is a miracle. Amen.

In the Darkness of the Night

Read John 3:1-13

There was a man of the Pharisees named Nicodemus, a member of the Jewish ruling council. He came to Jesus at night. (John 3:1-2)

Some people are afraid of the dark, especially if they have been attacked or burgled. But there are other forms of darkness that can surround you. Sorrow or doubt can become a "midnight" experience. To discover that you have been let down by those who swore you could trust them plunges you into darkness. In the same way sickness, worry, unemployment, guilt and confusion can drive you into darkness.

> *Only in Jesus Christ do we have the certainty of redemption, forgiveness of sins, admission to the family of God and the guarantee of eternal life after death.*
>
> ~ Luis Palau

Nicodemus came to Jesus in the dark, not just in the darkness of night but in the darkness of his doubt and confusion. The faith he upheld, and of which he was a leading figure, posed more questions than answers. He knew the rules, but he didn't know the God who made the rules. He might have been a shining light in the community, but he himself lived in darkness – a teacher who himself had to be taught. He came in the night so that no one would know that he met with Jesus. But Jesus turned on the light of truth and faith for Nicodemus and gave him a new beginning.

No matter what form of darkness has descended on you, do exactly what Nicodemus did: turn to Jesus Christ. Tell Him about your problems, fears, loneliness and unbelief. Open yourself to His wisdom, truth and might. Benefit from His strength, love and dominion over the powers of darkness. When you come to Jesus, you move from the darkness of night into the bright light of His truth and love.

Savior and Comforter, lead me out of the night of my confusion and into the dawn of Your light. Amen.

The Road to Forgiveness

Read Psalm 32:1-11

I confessed all my sins to You and stopped trying to hide my guilt. I said to myself, "I will confess my rebellion to the LORD." And You forgave me! All my guilt is gone. (Psalm 32:5 NLT)

We are not generalizing when we say that we are living in a world that is broken and torn apart by sin. There are so many perils surrounding us, so many sinister temptations around us and so many chains enslaving us.

Time and again we are forced into the darkness and we sit trapped, surrounded by the cold prison walls in which sin has incarcerated us. But there is a way out of this misery. It is the way leading to Jesus Christ. It is the way wherein we have to confess our sins in sincere repentance.

> *Success is to be measured not by wealth, power, or fame, but by the ratio between what a man is and what he might be.*
> ~ H. G. Wells

If you come to Christ with your tarnished life and confess your sins, then forget the failures and disappointments of the past and reach out for new life in Jesus Christ. Forget your disgrace and shame by accepting that you are a child of the King. Forget your defeats and follow Christ on the road to victory.

Keep your eyes fixed upon Him as the Perfecter and Finisher of your faith with the expressed conviction: "You are my hiding place; You will protect me from trouble and surround me with songs of deliverance" (Ps. 32:7).

Our merciful and eternally strong God is capable in all circumstances. If you faithfully fight sin in His powerful name you will taste victory. Then you can walk into the future bravely and with a song of deliverance in your heart.

How wonderful is the deliverance You provide, my Lord and Savior. I thank You that I can bring my sin and distress to You and leave singing songs of deliverance. Amen.

Where There's a Will ...

Read Mark 2:1-12

Some men came, bringing to Him a paralytic, carried by four of them. Since they could not get him to Jesus because of the crowd, they made an opening in the roof above Jesus and, after digging through it, lowered the mat the paralyzed man was lying on. (Mark 2:3-4)

There are people who will do anything to accomplish their goal: they will spare no expense; they refuse to get discouraged or unnerved and they do not allow problems to put them off. They simply sweep all objections aside and overcome every stumbling stone in their path. They never give up. These people are often looking to enrich themselves, or become more important or famous. It takes a very special kind of person to have this persistence and tenacity for the sake of someone else.

If Jesus Christ be God and died for me, then no sacrifice can be too great for me to make for Him.

~ C. T. Studd

The four men in today's reading were unstoppable in their desire to bring their friend to Jesus. He couldn't possibly do it for himself and they knew that they were his only hope. Even worse – Jesus would be gone the next day. For them it was now or never!

How determined are you to get to Jesus for help with healing, guidance, instruction, or forgiveness? What will you do to get your spouse, children, brother or friend to the only Person who can heal the root of evil that is harassing them? For how long are you willing to pray? How much are you willing to give? What stumbling blocks are you willing to overcome? How much energy are you willing to expend? Today there are many people who have faith in Christ because someone else cared long and seriously enough to make sure that they reached Jesus.

Savior and Redeemer, let me never give up until .... reaches You. Amen.

Substitutionary Faith

Read Mark 2:1-12

When Jesus saw their faith, he said to the paralytic, "Son, your sins are forgiven." (Mark 2:5)

Faith is a critical and crucial component of anyone's religious beliefs. Faith is necessary to know God, obtain His help and receive His love. You often hear someone say, "I wish I had more faith, because then everything would be so much easier." Sometimes we think that we can strengthen our faith like an athlete who trains longer and harder as the big race approaches. We assume that faith is a requirement God sets before He will work in and through us.

There is absolutely nothing in the story of the paralytic man who was lowered down through the roof to indicate that he had that "extra dose" of faith that we think was necessary before Jesus would

> *Faith is the deliberate confidence in the character of God whose ways you may not understand at the time.*
>
> ~ Oswald Chambers

heal him. Our reading today is actually quite amazing: "When Jesus saw *their* faith ... " He forgave the paralytic man's sins. The man himself didn't take a test of faith, but his friends did. How exciting it must have been for Jesus to look up and see the hole in the roof and the anxious faces looking down at Him expectantly, their hands sore and bruised from their efforts to accomplish their deed of faith.

In Jesus' eyes this faith was enough: simple, strong, self-assured and firm. The core of the story is: Jesus is ready and waiting to perform His deed of love, whether our faith is strong or not – even if we come in the strength of someone else's desperate hope which binds us to Him.

Redeemer, thank You for those people whose faith brought me to You in all my weakness and need. Amen.

Recognize Jesus in the Small Things

Read Luke 24:13-24

As they talked and discussed these things with each other, Jesus Himself came up and walked along with them; but they were kept from recognizing Him. (Luke 24:15-16)

Whatever it was that "kept them from recognizing" the glory of the risen Savior, accomplished its goal. When Jesus joined them on the road to Emmaus, their thoughts were consumed by the events of the previous few days and their emotions fluctuated between depression and vague hope. They knew that Jesus was dead, but a woman said that she had seen Him. What were they to believe? In these circumstances they sought the haven of familiar surroundings where they could bury their sorrow and talk and pray about their problems in seclusion.

> *The steady discipline of intimate friendship with Jesus results in men becoming like Him.*
>
> ~ H. E. Fosdick

The Stranger did all the talking while they walked toward their retreat. As they listened, they began to see things in a new light. Their sorrow lessened; their depression dissipated, and they began to understand more clearly that one's spiritual life has both mountain-top experiences and deep valleys.

In His own time and at a simple meal, Christ revealed Himself to them. His preparation for this revelation was a scriptural explanation about Himself. But it was only after He spent time with them and prepared them for it, that they understood.

It is still the same today. While you read His Word, and listen to Him quietly in your prayer time, Jesus waits to reveal Himself to you. Keep your mind clear, awake and receptive and you will recognize Christ in the unexpected and simple things He does.

Heavenly Savior, help me to recognize You in the simple and beautiful things in life while You walk beside me. Amen.

The Danger of Success

Read Luke 12:13-21

"Watch out! Be on your guard against all kinds of greed; a man's life does not consist in the abundance of his possessions." (Luke 12:15)

We live in a success-driven society. If someone in the business world achieves success and climbs higher on the corporate ladder, he is described as successful and he wins the respect and admiration of society.

Success is an indescribable experience. It is achieved through hard work and the acceptance of responsibility. It results in a deep satisfaction that can seldom be achieved in any other way.

However, one of the dangers of success is that, besides pride, haughtiness develops. Success then warps the individual's personality, leading to the denial of his humble beginnings. He can even refuse to acknowledge those who stood by him and helped him reach his high position.

> *It is not your business to succeed, but to do right: when you have done so, the rest lies with God.*
>
> ~ C. S. Lewis

Success must always be handled with caution, because no matter how successful you are, the possibility of failure is always present. Often this happens because of circumstances beyond your control. It's unsettling to think that however successful you are, there is always the possibility of failure. The crucial question is whether your success has equipped you to handle failure.

It is a wise person who builds his success on spiritual principles, and who regularly remembers, through prayer and meditation, that all achievements are a gift from God and should be used for His glory. Whatever may cross your path – success or failure – with God's help you will always be able to handle it through His wisdom and strength.

Faithful Master, let Your Spirit constantly remind me that I can accomplish nothing worthy without you. Amen.

Keep on Track!

Read Luke 9:57-62

As they were walking along the road, a man said to Him, "I will follow You wherever You go." (Luke 9:57)

When a new Christian has experienced conversion, he has a burning desire to serve the Lord in every facet of life and in every moment of the day. It is heart-warming and wonderful to see the enthusiasm of new Christians after they have been transformed and have dedicated their lives to the Lord's service.

However, at this stage it is crucial that new Christians guard against the attacks of the Evil One. They might be bubbling over with enthusiasm to serve the Lord, but if others don't share their enthusiasm, or if more mature Christians try to curb their enthusiasm, it is easy for the Tempter to dampen this enthusiasm through the weapons of discouragement and disappointment.

> *Some suffer great temptations at the beginning of their conversion, others toward the end, while some are troubled almost constantly throughout their life.*
>
> ~ Thomas à Kempis

In your walk with Christ and while you enthusiastically follow Him, always be aware of the devil and his subtle attempts to lead you off the path the Lord has prescribed for you. Be faithful and constant in your prayer life and open yourself to the guidance and influence of the Holy Spirit. He will give you the ability to remain faithful to Christ and to live within His will.

Lord and Savior, great and mighty, watch over me through the rough seas of life. Be my map and compass so that I will safely reach my eternal destination. Amen.

Jesus Is Calling

Read Matthew 4:18-22

At once they left their nets and followed Him. (Matthew 4:20)

The call to discipleship causes much introspection and sometimes sadness for those who feel that they have been called to serve the Master. Often they are consumed by doubt for various reasons.

The questions that trouble them are many and diverse. To name but a few: Do I have the ability for this? Will I be able to provide for myself and my family? Do I have the time for this?

We must remember that Jesus will never call a person without providing for him. He alone will give you the time and the abilities to stand in His service. All you have to do is be willing to surrender your life to Him and leave your worries and doubts to Him. Someone once said, "Jesus doesn't call the able, He enables those He calls."

> *God doesn't call people who are qualified, He calls people who are willing, and He qualifies them.*
>
> ~ Richard Parker

When the first disciples heard the Master's call, they gave up everything – especially themselves – so that they could follow Him. Immediately their lives gained new meaning and reached heights that were unthinkable until that moment. The living Christ offers the same wonderful and fulfilling life to you if you dedicate yourself to His service.

Savior, thank You that I heard Your call and followed You. Amen.

You are Never Alone

Read Matthew 28:11-20

"I am with you always, to the very end of the age." (Matthew 28:20)

The awareness of the presence of the risen and living Savior is a basic prerequisite for meaningful discipleship. We should always guard against our faith becoming a tradition that lacks vivacity and strength. It can so easily happen if we do not continuously experience the presence of the living Christ in our lives. It does not matter how long you have been following the Christian way of life, you must know Christ as a living reality.

> *The love of the Father is like a sudden rain shower that will pour forth when you least expect it, catching you up into wonder and praise.*
>
> ~ Richard J. Foster

Christ reveals Himself in your life as a result of your simple faith and because you have invited Him to take control of your life. Many people find it extremely difficult to give themselves entirely to someone they cannot see or hear.

If you believe His Word completely, which says that you can know Him at all times through the strength of His resurrection, new horizons of spiritual experience will open up to you.

Realize that Christ is with you every moment, firmly believe this and live like someone who is in His loving company every moment. Faith is a firm belief in those things we cannot see (Heb. 11:1). Believing that He is with you will give you strength to face the challenges of each day.

In prosperity and adversity, in joy and in sorrow, His delivering Presence will lead you to a life of abundant inner peace and strength. And this is not only for today, but also for tomorrow and the day after that, to the end of time.

I praise You for Your living Presence, O Lord! It fills my life with certainty. Do not let the world around me ever rob me of this wonderful privilege. Amen.

An Awakening Faith

Read Acts 3:11-21

By faith in the name of Jesus, this man whom you see and know was made strong. It is Jesus' name and the faith that comes through Him that has given this complete healing to him, as you can all see. (Acts 3:16)

For many people, spiritual awakening comes with dramatic suddenness. They might lead a self-centered, selfish and unloving existence, without ever thinking of people's needs around them. And then they come to stand before the challenges of Christ and they react in a way that surprises even themselves. The transformation of their lives can be likened to moving from darkness into light.

Being a Christian is more than just an instantaneous conversion – it is a daily process whereby you grow to be more and more like Christ.

~ Billy Graham

Those who have experienced such a dramatic life-change must never judge those who came to faith in Jesus in other ways. There are many believers who witnessed the Spirit in their own spirits, but who can't confirm the exact date of their conversion. From childhood, through the influence of Christian parents or dedicated Sunday school teachers, their faith has been awakened and they have served the Master with sincere love for as long as they can remember.

A faith that slowly unfolds might not have the impact of a sudden spiritual awakening, but there can be no doubt about its sincerity. Christian faith comes in different ways to various people. The way it comes is quite unimportant. People who claim that they have a living faith should demonstrate Christian qualities in their lives.

Holy Jesus, may the method of my conversion never blind me to the Christian qualities of people who were led to You in a different way.
Amen.

The Saving Love of God

Read Ephesians 2:11-21

But now in Christ Jesus you who once were far away have been brought near through the blood of Christ. (Ephesians 2:13)

In the dark days before the abolishment of slavery, the unfortunate victims of this cruel practice were bought for money by their masters. They belonged to the buyer completely, so much so that their lives were under his control and they were forced to obey and fear him.

As a Christian, you belong to God, but in stark contrast to the slave, you were bought and redeemed from sin and death through the blood of the Master, Jesus Christ. You belong to Him and obey Him out of love and not fear. Your desire to serve Him is born from the knowledge that He loved you so much that He laid down His life for you.

> *We find freedom when we find God; we lose it when we lose Him.*
>
> ~ Paul E. Sherer

When you meditate on the great sacrifice that Christ made on your behalf, you experience a burning desire to serve Him in every area of your life. The fact that you "live" is exclusively thanks to Him.

The sheer wonder of His grace is that Jesus leaves the decision up to you. Can you ignore this love?

O Love, inconceivably great, that You died for me, a wretched slave.
Amen.

Holy Extravagance

Read Mark 14:3-9

Some of those present were saying indignantly to one another, "Why this waste of perfume? It could have been sold for more than a year's wages and the money given to the poor." And they rebuked her harshly. (Mark 14:4-5)

There are people who constantly talk about what they do for the church and for God. Others tell you how much time they spend in prayer, or self-importantly about all that God has done for them. However, true love for Christ does not boast. It finds ways to shower Jesus with love, regardless of whether others see it or not.

To get an idea of what the woman's gift to Jesus in today's reading was worth, remind yourself about your yearly income. Then ask yourself how much you have given to Christ. It will probably surprise you to see how little you give. This woman must have completely emptied her savings to buy the perfume – all as a token of her love for Christ.

> *I have held many things in my hands, and I have lost them all; but whatever I have placed in God's hands, that I still possess.*
>
> ~ Martin Luther

Those who complained that it was an extravagant waste of money were correct in a sense. But love lives to give – and then give again! Love doesn't count the cost. It only thinks of the joy the receiver of the gift will experience. It can be said that the gifts that are given to God are extravagant, but they bring God joy. It also brings joy to the giver, if the gift was really meaningful. It is not good to waste, but it is good to shower God with love. He delights in it as much as He delights in our prayers.

Lord Jesus, may my love for You never have a price tag. Amen.

The Power of the Spoken Word

Read Proverbs 25:1-12

A word aptly spoken is like apples of gold in settings of silver.
(Proverbs 25:11)

A single word can make a difference in a person's life. This is why the way you say something is vitally important. Some people have a way with words. By choosing the right word at the right time they can radically change a person's life. The words a person uses can also have a devastating effect on another's life.

Sometimes people are in need of a sympathetic or inspiring word because showing sincere concern and understanding for a person can make a huge difference and brighten up their day. A word of appreciation or advice is never wasted; even constructive criticism or a loving reprimand can be advantageous to the recipient.

Kind words can be short and easy to speak, but their echoes are truly endless.

~ Mother Teresa

A person should never be afraid to talk, but at the same time you should choose your wording and timing cautiously through the power of the Holy Spirit. Avoid unnecessary flattery as well as harsh words; be sincere and speak with the love of Jesus in your heart. By doing this, you will endlessly enrich the person you talk to and yourself.

May the words of my mouth and the meditation of my heart be pleasing in Your sight, O LORD, *my Rock and my Redeemer (Psalm 19:14).* Amen.

Christ's Heart of Love

Read Matthew 9:35-38

When He saw the crowds, He had compassion on them, because they were harassed and helpless, like sheep without a shepherd. (Matthew 9:36)

Sympathy and compassion are outstanding characteristics of Christ's unique personality. They were a sign of His greatness, and not of weakness, and were at the center of His life and teachings.

Scripture emphasizes that ordinary people enjoyed listening to Jesus and traveled far distances to hear Him speak. The short report we have of His teachings reveals the depth of His wisdom and the uniqueness of the revelation of God. Yet, the spirit in which these words were spoken

You may call God love, you may call God goodness. But the best name for God is compassion.

~ Meister Eckhart

not only touched people's thoughts, but won their hearts. They were aware of His love for them and responded by giving their love to Him in return.

Because the eternal Christ lives today, His compassion towards people is as real as it was when He walked in Galilee. When we read the gospel story and rejoice in the truth that is revealed, our hearts are warmed by the reality of His love for us.

If you feel that life has treated you unkindly, or if you have failed and are filled with despair; if you don't know where to turn to for fresh inspiration and strength, remember the compassion of Jesus. He is with you in your misery. He encourages you through the power of His love to stand up and start rebuilding your life.

Compassionate Master, may Your indescribable love renew my life so that I can rejoice in Your ways. Amen.

"If You Are Willing ... "

Read Mark 1:40-45

A man with leprosy came to Him and begged Him on his knees, "If You are willing, You can make me clean." (Mark 1:40)

People who are seriously ill often become desperate. When one method of medical help fails to bring about healing, the patient becomes depressed and will then resort to trying alternative medicines in an attempt to get healing.

Leprosy was a feared disease. Besides the horrendous physical effects, the person was cut off from all contact with people in order to prevent the disease from spreading. The man in today's reading heard about Jesus' healing powers and was convinced that Jesus could heal him. He just didn't know if Jesus would. No one else would dare to touch him. For him life wasn't worthwhile, therefore he "begged Jesus on his knees."

> *We turn to God for help when our foundations are shaking, only to learn that it is God who is shaking them.*
>
> ~ Charles C. West

Jesus always reacted when people threw themselves before Him. Those who came in their emptiness, desperation and sickness, who had no pretences about their ailments, always touched a deep chord in Jesus' heart.

This is always the way we must come to Jesus. Don't come and plead on the grounds of your good deeds, your religious ties, your high degree of education, your money or your reputation. Come as you are – lost, depressed, lonely, confused, helpless, guilty and foolish. Forget about the failures and foolish mistakes, the unanswered questions or the gnawing doubt. Come as you are and cast yourself on the grace of Jesus. He can and wants to make you whole.

"Just as I am, Thou wilt receive, wilt welcome, pardon, cleanse, relieve, because Thy promise I believe, O Lamb of God, I come!"

Amen.

The Compassion of Jesus

Read Mark 1:40-45

Filled with compassion, Jesus reached out His hand and touched the man. "I am willing," He said. "Be clean!" (Mark 1:41)

A group of Christian pastors sat talking on the deck of a passenger ship. They didn't notice anything when a member of the crew walked past. Suddenly an older pastor jumped up, hurried to the crew member and called him back. The pastor pointed to the man's hand and they saw that it was heavily bandaged. After a moment's discussion, the crew member carried on walking and the pastor sat down again. He had noticed the crew member's bandaged hand as he walked past and asked about his injury. It was an act of compassion – unasked for, unnecessary, intuitive and beautiful.

God does not comfort us to make us comfortable, but to make us comforters.

~ J. H. Jowett

Jesus was motivated by compassion. It wasn't simply one of His character traits – He was *filled* with compassion. Compassion made it necessary for Him to heal the sick, to feed the crowds, to still the storm, to forgive a dying thief and to visit a tax collector's house.

There is a bumper sticker that says, "Practice random deeds of compassion." Every day there are people in need around you who are in need of compassion: the poor, sick, lonely, troubled, and grief-stricken. Everyone needs compassion and understanding. You don't have to be qualified to do something to alleviate their need. If your thoughts are centered on Christ, you will notice the needy and do something constructive for them.

Lord Jesus, help me to follow Your example and to see the need around me and to do something about it. Amen.

The Forgiveness of Sin

Read Mark 2:1-12

"I tell you the truth, all the sins and blasphemies of men will be forgiven them." (Mark 3:28)

A woman went to her doctor with an abscess on her leg. After months of unsuccessful treatment, a friend urged her to go to a pastor who offered counseling and healing. The pastor listened to her problem about the abscess and all her other complaints. Then he asked, "If God was here, do you think there is something that He would need to know about you?" After a long silence she described an incident that had happened years previously about which she was very embarrassed. When she was finished speaking, the pastor said, "You were honest with God. Now God is cleansing you. He forgives you." He prayed for her, laid hands on her and served Communion to her. They made an appointment to meet again in two weeks' time. Two days before the appointment, she phoned the pastor and said, "Can you believe it? My abscess is gone; it has been completely healed!"

> *It is always the case that when the Christian looks back, he is looking at the forgiveness of sins.*
>
> ~ Karl Barth

Feelings of guilt are a destructive element of the human heart. They can even lead to physical disorders. In all probability, the lame man had also committed some sin, and experienced the results of the terrible guilt in his body. Jesus had the insight to see this and directly addressed the heart of the problem.

If you are struggling with the memory of unforgiven sin, speak to Christ. You might not be experiencing a physical disorder, but your thoughts will be negatively affected and your relationship with Christ will be seriously harmed.

Holy Jesus, stand by those who are carrying a heavy burden of sin, so that they can confess their sin to You and receive forgiveness.

Amen.

How Presumptuous Can One Be?

Read Mark 2:1-12

Some teachers of the law were sitting there, thinking to themselves, "Why does this fellow talk like that? He's blaspheming! Who can forgive sins but God alone?" (Mark 2:6-7)

Proud people make the mistake of thinking that they are the center of the universe. Because they aren't God and can't see the whole picture as He does, they scale the world down to fit into their own limited awareness where they are in the center and everything else revolves around them. By doing this they are creating a godly image for themselves. This is what the Bible means with the word "sin." People challenge God.

Sin – shall we call it our pride, or our laziness, or shall we call it the deceit of our life? Let us call it the great defiance which turns us into the enemies of God and of our fellow men – even of our own selves.

~ Karl Barth

This is what the teachers of the law thought that Jesus was doing. Since all sin is against God, it is obvious that He is the only One who can forgive sin. They also took it as self-evident that the lame man was being punished by God for his sin. In their theology, comparing yourself to God was blasphemous. They never considered the fact that Christ *was* God. If the man was healed, then his sins were forgiven. If his sins were forgiven – and only God could do that – then Jesus must be God! This is exactly what Jesus told them.

Jesus also comes to you and me as the true God. He comes in your weakness and offers you strength; He comes in your sickness and offers you healing; within your restrictions He offers you space to live. What a great God we worship!

Savior, help those who have preconceived ideas that make it difficult for them to truly know You. Amen.

Jesus Knows!

Read Mark 2:1-12

Immediately Jesus knew in His Spirit that this was what they were thinking in their hearts. (Mark 2:8)

We often look into someone's face and see pain, confusion or fear and then wonder what that person is thinking about. It happens that people who have been in an intimate relationship with each other for years can sense what the other is thinking without saying anything.

Jesus had deep insight into people and could penetrate their thoughts. In this incident, the teachers of the law were secretly accusing Jesus of blasphemy and He knew of the evil in their hearts.

> *The going on to perfection, includes both an increase of knowledge, and the greatest holiness of life.*
>
> ~ Jacob Boehme

Jesus also knows what is in your heart. He sees behind the facades of friendship and the masks of kindness that you put on for other people so that they will like you. When you have deep contempt for what someone said or did and you display an attitude of pious friendship to him, Jesus knows. When you cover up a bad deed with lies and pretend that it was done for the sake of some noble deed, Jesus is aware of it. You can never deceive God – you can only fool yourself in the process.

At the same time, Jesus sees the good deeds you do that no one is aware of. He knows the intentions of your heart and sees the love when you forgive someone who has hurt you. If you act with mixed motives, Jesus also sees the good ones. He knows and He understands. He accepts that with all your hidden mistakes and frivolous jealousy, you are really honest and loving inside.

Redeemer and Savior, know my thoughts and help me to reveal the attitude that was also in You. Amen.

Get Up and Go Home!

Read Mark 2:1-12

He said to the paralytic, "I tell you, get up, take your mat and go home." He got up, took his mat and walked out in full view of them all. (Mark 2:11-12)

We often make an elaborate and complicated case out of a simple issue. This is especially true of our faith. We imagine that we have to perform all sorts of difficult tasks to force God to love us. Some of the prerequisites we set are regular church attendance, obedience to the Ten Commandments, doing good deeds and working in the church.

All that the lame man did was allow his four friends to take him to Jesus. He was passive through-out the whole operation. Because he was very sick, he had nothing to recommend him to come to Jesus – except his sin, for which he had to receive forgiveness. In contrast, the teachers of the law were the distinguished ones – they knew it all. In the first place, they were apparently there to spy on Jesus. But the man whose sins had made him sick, received the word from Jesus that completely healed him. It was really so simple. But the teachers of the law got caught in an argument and had to be reprimanded by Jesus.

There is no love without hope, no hope without love, and neither love nor hope without faith.

~ St. Augustine

Don't make it more difficult for yourself than it really is. The message of this story is simple: come to Jesus just as you are – with your emptiness, worry, weakness, helplessness, ignorance, need, failure or guilt feelings. Fall upon His grace and love – totally, unreservedly, completely!

Lord Jesus, words fail; I am silent before Your holy face. Amen.

Jesus at the Tax Collector's Booth

Read Mark 2:13-17

As He walked along, he saw Levi son of Alphaeus sitting at the tax collector's booth. "Follow Me," Jesus told him. (Mark 2:14)

Nobody enjoys paying income tax, but we all have to do it. We admit that tax collectors are a necessary evil.

The people in Jesus' time hated tax collectors. They collected money for the Roman authorities. This task was sold to certain individuals after it was determined how much was to be paid. The collectors added their own percentage. Tax collectors were rich and the people saw them as deceivers and lapdogs.

The responsible person seeks to make his or her whole life a response to the question and call of God.

~ Dietrich Bonhoeffer

Jesus called a tax collector to be His disciple. Jesus didn't want to reflect the reigning judgment of the tax collector and instead He saw him as a person. He didn't allow His judgment to be hampered when He chose Levi as a student. He didn't see the hated person of public opinion, but the qualities of a man who could become a new being filled with passion, love, hope, and faith for the gospel message.

However inexperienced and unworthy you might consider yourself, however different you might be from the ordinary churchgoer or believer, however amazed and perplexed other people might be about you, Jesus looks at the good things that lie concealed deep in your heart. He sees the qualities in you that He can bring to the fore. He won't allow someone else to make this choice for Him. He also says to you, "Follow Me!"

Savior and Redeemer, I know that I am not what other people are, but if You need me, I want to say with Isaiah, "Here I am, Lord."

Amen.

To Leave Everything Behind

Read Mark 2:13-17

Levi got up and followed Him. (Mark 2:14)

Some people are "all-or-nothing" and others work slowly, bit by bit. If you have to change something, you either do it all at once, or you gradually adjust to it.

Even though the Bible implies that Jesus and Levi (known as Matthew) met here for the first time, it is possible that they had already seen each other before, while Jesus was busy in the area. Matthew may have been part of the crowds who listened to Jesus' teachings. He was immediately ready to go with Jesus. For him it meant leaving behind the familiar life of a tax collector where he was a well-known, rich man with a good income and an uncomfortable place in society. This is what he was used to.

> *There are no crown wearers in heaven who were not cross-bearers here below.*
> ~ Charles H. Spurgeon

To follow Jesus meant to risk everything he owned in order to set out on a new, uncertain and dangerous path with Jesus. He had to walk out into the unknown, follow a new lifestyle without knowing what the reward would be or where it would all end. When he left everything behind that day, he didn't know where the path would lead.

To follow Jesus doesn't necessarily mean that you must leave your normal day job. But it does mean that you must give up your own interests, your truths, and your own small world of conventional ideas and theories. Only one thing makes it worthwhile – to know Jesus. To know Him has its own reward. The day you leave everything behind and follow Him, you have a life-long pilgrimage ahead of you – and after this life, there is still more to come.

Heavenly Father, help me not to cling to the past, but to walk out into the future You have prepared for me. Amen.

When You Can't Afford It

Read John 6:1-10

Philip answered Him, "Eight months' wages would not buy enough bread for each one to have a bite!" (John 6:7)

You might have on occasion said, "If I only had more money I could do that or buy this." Maybe you have envied those who can afford to do and buy anything they want.

Philip was the disciple whose budget could not be stretched to feed the crowds. Quite fittingly, his judgment was based on precise calculations. But neither Philip's mathematics nor anyone else's will ever be enough to calculate the extent and power of God's grace.

> *Faith is the conviction that God knows more than we do about this life and He will get us through it.*
>
> ~ Max Lucado

Mother Teresa was one of the greatest Christians of all times. She once began to build a convent with just a few dollars in her hand. Someone said to her, "Not even Teresa can do something like this with so little money."

"Completely true," replied Teresa, "but God can do anything with little money."

You are wise if you don't spend outside of your financial budget. Live within your means, but at the same time know that God has unrestricted resources at His disposal. Many believers have called on this resource and the results have been amazing. Churches have been built, business ventures have been started, missionary outreaches have been established, the sick have been healed, and the crowds have been fed. God's balance sheet always shows a surplus.

Faith in You, my God, exceeds my greatest expectations. Amen.

No Man Is an Island

Read Romans 14:1-11

None of us lives to himself alone. (Romans 14:7)

If we lead a normal life, we come into contact with other people all the time. At home, at work, on the sports field, and in spiritual areas we are continuously confronted by the challenge of relationships.

There are people who we like and there are people who we dislike. It is precisely those people who you do not like that present a challenge to you as a Christian.

Ensure that your attitude is not based on jealousy. This sin has destroyed more relationships than we will ever know. Open yourself to the Holy Spirit and make sure that there is nothing in your life that can cause friction. If there is tension in your relationship, try and determine your role in the unhappy situation.

> *Use your head to handle yourself, your heart to handle others.*
> ~ Anonymous

Perhaps you have been aware of the faults and weaknesses of the other person for such a long time that you no longer expect anything good from them. When you see each other serious conflicts occur, and before either of you have said anything, there is a mutual feeling of antagonism present.

As a Christian, it is your duty to defuse such a tense situation. Pray for the cleansing power of the Holy Spirit. Seriously pray to be saved from the spirit of antagonism and accept others in a spirit of good will.

If you persevere lovingly, you will conquer this destructive spirit and through your attitude you will bring forward the best in others. Only God, through the love of Jesus Christ, can enable you to do this.

God of love, with Your help and mercy I am going to build every relationship in my life with a positive attitude. Amen.

Growth Is Essential

Read 2 Peter 3:14-18

Grow in the grace and knowledge of our Lord and Savior Jesus Christ. (2 Peter 3:18)

The Christian's spiritual life may never stagnate, since this can so easily cause dreariness. If you are not continuously growing towards a more intimate relationship with Christ, you are allowing your love for Him to cool down and your communion with Him to fade away.

Do you know Christ better now than you did a year ago? An honest answer to this question will indicate the direction that you are moving in spiritually.

Peter encouraged the disciples of the early church to grow in the grace and knowledge of Jesus Christ. Grace is a gift bestowed on us by the Holy Spirit. As your experience with the risen Lord deepens and grows richer, His nature is reflected in your life and is directly linked to your commitment to God.

> *Don't go through life, grow through life.*
> ~ Eric Butterworth

A disciple who lives according to Christ's example is never too conscious of this development taking place in his life. On the contrary, he will deny it since he is very much aware of his own shortcomings. Nevertheless, it can be proof of his spiritual growth.

Growing in the knowledge of Christ can be understood only in view of the knowledge God gives His disciples through the Holy Spirit and through His Holy Word. The Christian reacts to this knowledge and grows in his resemblance to his Perfect Example – Jesus Christ.

Help me, my Redeemer and Example, to grow through grace in such a way that the world will see something of You in me. Amen.

July

The Great Teacher

The crowds were amazed at His teaching, because He taught
as one who had authority, and not as their teachers of the law.
~ Matthew 7:28-29

The mediocre teacher tells. The good teacher explains.
The superior teacher demonstrates.
The great teacher inspires.
~ William A. Ward

Holy Teacher,
We praise and thank You for the
loving teaching we receive from You.
We thank You that through Your teaching
You train us in our most holy faith
and show us the way to Eternal Life.
Through Your teaching You have taught us
how to live here and now:
in our relationship with the Trinity;
our fellow man;
and the Evil One and sin.
You came to teach us about
redemption and freedom from sin.
Your teachings on prayer have improved and
strengthened our relationship with the Father.
Thank You for never being disheartened
by our foolishness and stubbornness.
We praise Your name because through
Your teachings we can grow to maturity
and our lives can find depth and
meaning to the honor of Your name.
Make us faithful in our research
and application of Your teachings,
so that we can be equipped for
the spiritual battle each day holds.
We pray this in the name of our
Teacher and Redeemer,
Jesus Christ,

Amen.

Beware of Thieves and Robbers

Read John 10:1-11

"I tell you the truth, the man who does not enter the sheep pen by the gate, but climbs in by some other way, is a thief and a robber."

(John 10:1)

Due to the high crime rate in many countries, people must constantly be on the lookout for thieves and robbers. They steal money, keys, vehicles and household goods. Stock farmers must continually guard their cattle and sheep from thieves.

In the parable of the Good Shepherd, Jesus warns His disciples against the thieves and robbers who steal sheep. *They* are the sheep and they are attacked by those who want to rob them of their faith. Some thieves would even try to kill them to achieve this, and others would try to undermine their faith in Jesus.

> *The world was never conquered by intrigue, it was conquered by faith.*
>
> ~ Benjamin Disraeli

We must still earnestly guard against those who try to rob us of our faith. Some people write books claiming that the Bible is just one big lie and that Christianity is a concoction the apostle Paul thought up. They assert that Jesus was just an ordinary teacher, like any rabbi of His day. They argue His miracles away and place doubt on everything that Jesus taught. They spread distrust and suspicion to undermine the Church of Christ. They are even trying to eradicate Christianity completely.

Recognize these people for what they truly are. Refuse to listen to their half truths and untruths. Don't allow the robbers to steal Jesus Christ's flock and don't allow your own faith to be undermined. Learn to discern real gospel truths and don't be misled by substitutes. Keep a firm grip on your faith by walking with Jesus every day.

Savior and Lord, help me to know the truth and to resist those trying to rob me of my faith. Amen.

The Correct Way

Read John 10:1-11

"The man who enters by the gate is the shepherd of his sheep." (John 10:2)

The times in which we live require people to almost be security specialists in order to survive. This is because the world is full of thieves, deceivers and terrorists. We have cards, passwords, codes and electronic equipment to protect our lives.

In early Israel, sheep were kept at night in a walled enclosure which was situated at the entrance to the house. There was only one gate and the guard kept watch there. He knew the shepherd and allowed him to enter and exit. Robbers had to climb over the wall to perform their evil deeds. The shepherd's behavior is what we would call insightful today. The robbers behaved mysteriously and suspiciously.

> *The gospel is so simple that small children can understand it, and it is so profound that studies by the wisest theologians will never exhaust its riches.*
>
> ~ Charles Hodge

The parable, of course, is about Jesus who is the true Shepherd. He acts with love and care, and He is open and transparent in all His actions. He comes through the gate because He has the interests of the flock at heart. He can be trusted to the utmost. There is an invisible unity between the Shepherd and His flock.

You can also trust Jesus, because He comes to you and includes you in His flock in love. He will always act in your best interests. He doesn't come to gain advantage from you, to terrorize you or to use you for His own selfish motives. He works to increase the flock, of which you are one. He protects you from the evil intentions of those who are trying to rob you of your faith and He gives you the truth, guidance and love. It is of crucial importance that you ensure you are safe inside His flock.

Thank You, Lord Jesus, that I am safe and secure within Your flock.
Amen.

Be Careful Who You Follow

Read John 10:1-11

"They will never follow a stranger; in fact, they will run away from him because they do not recognize a stranger's voice." (John 10:5)

Advertisers usually promise to make your wildest dreams come true. According to them, you will win the heart of a one-in-a-million life partner if you buy their product, whether it be face cream, deodorant, shoes, shirts, weight-loss pills, or cars. They promise instant wealth, perfect holidays, career success, happy families, popularity, and perfect health. If you believe what some advertisers say, then you'll believe anything.

The parable of the Good Shepherd follows the story of the man who was born blind. The religious leaders who attacked the man and tried to undermine his faith in Jesus are the thieves and robbers in the parable. The blind man who received healing didn't listen to the unfamiliar voice. He was rejected by one flock, but the Good Shepherd found him and brought him back to the true flock.

If you have been tempted into evil, fly from it. It is not falling into the water, but lying in it, that drowns.

~ Anonymous

In later years there would be other thieves and robbers. Some of them were the false teachers within the church. Others were heathen religious leaders who tried to mislead Christian believers. There were also political leaders who regarded Christianity as a threat to the state.

Be very careful and listen to the right voices. Don't listen to those who promise you heaven on earth; whether it be through consumer products, instant wealth or a political paradise. Listen to the voice of the Good Shepherd, otherwise you might be led onto strange paths and get totally lost.

Savior of Your flock, protect Your people from false promises that solely seek to undermine their faith. Amen.

Do You Understand?

Read John 10:1-11

Jesus used this figure of speech, but they did not understand what He was telling them. (John 10:6)

A good novel or play often has an underlying theme or message it wants to convey. Behind the events and people portrayed, it might be saying, "Crime doesn't pay!" or "Evil destroys itself!"

The stories about Jesus and the stories He told all have messages. However, sometimes these messages are not so clear and not everyone can grasp their deeper meanings. The parable of the Good Shepherd asserts that there is only one Redeemer. He comes of His own accord and in love; His flock hears His voice and follows Him. They know that He loves each one individually and by following Him they no longer have to walk in darkness.

> *The purpose of Christianity is not to avoid difficulty, but to produce a character adequate to meet it when it comes. It does not make life easy; rather it tries to make us great enough for life.*
>
> ~ James L. Christensen

On the surface, this parable is about shepherds and sheep in Israel. In reality, it is about you and me. The Redeemer comes to us, calls us by name and asks us to follow Him. It's only when you hear Him call you by name that you realize what is happening. The parable speaks to you personally and asks whether you have heard His voice and reacted to it.

In response to this parable, you can shrug your shoulders and regard it as a simple story about sheep and shepherds in Israel. Or the true message can penetrate through to you as personal, and then you can attain eternal life through your Savior, Jesus Christ. It is good to listen to stories, but it is much better to take the message to heart and allow the story to totally change your life.

Holy Master, give me the grace to hear what You want to say to me.
Amen.

How "Good" Are You?

Read John 10:1-11

"I am the Good Shepherd. The good shepherd lays down his life for the sheep." (John 10:11)

We use the word *good* in a variety of ways. Sometimes we use it to describe proficiency. A coach will encourage a player by saying, "Good job! Well done!" A parent will use the word to emphasize obedience, "Be a good girl/boy, and do as I say." We also sometimes describe a doctor as "good" and by this we aren't necessarily referring to his skills or that he obeys the Ten Commandments. We admire him because he continues, despite the numerous people who don't pay their accounts; because he has gone to see dying patients on cold nights; because he has tried to help and because he has served the community in a variety of unselfish ways. There is something strong, dedicated and compassionate about him that makes him a "good" doctor.

> *To make the improving of our own character our central aim is hardly the highest kind of goodness. True goodness forgets itself and goes out to do the right thing for no other reason than that it is right.*
>
> ~ Lesslie Newbigin

It is in the same sense that Jesus was a "Good Shepherd." He was good in His selflessness; in His care; and in His single-minded commitment to the mission He was sent to fulfill. He went around and did "good" to all people because He was filled with compassion and care.

You possibly obey the Ten Commandments, but how "good" are you in the sense of beauty and attractiveness of character? Other people will feel drawn to the Good Shepherd through the way you reflect the goodness of Jesus.

Lord Jesus, let Your beauty and goodness be reflected in my life.

Amen.

The Good Shepherd

Read John 10:1-11

"I am the Good Shepherd. The good shepherd lays down his life for the sheep." (John 10:11)

There are good and bad people on every level of life. There are good plumbers, bus drivers and gardeners; but there are also bad ones.

Jesus spoke about evil shepherds who were thieves and robbers and were worse than bad shepherds. But He was the Good Shepherd who was willing to lay down His life for the sheep. The sheep would live, but they wouldn't only live, they would live abundantly (see John 10:10). But this abundance of life would only come because the Good Shepherd was willing to lay down His life for the sheep. He thought more about the flock than He thought about Himself.

> *Beloved, let the fact of what our Lord suffered for you grip you, and you will never again be the same.*
>
> ~ Oliver B. Green

The abundance of life that Christ offers to believers comes through the death of Jesus, the Good Shepherd. While the powers of death are everywhere around them, they are granted life because of the death of Christ. The Good Shepherd grants life, and not only in the sense of protection from death. He grants abundant life, which is a life of greater depth. This is God's quality of life.

You are one of the sheep for whom Jesus laid down His life. He really wants you to have this abundant life. It pains Him to see how you drift around, satisfied with a half-empty existence. He sincerely loves you and desires to fill your life with the joy, hope and peace that He alone can give. He wants to reform you and elevate your life to a new level. Why be satisfied with a bad shepherd when the Good Shepherd is available?

How will I ever be able to thank You enough, Lord Jesus, for laying Your life down for me? Amen.

Sheep Who Become Shepherds

Read John 10:12-21

"The hired hand is not the shepherd who owns the sheep. So when he sees the wolf coming, he abandons the sheep and runs away. Then the wolf attacks the flock and scatters it. The man runs away because he is a hired hand and cares nothing for the sheep." (John 10:12-13)

The parable of the Good Shepherd has more than one meaning. It presents Jesus as the Good Shepherd. Then it tells about the people who attack the flock in order to undermine their faith. It also has a third meaning: it warns people about shepherds who set out with bad motives and then denounce their high calling.

There is a Good Shepherd who is the great Shepherd of the flock – Jesus Christ. But He also appoints deputy shepherds who help to protect the flock – pastors and leaders in the Christian community.

Faith is not the holding of correct doctrines, but personal fellowship with the living God.
~ William Temple

The flock is not only the target of attacks from outside, but also from attacks by false shepherds within the flock. Christ only has human hands to help Him and many of those hands are soiled by bad motives, love of money, the desire to rule, and the urge for self-glorification.

One of the greatest problems in Christianity is the total fragility of the human leaders. From the time of Judas's betrayal and Peter's denial, this flaw of Christian pastors and leaders has created opportunities for enemies of the faith to belittle Christ. Try to understand the true human struggle your own pastor has. Pray for them where they might be tempted in their service. Give your love and encouragement wherever you can. Then you will be one of Christ's flock who is becoming a shepherd.

Savior of Your flock, strengthen the faith of those who serve as pastors and leaders. Amen.

A Firm Foundation

Read John 10:12-21

"I am the Good Shepherd; I know My sheep and My sheep know Me – just as the Father knows Me and I know the Father." (John 10:14-15)

A young groom said the following on his wedding day, "I want to thank my parents for everything they have done for me and given me. The most precious thing they have given me is their love for each other." Seen from a human perspective, the most important thing in life is relationships.

The most fundamental thing in the Christian faith is not our love for God, or His love for us – it is the Father-Son relationship between God and Jesus Christ. As the Good Shepherd, Jesus knows His sheep and each one is as important to Him as if there was only one to love. They know Him and trust Him. But more important than that knowledge is the unshakable foundation upon which all other things in the Christian faith are built – the knowledge and mutual trust that the Father has in the Son and the Son has in the Father.

> *There is no other method of living piously and justly, than that of depending on God.*
>
> ~ John Calvin

Your faith, your conversion, your growth as a disciple, your obedience to Christ, your walk with God, and your fellowship with other Christians are all beautiful and necessary aspects of knowledge of Jesus and service to Him. But underneath this is the deep and lasting foundation upon which it is all built – Jesus and God, God and Jesus. On this side of eternity we might not realize the importance of this completely. But when we reach eternity, we will see how it rules all other things.

Holy Jesus, even though I can't completely understand this deep mystery, I still place my trust in You. Amen.

A Precious Sacrifice

Read John 10:12-21

"I lay down My life for the sheep." (John 10:15)

Sometimes the Christian life is wrongly presented as one long joyride. Then there are people who think that Christianity is a springboard to achieve worldly success. Others regard it as a queue you have to stand in to receive blessings. Many who find comfort during difficulties over-emphasize the "soft-cushion" aspect and only expect comfort during testing and problems.

If Christianity rests on the foundation of the relationship between Father and Son, the heart and core of this is the self-sacrificing deed of Jesus Christ on the cross. The most important moment of Jesus' whole ministry was when He died on Golgotha in obedience to the Father. This was also one of the functions of a good shepherd.

> *The lives that are getting stronger are the lives in the desert, deep-rooted in God.*
> ~ Oswald Chambers

With wild animals in the area and thieves who were on the prowl, the life of those early shepherds was not easy. They could die at any moment.

Jesus, the Good Shepherd, was willing to die on behalf of His sheep. The whole life of the Christian faith revolves around this event. He paid the highest price on Golgotha and is the Cruci-fied One for eternity. He laid down His life for the sheep – those who were present then and those who would become part of His flock thereafter.

Christianity is costly. Any thought of the Christian faith which disregards this aspect distorts the true character of discipleship. The Shepherd who laid down His life for the sheep, calls His flock to be a suffering, serving, unselfish community who is willing to pay the price. May He, the Good Shepherd, through His grace, enable us to achieve this.

Savior, grant that we will restore the cross to its central place in our faith. Amen.

The Wider Horizon

Read John 10:12-21

"I have other sheep that are not of this sheep pen. I must bring them also. They too will listen to My voice, and there shall be one flock and one Shepherd." (John 10:16)

Few people risk looking beyond the borders of their own small world. Despite the window on the world that TV presents to us every day, most people's thoughts are occupied by the issues closest to them. Few Christians reach out or pray outside the borders of the congregation they belong to.

God never intended His church to be a refrigerator in which to preserve perishable piety. He intended it to be an incubator in which to hatch out converts.

~ F. Lincicome

The Good Shepherd did not only focus on the small flock around Him. He saw a vast horizon that confirmed the Father's love for the world. When He referred to "this sheep pen," He probably meant the people of Israel. Small groups of Gentiles joined synagogues outside of Israel and it was on these converts that the first apostles focused their attention. But Jesus knew that there were "other sheep," some in Greece, Syria, Egypt, Rome and elsewhere. He had laid down His life for them too. This was not a small, isolated movement – it had a global impact. When the Holy Spirit was given to the church at Pentecost, the disciples began to spread out toward the ends of the earth.

Don't allow your faith to become a strictly personal issue between you and Jesus. Always remember that your local congregation is only a small grouping within a mighty fellowship; some on earth and some in heaven. To believe in Jesus places you in a global community and joins you to believers in Brazil, Italy, Bolivia, Tonga, Tasmania, and Norway.

Heavenly Father, bless and multiply Your family throughout the world. Amen.

One Flock and One Shepherd

Read John 10:12-21

"There shall be one flock and one Shepherd." (John 10:16)

Christians have divided themselves into many groups and denominations. They reveal different forms of discipleship, teachings and systems. Sometimes they agree with each other, but often they differ greatly.

Jesus hoped and wished for "one flock and one Shepherd." Despite all their differences, Christians worldwide acknowledge Christ and worship Him as Lord and God. Above all other Christian heroes and leaders, Jesus remains the great unifying Shepherd. Christians seek His will, follow His teachings and find life through His redemption. He is their Savior, their hope, their comfort, and their joy.

> *If we focus on our differences, our focus is on each other. If we focus with unity, our focus is on God.*
>
> ~ Anonymous

You also belong to this "one flock." Look beyond your denominational loyalty and acknowledge Jesus as your Shepherd – as He is for all Christians from any kind of church. Jesus said, "There shall be one flock." He used the future tense, which indicated a vision for His disciples that lay beyond their lifetimes – and possibly beyond ours too. The Bible looks forward to a coming Kingdom, a great church and a flock that is one in Christ.

In heaven, the differences and divisions will fall away and Christ will be all and in all: "He tends His flock like a shepherd, He gathers the lambs in His arms and carries them close to His heart; He gently leads those that have young" (Isa. 40:11).

Pray for Christ's flock all over the world. Rejoice in His unifying love. Love your fellow Christians, whatever differences you might have. Look forward to that final gathering of the scattered flock.

Good Shepherd, gather Your flock and bind us together in You.

Amen.

Give and Receive

Read John 10:12-21

"The reason My Father loves Me is that I lay down my life – only to take it up again." (John 10:17)

In many areas of life, you can only receive after you have first given. Students devote years to dedicated study and then receive good positions in life. Gardeners perform many hours of dedicated labor before the beautiful flowers they dream of begin to bloom.

Jesus knew about this principle. He sacrificed His life in complete obedience to the Father. He used His life to serve others, as the Father had commanded Him. In the end, He sacrificed His life. But His death was certainly not the end. He received His life back when He rose from the dead. His new resurrected life was trans-

> *Shared joy is a double joy; shared sorrow is half a sorrow.*
> ~ Swedish Proverb

formed and glorified. What He received in return was a greater dimension of life than the one He had given up. His death and resurrection brought life and redemption to you and me. The Good Shepherd gives His life and then receives it back again – and He also gives it to the sheep of His flock.

Accept the life that Jesus offers to you. Receive it in its complete fullness, love and power. If you give it away with the same love that Jesus gave you, you will multiply your ability to receive. The more you receive, the more you will be able to give away. Give it with love, hope, encouragement, friendliness and care.

Just give – and then give again. You will be amazed at how much you will receive in return.

Savior and Redeemer, make me more concerned about giving than receiving. Amen.

Are You One of the Crowd?

Read John 10:22-42

The Jews gathered around Him. (John 10:24)

Many people think that Christianity is a private issue. They believe that it's just them and God and no one else is allowed in the picture. It *is* a personal relationship – but it's much more than just that.

Every sheep is part of the flock. Every believer is part of the fellowship. The Israelites were God's people. They gathered in the synagogue every Sabbath to hear the interpretation of the Scriptures. Jesus also met God there. People gathered around Him when He taught in the temple; when He was born; when He told His parables; when He healed the sick; and when He miraculously multiplied the bread and fish. Christianity is a shared experience. We meet Christ through meeting with those who gather together with us.

> *No Christian and, indeed, no historian could accept the epigram which defines religion as 'what a man does with his solitude.'*
>
> ~ C. S. Lewis

Even in the most difficult times, Christians feel drawn to each other. Some gather in huge church congregations. Others gather within prison walls; houses; hospitals; universities; military barracks and in work places. In Africa many congregations gather together under trees in the open air. Jesus stands central in all these gatherings! People come together to learn, to worship, to pray, to empower each other, to comfort and to give hope.

Not all Christians can come together, though. There are the sick and isolated who meet God in seclusion. One day you will be part of the great assembly of angels, archangels, and the crowds in heaven who will all gather around Jesus.

Lord my God, strengthen me through my fellowship with other believers. Amen.

Don't Nurse Old Wounds

Read Matthew 18:21-35

Then Peter came to Jesus and asked, "Lord, how many times shall I forgive my brother when he sins against me? Up to seven times?" Jesus answered, "I tell you, not seven times, but seventy-seven times." (Matthew 18:21-22)

To say that you will forgive but not forget means that you nurse old wounds and allow yourself to be poisoned by bitterness and hatred. It is terribly sad that people don't realize the dam-age they do to themselves when they foster disputes that should have been buried decades ago. Simmering hatred or growing bitter-ness has a disastrous effect on the one who nurses them. The spirit becomes small and mean and eventually thoughts become twisted – nothing is seen in its true perspective anymore. Atti-tudes become petty and warped.

> *The man who is truly forgiven and knows it, is a man who forgives.*
> ~ Martyn Lloyd-Jones

No one can afford to accommo-date an unforgiving spirit. Its companion is hatred, and together they cause unhappiness and internal defeat. Because of this, Christ's teachings were not unrealistic or removed from the hard facts of daily life. They were the peak of common sense and sound reason.

If you agree with what Jesus taught in principle, but at the same time feel that it is beyond your ability to forgive, remem-ber that Jesus not only called you to live right, but that He en-ables you to do what you can't do in your own strength. The indwelling Holy Spirit equips you to do this.

Thank You, Teacher and Lord, that Your indwelling Spirit enables me to forgive and forget. Amen.

Give and Receive

Read Acts 20:28-38

You should remember the words of the Lord Jesus: "It is more blessed to give than to receive." (Acts 20:35 NLT)

Some people do good deeds because it makes them feel good. They love it when people express their appreciation and are devastated when their kind-heartedness is not appreciated. To a greater or lesser extent, all good deeds serve a useful purpose. But those that are inspired by self-interest fall short of the enduring power that is born from unselfish actions.

Life is the repetitive process of give and take. Children accept parental care. Privileges are often granted to them without the accompanying responsibility. In the family, and in many other relationships, a lot is simply accepted without any of it actually being appreciated.

Blessed are those who can give without remembering and take without forgetting.

~ Elizabeth Bibesco

Give of yourself by discovering a need and helping to alleviate it. This need is not costly in financial terms. A sure road to happiness is to look past your own problems and to reach out a helping hand to alleviate the needs of others. Give of your time and listen, sympathize, encourage and place renewed hope in the heart of a discouraged fellow pilgrim. Remember the times when you were discouraged, upset and despondent and someone else held out a helping hand to you. Never pass by an opportunity to do something good for someone else. Your reward will certainly not pass you by!

It is only that which you give away that can enrich you; but nothing that you can ever give can equal God's unlimited acts of kindness. He gives His all – how do you receive Him?

Gracious Father God, we worship and praise Your name for Your perfect Gift to a humanity in need. Amen.

From Death to Life

Read John 5:18-29

"I tell you the truth, whoever hears My word and believes Him who sent Me has eternal life and will not be condemned; he has crossed over from death to life." (John 5:24)

Are you truly living or are you simply "existing" from day to day? For some people living means going completely overboard, and for others it means the accumulation of money and possessions, or the ability to avoid work, tension and pressure. There are people who don't really know who they are, why they are here and where they are headed. Do you know for sure?

> *It is always easier to fight for one's principles than to live up to them.*
>
> ~ Alfred Adler

When you give yourself to Jesus Christ in faith, you cross over from death to life. You no longer live for your own selfish interests. The pastimes and things that you used to value are no longer that attractive and the goals you used to strive for don't seem so important anymore. Instead of blaming other people for your problems, you do everything you can to help them with theirs. Instead of trying to grasp everything in sight, you try to give everything you can and you find joy in your generosity. While you used to complain about trifling irritations, you now accept difficult times and suffering as ways to glorify God through sharing in Christ's suffering.

Before you "crossed over," you were number one in your limited little world, but now you have placed God and Jesus first in your life and you see yourself in relation to them. Your body used to be a source of pleasure, now it is the temple of the Holy Spirit. Previously, you tried to get God to do everything you wanted, now you find joy and meaning by doing what God desires from you. "Cross over" from death to life!

Thank You for life, Lord Jesus. Grant that I may live life to the full every day. Amen.

On the Other Side of Death

Read John 5:18-29

"I tell you the truth, a time is coming and has now come when the dead will hear the voice of the Son of God and those who hear will live." (John 5:25)

Some people claim that everything is over when you die. Others suggest that the spirit leaves the body and that the spirit is indestructible. Therefore, you will lead a "spiritual" existence after death. There are also people who refuse to think about death and believe it is too gruesome to consider. They claim that life is ruthless and cruel enough as it is, and that it doesn't help to think about what happens afterwards.

From the New Testament we learn that, just as Jesus rose from the dead, so too will every believing follower of Jesus. In our reading for today, Jesus predicts that

> *Every man must do two things alone: he must do his own believing and his own dying.*
> ~ Martin Luther

He will come again and initiate a new resurrection where those who believed will be brought back to a fuller and richer life in His company.

Because Jesus is "the Resurrection and the Life," death is not a somber entrance hall – it's also not the end. It is only the "end of the beginning." For believers in Christ, this life is only preparation and practice for the glorious life with Him on the other side of the grave.

Even more important is that our lives here and now determine the hereafter. What you do or don't do now; how you believe or neglect to believe; if you grow in love or allow your love to wither; if you partake in worship, demonstrate compassion or help to build up the fellowship of believers – these are the ways you prepare for eternal life. The choice is exclusively yours – use it!

Savior, help me to be ready when the time arrives for me to die.

Amen.

Christian Love Overcomes All

Read John 14:1-31

"If you love Me, you will obey what I command." (John 14:15)

Christianity is moving through difficult times. The appearance of many sects that all claim to have the authority of Scripture; the substitution in some areas of Christian thought; the swapping of a living gospel for one that is social and political; the infiltration of forces into the church that work toward its downfall – these all work together to confuse disciples who find it increasingly difficult to know what to believe or accept.

We thank God that in the midst of all this reigning religious confusion, there is a solid core of believers whose first love is the living Christ. Even though they might appear to be divided in their dogma; irreconcilable in their traditions and roots; and they are divided by racial and cultural differences, there is a great love for

We look forward to the time when the power to love will replace the love of power. Then will our world know the blessings of peace.

~ William Gladstone

Christ in their hearts. It is this love that forms the core of the true church of God.

Christian love must be revealed in a practical way. A social love is a contradiction because true Christian love cares for the lonely, the grieving and the underprivileged. This is the spirit that is inspired by the love of Christ and which distinguishes between Christian love and pure socio-political propaganda.

If you belong to the group that truly loves Christ, you will be able to overcome all obstacles and your insight will be so expanded that you will be free from narrow-mindedness. You will no longer judge fellow Christians based on their dogmatic statements, but on the depth and quality of their love.

Holy Savior, grant that Your Holy Spirit and the Law of love will control my life. Amen.

The Greatest of All!

Read John 14:15-31

Jesus replied, "If anyone loves Me, he will obey My teaching. My Father will love him, and We will come to him and make Our home with him." (John 14:23)

Most people want the best out of life, but few are willing to sacrifice their best for it. This is not because of selfish motives, but because they have never bothered to discover what the best is for them. They accept what life offers and never ask, "What is the best life can offer me?" or "What does life still ask of me?"

What you regard as the best for you is determined by standards you set for yourself, because you will never rise above them. If you have a low level of expected achievements, your life will be unproductive. But if your best faith, energy and concentration are required, then you will be enriched in every area.

> *Faith is the sturdiest of all the virtues. It is the virtue of the storm, just as happiness is the virtue of the sunshine.*
>
> ~ Ruth Benedict

Most people are satisfied to limit their goals to their intellectual horizons. They limit their goals to personal ambitions and don't accept the Person and teachings that Jesus Christ offers them, namely the best of all – God Himself!

When you taste the power of God in your life through the indwelling Christ, then you reach the best that life can offer you. He gives guidance in confusion; strength in weakness; comfort in times of sorrow; satisfaction with everyday life; and confidence when our self-confidence fades. He also gives an awareness of the eternity of life – the realization that the individual life is not brief, but an integral part of God's eternity. If you have God, you have the best of all!

Eternal God, it is wonderful to realize that You live in me and I give You all the honor. Amen.

Experience of the Christian Faith

Read John 15:1-8

"Remain in Me, and I will remain in you." (John 15:4)

Even though creeds and dogmas are essential to the interpretation of the Christian faith, at their best they are simply attempts to explain the unexplainable. Just as God can't be completely analyzed, so the relationship of the human soul to God can't be understood. Even though this experience touches on the mystical, it is still very real. You might know God and at times be deeply aware of His Presence, especially in times of prayer and meditation, but still find it difficult to adequately explain this experience.

> *Our first place of victory is in believing the truth concerning our relationship with God. We come to believe He is our Helper in the healing of our souls!*
>
> ~ Francis Frangipane

Not being able to explain the awareness of the indwelling Presence of Christ is certainly not reason enough to reject it or to set it aside as only a personal emotional experience.

The living Christ has invited you to live *in* Him. The only way to do this is to accept His invitation in faith. Confirm your trust: "Lord, I now live in You. I invite You to live in me." Now be assured that this has happened and that it will continue to happen as an ongoing process.

To realize that the Spirit of the living Christ is within you is to discover a totally new attitude toward life. You will start to see things from God's viewpoint and even in the darkest moments of life, you will be aware of His guiding influence. When defeated, you will not lose the vision of victory. Your relationships with others will contain understanding, trust and hope. You can't claim to have the Spirit of the Master or to be owned by Him unless you change your old attitudes and habits.

Holy Jesus, draw me nearer and nearer to Yourself. Amen.

Follow Christ

Read Psalm 31:1-13

You are my rock and my fortress, for the sake of Your name lead and guide me. (Psalm 31:3)

When you commit yourself unconditionally to Christ, it is the most significant decision of your entire life. You may be guided onto strange and exciting paths since God undoubtedly guides those who swear obedience and faithfulness to Him.

When you subject yourself to His guidance, wonderful things will start happening in your life. Where life probably seemed like a dead end before, doors now open in remarkable ways. Problems that you feared previously now shrink to trivialities and you become aware that you are not alone on the path.

The experience and perception of Christ's guidance elevates life beyond the world of theological

> *Don't try to hold God's hand; let Him hold yours. Let Him do the holding, and you do the trusting.*
> ~ Hammer W. Webb-Peploe

speculation. It finds practical application in the harsh realities of our daily lives. This is faith in action!

There will be times when doors slam shut or close quietly and it would be wise not to try to force them open. When Christ wants you to travel a certain path and you are receptive to what He expects from you, you will always get a clear indication of the direction you must follow.

Experiencing the presence of the great Guide is an exciting and satisfying event. You will know no greater joy on your entire journey. It will lead you to "green pastures" and "quiet waters."

It is only when you are guided by Christ that you learn to understand the true wealth and deep satisfaction of your partnership with Him. Then your heart sings, " Jesus is the source of all my joy!"

Guide and Perfecter, guide me on my path of life so that I can reflect whose follower I am. Amen.

Christ's Invitation

Read John 6:30-40

"All that the Father gives Me will come to Me, and whoever comes to Me I will never drive away." (John 6:37)

Sometimes people struggle to completely surrender their lives to Jesus Christ. They know they must do it (and they even want to do it), but there are various factors that prevent them from coming to the point of full surrender to Him. They think of the things they will have to give up. They also know that sin and the living Christ can't both reign in their lives.

When Jesus calls, "Come to Me!" He offers them a full and satisfying life that reveals their sins in the right light. Sincere repentance is then necessary.

> *Lord, make me according to Thy heart.*
> ~ Brother Lawrence

Many people find it embarrassing to react to an emotional evangelical appeal. Their proud attitude prevents them from having the greatest experience they will ever know. The "come to Jesus-school" might possibly be mocked, but even so, it is still the greatest challenge a person can respond to.

Then there are those who have disappointed Jesus so many times with their efforts to follow and serve Him that they think to risk it again will be to make a mockery of the invitation.

Every Christian has experienced bitter defeat in his spiritual life at some point. No matter how many times you have disappointed the Master, His invitation still stands. He calls, "Come to Me!" and when you return to Him, He gives you a festive reception.

I thank and praise You, Holy Savior, for Your love that will never leave me. Amen.

The Moment of Truth

Read John 18:28-40

"I came into the world, to testify to the truth. Everyone on the side of truth listens to Me." (John 18:37)

Many people refuse to come to a standstill and deal with their personal issues. Deep down in their hearts various questions arise, but they refuse to listen to or handle them. Usually every possible effort is made to avoid these questions. However, they keep cropping up with tedious regularity and demand answers.

Questions most people have asked in one form or another are: "What is truth?"; "Is my life governed by blind fate?" or " Can I really know God?"

These and other important questions need to be answered. There are no instant answers to these questions. Many students have devoted a lifetime to searching for the answers and trying to explain them.

Christ is the key which unlocks the golden doors into the temple of Divine truth.

~ A. W. Pink

When you reach the moment of truth in your life and admit that the questions that touch the core of life are far beyond your understanding, the wise and constructive thing to do is to place yourself under the instruction of Jesus Christ.

Accept His wisdom and guidance for your life. It requires the discipline of prayer, meditation, Bible study and self-discovery. He teaches you and guides you through your daily life.

You will soon find that though you may not discover all the answers immediately, you will develop the awareness that God is guiding you to a more complete and richer understanding of life. Then your struggle with the vital questions will not be in vain.

Perfect and all-knowing Lord, because You control my life, I leave all the unanswered questions in Your hands. Amen.

The School of Love

Read Mark 10:13-16

"Anyone who will not receive the kingdom of God like a little child will never enter it." (Mark 10:15)

Most small children are pure, innocent and loving. They are teachable and are easily guided. Jesus Christ set these qualities as the conditions for access to the kingdom of God.

Teachers will tell you that up to a certain age children believe that the teacher is flawless and can do no wrong. Children have the same trust in most adults, especially their parents. There are many aspects to consider if one desires a complete understanding of a child's faith.

> *Learn to follow counsel, serve faithfully, and magnify your calling, for God's kingdom is a kingdom of order.*
> ~ Anonymous

Unfortunately evil and sinful things are also taught to children. They follow the examples we set for them. If these include prejudice, violence, hatred, selfishness and other negative qualities, then they believe that this is how they should live. If they are strengthened in their faith and have examples of love, nobleness, integrity and sympathy, they will then follow this example.

It is no wonder that adults have to learn afresh how to love. The world in which we live is not a loving place, but the true world, God's world, is a place of love. The love of Jesus Christ was not a weak, emotional love, but something more powerful that could achieve great deeds.

We should purposefully focus on loving more every day; we should enroll in Jesus' school of love so that He can love through us. We should learn to be tolerant and allow others to differ from us. We should always be filled with compassion and be prepared to reach out to someone in need. Give other people a sense of self-worth by expressing appreciation for them.

Teach me daily, O God, to love with a pure and sincere heart.
Amen.

A Solid Foundation

Read 1 Corinthians 3:9-23

No one can lay any foundation other than the one already laid, which is Jesus Christ. (1 Corinthians 3:11)

Over the years people have held differing opinions regarding the education of children. Academic experts have researched and compiled volumes, teachers have used their practical experience in the classroom to base their ideas on and parents have experienced all the trials and tribulations of family life.

Every generation is convinced that they will carry out the task better than the previous one, and every child is sure that he will handle the situation better than his parents did.

There is, and will always be, just one method of ensuring that your child is educated in such a way that he is able to face the un-

> *The ultimate ground of faith and knowledge is confidence in God.*
>
> ~ Charles Hodge

certain future with confidence and has a balanced outlook on life. That is making sure your child's life is based on the steadfast foundation of Christian faith. This means that you too must lead a Christian life.

When your child's life centers around Christ, he will be filled with love, joy, peace, patience, kindness, goodness, gentleness, faithfulness and self-control while growing up and through the rest of his life (See Gal. 5:22-23).

Jesus shares all these things with His children through His Spirit. What better way can you equip your child to enter an ever-changing world? Your child will have a solid foundation upon which to build his life.

Father, by building my life on the Rock, I will ensure that my children will also find fulfillment in life. Thank You for entrusting them to me with this glorious purpose. Amen.

The Test of Solitude

Read Mark 1:32-39

Very early in the morning, while it was still dark, Jesus got up, left the house and went off to a solitary place, where He prayed. (Mark 1:35)

The Master had a very busy ministry. The crowds followed Him wherever He went. He was aware that healing power flowed out of Him. The only way He could maintain and replenish His spiritual strength was to guard His valuable relationship with His heavenly Father. To do this He had to spend time alone with God. He got up early, before dawn, and spent time in fellowship with God in the silence of daybreak.

> *Language has created the word 'loneliness' to express the pain of being alone. And it has created the word 'solitude' to express the glory of being alone.*
> ~ Paul Tillich

Many people today find it difficult to separate themselves from others and be alone. They have to be part of a crowd where they can lose their identity and become part of the thrill of the moment. This is true of religious people too. They are strong when they are involved in an emotional act of worship, but when the excitement of the moment has passed, they stand alone. What then? Many become so frantically active in the service of God that they lose sight of the God they are serving.

Christianity flourishes in fellowship and sharing in Christian brotherhood is essential for spiritual growth. But it is when you are alone that your faith is tested. When you stand alone without the support of any emotional outpouring and God calls you into fellowship with Himself – then the true quality of your Christianity is revealed. While you spend time in God's Presence, these moments become times of spiritual strength and renewal.

Gracious Master, grant me the desire and determination to regularly spend time in solitude with You. Amen.

Gathering Together

Read Mark 2:1-12

So many gathered that there was no room left, not even outside the door, and He preached the word to them. (Mark 2:2)

People gather in crowds for different reasons. Sometimes it's for entertainment, like at sports games or music concerts. They gather to see and hear a famous person. Sometimes they just enjoy being part of a crowd. At other times they come together to celebrate a big occasion. They also come together to listen when they know that someone has an important message that can influence their lives and existence.

That is why people gathered in the fisherman's house in Capernaum. They wanted to listen to Jesus and receive the words of Life from Him. They knew that He had a message that would touch the depths of their souls. They knew that when Jesus preached, God was speaking. Sometimes He performed great works. Little did the crowds of that time know that the words and actions of that day would be retold through the ages and would bring life to millions of people.

> *The Word is the face, the image, the presence of God in those to whom He brought light and made Himself known.*
>
> ~ Clement of Alexandria

They listened to Jesus because He answered their questions. They accepted His teachings because they knew it would give direction to their lives. They listened to His words because they brought joy and hope to their hearts. They accepted His preaching because it brought them face to face with God. They yearned for His words because they brought healing; they waited for His word of forgiveness; His insight into the truth, and the proclamation of the kingdom of God. They knew that His Word was not simply a passing thought, but an everlasting truth that would stand till the end of time.

Holy Lord Jesus, gather the people of the world and make them people of the Word. Amen.

Beware of Harboring Vengeful Thoughts

Read Matthew 6:5-15

"If you forgive men when they sin against you, your heavenly Father will also forgive you. But if you do not forgive men their sins, your Father will not forgive your sins." (Matthew 6:14-15)

Don't allow a grievance to develop into long-term disapproval. If you do this you might discover that it becomes part of your personality and that it sours your attitude toward life.

What many people don't understand is that harboring a grievance against another person does unspeakable damage to yourself. It is an accepted belief that certain physical ailments have their roots in a bitter and unforgiving spirit. Forgiveness, besides its religious implications, is a healing emotion that makes a positive contribution to your own health and happiness.

> *When you forgive, you in no way change the past – but you sure do change the future.*
>
> ~ Bernard Meltzer

When Jesus commanded His disciples to forgive their enemies, He gave them the rules for a healthy life. To forgive those who have let you down is essential for developing a new relationship with God. Without forgiveness, a healthy relationship with God can't exist. When this unit is broken down, or didn't exist in the first place, you miss one of the most enriching life experiences.

To know God as far as it is humanly possible is to live an abundant and happy life, and it is precisely for this reason that Jesus Christ came to earth: to forgive us so that we can forgive our enemies and share His unity with the eternal Father. Don't allow an unforgiving spirit to rob you of the spiritual riches that are your rightful inheritance.

Savior, as You have forgiven me, give me the grace and strength to forgive others so that I can enjoy the abundant life that is my spiritual inheritance. Amen.

Is It from God?

Read Acts 17:16-34

Then they took him and brought him to a meeting of the Areopagus, where they said to him, "May we know what this new teaching is that you are presenting?" (Acts 17:19)

Old habits are hard to change and this is applicable to the church as much as it is to any other area of life. Over the years people have become used to traditions, customs and methods. They are inclined to regard any change with disapproval and even suspicion. This happens to such an extent that it causes friction and even a split.

When you notice signs of change in your congregation; when new methods replace the old tried-and-tested ones, it will be worth your while to think about these things and to analyze them

> *Don't fear change; embrace it.*
> ~ Anthony D'Angelo

before you air your opinion. It is advisable to consider each new idea and to search for the reason for its implementation. Did the old methods fail? Is the new idea an improvement? Or is it just a few people's gimmick? It can also simply be for the sake of change.

Remember that Jesus Christ's methods were revolutionary in relation to the religious practices of His day. Events, however, proved that He was correct. When you are confronted with change, you must first investigate it in relation to God and His Word. If it fits in with Christ's teachings, if it glorifies God and keeps Jesus as its focal point, then you dare not totally reject it. However, if it doesn't fit in with these criteria you can be sure that it doesn't play a role in the advancement of the gospel.

Faithful Savior, thank You that I may strive to glorify Your name in all things. Amen.

A Practical Religion

Read Matthew 7:21-29

"Not everyone who says to Me, 'Lord, Lord,' will enter the kingdom of heaven, but only he who does the will of My Father who is in heaven." (Matthew 7:21)

The difference between sincerity and religious hypocrisy is not always noticeable. It is possible to be intensely religious, but not have the spirit of consecration. It is possible to be faithful in a routine of worship; to enjoy Christian fellowship; to drop Christian phrases and to refer to Christ in loving terms – and not have the Spirit of Jesus.

Jesus reveals God's truths in a way that makes it easy for people to understand. He knows about the testing, temptations, failures and disappointments that people experience. But if His teachings are applied in the power of the Holy Spirit, it gives sense and meaning to their lives.

> *Take away love and our earth is a tomb.*
>
> ~ Robert Browning

In this day when religious theories and philosophies abound, some people are busy propagating their own unique kind of religion and theology. They forget that what they proclaim is of little importance if their lives are not a practical expression of their theory.

You might allege that Jesus is your Friend, but for this friendship to be meaningful there has to be a practical application of it in your daily life. It means that you must love God with your heart, soul and mind and in the power of this love, you must love your fellow man. As a Christian, you are called to practically demonstrate this holy love in the world you live in.

Lord Jesus, through Your Spirit, help me to develop a practical faith of love. Amen.

Who Is in Control?

Read 1 John 2:1-17

We know that we have come to know Him if we obey His commands.
(1 John 2:3)

We sometimes wonder who is in control of certain activities. If an ugly confrontation arises during a sports match, we ask, "Who is in charge?" Is it the referee? Or the captains? Or the fighting players?

The question can also be asked, "Are you in control of yourself?" Are you under the control of your baser instincts like envy, lust and pride? Are you driven by success, or by your love for God?

It is possible to determine whether you know Jesus by seeing whether you obey your own requirements or God's. People often declare that they have had a spiritual experience, but it is the way in which they live that tests the depth and sincerity of that experience.

It does not require great learning to be a Christian and to be convinced of the truth of the Bible. It requires only an honest heart and a willingness to obey God.

~ William Barnes

The sincerity of our faith is not measured by the apparent success of our work for God. Nor by how popular we are or how much we are praised by people. It is determined by the standard of our obedience to God's commandments and Jesus' requirement that we love our fellow man.

Ask yourself: Does Jesus own the central place in your life? Do we find our greatest joy in being obedient to Him, even at our own discomfort? Whose interests do we serve? Who is in control?

Control my entire life and being, Lord, so that I might live to Your honor. Amen.

August

Follow Him

Not only was the Teacher wise, but also
He imparted knowledge to the people.
~ Ecclesiastes 12:9

Learning is not attained by chance. It must be sought
for with ardor and attended to with diligence.
~ Abigail Adams

*R*edeemer and Savior, Jesus Christ,
Thank You for coming to this earth
to live among us and to teach us
to find the path to life.
You said, "I have come that they may
have life, and have it to the full" (John 10:10).
Thank You for every lesson You
taught us during Your earthly stay:
Lessons through Your perfect example
and Your enriching parables
that can even be understood by the most simple.
Life is sometimes dark, but You bring the light;
Life is sometimes lonely, but You are always with us;
Life is sometimes puzzling, but You
bring sense and meaning to it.
In this month, lead us through Your life and teachings.
Be our Good Shepherd who leads us to
green pastures and quiet waters.
Thank You that we can belong to the flock
that cost You dearly and therefore
experience life every time You act or teach us.
Make us willing learners in Your
preparatory school for eternal life.
We pray this in the name above all names – Jesus our Savior,

Amen.

Focusing on Trivialities

Read Mark 2:23-28

One Sabbath Jesus was going through the grain fields, and as His disciples walked along, they began to pick some heads of grain. The Pharisees said to Him, "Look, why are they doing what is unlawful on the Sabbath?" (Mark 2:23-24)

Many people are under the erroneous impression that Christianity imposes a set of rules and regulations on them. There are certain things Christians "simply don't do" and there are other things Christians "must do." Most other religions have similar codes of behavior that they uphold.

The Ten Commandments that God gave Israel served to direct the children of Israel. Through the ages, teachers have tried to help learners by showing them which actions do and do not break the Law. This culminated in more than six hundred rules and regulations. Picking heads of grain was regarded as harvesting – which was work – and to work on the Sabbath was forbidden. Jesus knew that the Law was meant to bring life, not to make people distressed and miserable and overload them with guilt.

> *If the Spirit of grace is absent, the law is present only to convict and kill.*
>
> ~ St. Augustine

Christianity is not a set of regulations, rules and laws. It means to follow Jesus and to know that He loves you, to love Him in return, and to transform that love into love for your fellow man. It does, however, include a few disciplines, but love always rises above the law. Laws are too small, narrow-minded and soul-destroying. They lead you away from the true issue – God! God fills your heart with His love and not with His laws and makes a worthy person out of you. He doesn't want you to be a slave to the Law. He wants to free you to live, grow and love.

Lord Jesus, fill my heart with love so that I will truly love. Amen.

What Is the Sabbath Day For?

Read Mark 2:23-28

He said to them, "The Sabbath was made for man, not man for the Sabbath." (Mark 2:27)

During the Second World War there came a time when the English army urgently needed ammunition. It was decided that the factories producing the ammunition would work seven days a week to increase their production. Initially there was a rise in production, but after just a few weeks the production dropped to less than when they worked six days a week. The experiment was stopped and the factories returned to working six days a week. Production again rose to its previous level.

> *The Sabbath is God's special present to the working man, and one of its chief objects is to prolong his life, and preserve efficient his working tone. The savings bank of human existence is the weekly Sabbath.*
>
> ~ William G. Blaikie

God knew a few things when He commanded, "Remember the Sabbath day by keeping it holy. Six days you shall labor and do all your work, but the seventh day is a Sabbath to the LORD your God" (Exod. 20:8-10). Jesus was saying that God gave us the Sabbath (which is Hebrew for *rest*) as a gift and for our own benefit. It was meant to enrich human life.

Christians don't honor the Sabbath – which is on Saturday – but the Day of the Lord – which is Sunday – the day of Christ's resurrection. This is a day to celebrate Christ's sovereignty, to rest and refresh ourselves, to renew relationships, to spend some time alone and meditate on all the wonderful gifts God has given us. Don't make it a burden or a torturous experience. Rejoice and be glad in it. Worship God and find new direction for your life from Him. Open yourself to the Spirit and begin to truly live.

Let Your disciples throughout the whole world rejoice in Your resurrection and Your glorified Presence among us. Amen.

What Is Your Answer?

Read 1 Peter 3:13-22

Always be prepared to give an answer to everyone who asks you to give the reason for the hope that you have. (1 Peter 3:15)

You probably feel that you don't know enough about the Bible to get involved in religious arguments. It is a broad subject with many pitfalls that are to be avoided. Furthermore, few unbelievers are convicted through clever arguments.

In spite of this, Peter told the early believers to be ready with a meaningful response if they were asked why they believed in Jesus Christ. He didn't command them to run off and obtain degrees in theology. He knew that there would be sincere people who wanted to know more about their new faith and their confidence in the future.

> *Be careful how you live; you will be the only Bible some people ever read.*
> ~ William J. Toms

The future was a real factor for Peter's believers because they could be killed for their faith at any moment. Some people were amazed that Christians could face death so courageously, but they knew that they would be with Christ after they died.

We must also know the reason for the hope that lives within us. You don't have to be clever to give a simple, direct answer when asked. "I believe in Him because He has carried me in love over the years," would be a good starting point. Knowing the Bible better will take you a step further. Always be ready to share your faith with someone else because it could be the turning point in that person's life.

Teach me, faithful Savior, to always be ready to answer questions about my faith. Amen.

Gentleness and Respect

Read 1 Peter 3:13-22

Do this with gentleness and respect. (1 Peter 3:15)

Christianity today tends to think of Jesus in terms of how He has helped us. We primarily think of Him as our Friend, Redeemer, Helper in need, Shepherd, Healer, Advisor and Guide. We call Him "Lord" but hopelessly underestimate His glory.

The New Testament Christians could never have done this. They were forced to declare, "Caesar is Lord!" By doing so they would be pledging their highest allegiance to a politician, who was just an ordinary human. They knew that they couldn't declare, "Jesus is Lord" and simultaneously say the same of the Caesar. They refused to acknowledge that Caesar was Lord and for this reason they were persecuted and killed.

> *Now sinner, whether thou knowest it or not, thou are indebted to Him that did hang upon the tree, for the breath that is now in thee.*
>
> ~ Charles H. Spurgeon

To exalt Jesus as Lord and to declare this was to sacrifice your life for your faith. For this they were burnt at the stake. To make Christ Lord of your life at that time meant more than simply using the name "Lord" as a comfortable crutch to lean on.

Christ offers to be your Friend and Helper. But at the same time He expects to be "Lord" of your life. This means that you allow Him to take full control of your life and to direct your life every moment. It means to submit to Him in loving obedience and to accept that He now gives the commands. He becomes the object of your greatest loyalty – above political rulers, before your spouse, before your boss and before your community. Make sure who is "Lord" of your life.

Jesus Christ, my Redeemer, You are Lord of my life, both now and forevermore! Amen.

When You Have to Walk Alone

Read Hebrews 13:1-6

God has said, "Never will I leave you; never will I forsake you." (Hebrews 13:5)

Christian fellowship is essential for spiritual growth. To belong to a warm, caring fellowship inspires us and strengthens our daily walk with the living Christ. To try and walk the Christian way alone, without the support of living Christian fellowship, is to become prey to spiritual failure. You need the support of fellow Christians to help you as you carry your cross.

If, however, your spiritual dynamic depends on enthusiastic or emotional gatherings, the day will come when you realize that you don't possess a living faith, but rather a masquerade of a religion that will let you down in a time of crisis. Then you will realize that you have to depend on God and not on the support of His people.

> *It is morally impossible to exercise trust in God while there is failure to wait upon Him for guidance and direction.*
> ~ D. E. Hoste

You have to accept full responsibility in every area of life. No one else can do it for you. When you have to make choices and decisions, you alone are responsible for the consequences and you have to walk your chosen path. Choose very carefully because you can't digress from the path you have chosen.

When you set out on the final journey of life, you have to travel alone. No one can accompany you. You have to walk that path alone, and yet, you are not alone because the Master has promised to be with you as you enter the great unknown. As a disciple, you have the privilege of knowing Him as the Companion who will stand by you until the end of your life – and beyond!

Faithful Savior, even though I sometimes have to walk alone, You are my constant Companion. I thank You for this! Amen.

True Christianity Balances Life

Read James 4:1-10

Humble yourselves before the Lord, and He will lift you up. (James 4:10)

All Christians desire to live balanced lives. They hope to remain calm in the midst of chaos; to think clearly when conflicting standpoints fight to win their trust; to see both sides of every problem and to refrain from mean-spirited criticism.

Unfortunately this experience proved that it is easy to nurture an ideal, but very difficult to live it out in practice. What you must do and what you are often causes inner pressure and throws you spiritually off balance. It makes life confusing.

Make sure that the thing you are living for is worth dying for.

~ Charles Mayes

It is very important to accept that life must have a spiritual foundation and that it can only be lived successfully if this fact is accepted. This foundation is more than intellectual approval of a creed or dogma – no matter how much it might express the truth. It is accepting the living Christ in your life and allowing Him to express Himself through your actions and thoughts. The glorious fact that Jesus Christ lives makes Christianity the most powerful and dynamic force in the lives of modern disciples.

It is only when you start a relationship with the living Christ through love, grace, daily prayer and meditation that your thoughts can turn toward Him and you can become aware of His guidance and accept His practical way of living. In this relationship the battle of your life becomes subjected to your living Lord and your life becomes balanced and Christ-inspired.

I rejoice, Lord Jesus, that through Your grace and love I can live a well-balanced life. Amen.

Love That Conquers

Read Philippians 2:5-14

Your attitude should be the same as that of Christ Jesus. (Philippians 2:5)

The sad fact is that we live in a world where the attitude and behavior of many leave much to be desired. Corruption, scandals and violence are the order of the day and decent, right-minded people are astounded by the decline of standards and the degeneration of behavioral patterns.

The normal human reaction to this is the temptation to handle the situation with similar attitudes and to fight fire with fire. However angry you may be about present circumstances – especially if you have been a victim – as a Christian, you can't allow yourself to stoop to their level. It might give you temporary satisfaction, but it isn't a lasting solution to the world's problems.

> *Love of God is the root, love of our neighbor is the fruit of the Tree of Life. Neither can exist without the other, but the one is cause and the other effect.*
> ~ William Temple

Jesus Christ clearly demonstrated that His way was the best and always will be. The only way to handle evil is through the path of divine love.

Love is not a sign of weakness, as some would have you believe. If we consider Christ's courage and endurance on the cross, nobody can dare to call Him weak. As it was then, so it is now: only the forgiving love of Christ can and will conquer the powers of evil.

Father God, You are love. This is clearly spelt out on the cross.

Amen.

To Find God!

Read Ephesians 4:1-10

There is one Lord, one faith, one baptism; one God and Father of all, who is over all and through all and in all. (Ephesians 4:4-6)

Through the ages people have searched for God. They saw His majesty in the heavens; studied His handiwork in nature; and experienced His timing through the galaxy. God was "out there" the whole time. He was Someone separated from the human race, introduced as a kind-hearted old gentleman who was quick to forgive and slow to judge. In moments of testing He was asked for help and comfort – but He was always the One placed apart from the human race.

> *Before I began to think and consider the love of God and the mercy and compassion of God, I must start with the holiness of God.*
> ~ Martyn Lloyd-Jones

The coming of Jesus totally changed this concept of God. The living Christ teaches us that the eternal God is not a distant Godhead who lives far away from us, but rather the Holy One who makes His home in a person's spirit.

Jesus, who is in perfect harmony with God, invites people to the same relationship. Jesus said, "I am in the Father and the Father is in Me." Then He invited His followers to abide *in* Him.

If you want to come to a full understanding of the Presence of God, you have to look at your own spirit and realize that you can't come to a full understanding of the outer God until you discover Him who lives inside you. Be still and know that He is God and confirm this reality in your own life. Then you will experience His living Presence with glorious certainty.

Master and Savior, come through the Holy Spirit and make me aware of the indwelling Presence of the eternal God every day. Amen.

Tell Me a Story!

Read Mark 4:1-9

He taught them many things by parables. (Mark 4:2)

When you were a small child you probably enjoyed bedtime stories and regarded this as the best part of the day. When the one story was finished, you pleaded for another. And when you were safely tucked up in bed, your parents would switch on the TV and watch – a story!

The whole Bible is the story of God's dealings with His people and with the world. The Gospels tell the story of Jesus' life, crucifixion and resurrection. Acts and the Letters of the Apostles tell the story of God's ongoing activity through His church. Jesus didn't come to proclaim a philosophy, or to lay down a set of rules. He didn't bring a political system to life. He told stories. And the things He did resulted in stories that have been told over and over again. We still tell these stories and they continue to spark the imagination of young and old alike.

> *I wonder what hours of prayer and thought lie behind the apparently simple and spontaneous parables of the Gospel.*
> ~ J. B. Phillips

The stories Jesus told were stories about life. They are about people – working people; foolish people; clever people; strong people; and sinful people. They are also about God – a loving God; a wise God; a sovereign God; a strong God and a kind-hearted God.

You also have a story. Indeed, you *are* a story! If you believe in Jesus Christ and follow Him, He helps you write a new story – the tale of human struggle, failure and growth, with the glory of God, the grace of Jesus and the tender touch of the Holy Spirit. When you eventually stand before God, He will say, "Tell Me your story!" What will your story be like?

Help me, Good Shepherd, to write a story with my life that will gladden Your heart. Amen.

On the Shore at the Water's Edge

Read Mark 4:1-9

Jesus began to teach by the lake. The crowd that gathered around Him was so large that He got into a boat and sat in it out on the lake, while all the people were on the shore at the water's edge. (Mark 4:1)

In court great emphasis is placed on what the witnesses say. Some are regarded as "good" witnesses, others as "trustworthy" and others as "unreliable." The manner in which they tell their story, whether they appear honest or devious, and how their story survives under cross-examination are all factors the judge takes into account when he decides to accept or reject a witness.

If you were arrested for being a Christian, would there be enough evidence to convict you?

~ Anonymous

The Gospels consist of stories that were told by witnesses about the actions and words of Jesus Christ. Mark wrote about what Peter told him – and Peter was there. Therefore, Mark's story is authentic. In our reading for today we see details that could only have been observed by an eye-witness. Peter remarked that Jesus "sat in" the boat to teach the people. He remarked that the people were on the shore. Such facts are not simply made up. You can believe and trust the Gospels. You can have faith in Jesus on the basis of the trustworthiness of those who recorded Jesus' first actions. God entrusted the truth of His eternal Message to ordinary people.

Jesus never wrote a book, because the people who saw and heard Him and conveyed the message were living embodiments of the truth. And you are too. Jesus conveys the same message through your life and personality, and for this reason you must be a trustworthy witness.

Holy Jesus, may my life proclaim Your truth and love. Make me a trustworthy witness. Amen.

Be Prepared to Suffer

Read 1 Peter 4:1-6

Since Christ suffered in His body, arm yourselves also with the same attitude, because he who has suffered in his body is done with sin.

(1 Peter 4:1)

Above the west door of Westminster Abbey in London are ten small statues, each one in its own slot. They all represent people who died for their faith in Jesus Christ during the twentieth century. One is a South African, Manche Masemola. She was born into the Pedi tribe and grew up in an environment where Christianity was regarded with aversion. She became a Christian during a missionary outreach in her area. Every form of physical persecution, including violence, was used to make her abandon her faith. She said to a priest, "I will never deny my faith, even if they behead me. I will be baptized in my own blood." Her parents took her to an isolated place and she was beaten to death.

> *When the Christians, upon these occasions, received martyrdom, they were ornamented, and crowned with garlands of flowers, for which they, in heaven, received eternal crowns of glory.*
>
> ~ John Foxe

You will hardly be called to such martyrdom. But you can ask yourself some serious questions about how far you will be willing to go to obey Christ. If a romantic relationship required you to sacrifice your faith, would you be willing to do it? If your superiors at work required you to abandon your faith, would you do it? If the only job you could find required you to sell drugs, would you let your faith fit in with it? Followers of Jesus all over the world make these kinds of decisions daily. How prepared are you to suffer for Christ?

Holy Spirit of God, thank You for helping me to calculate the cost of my discipleship. Amen.

The Great Commission

Read Matthew 28:11-20

"Go and make disciples of all the nations." (Matthew 28:19)

Many businesses believe in the saying, "If you aren't growing, you're dying." They are continually on the lookout to buy similar companies and expand their own activities so that their profits increase.

Jesus commanded His disciples to become apostles. Earlier He had invited them to "Follow Me!" and now He sends them to "Go and make disciples of all the nations." Their task was commissioned to them by One who received His authority from God. From that moment on the church of Christ knew that its mission was to make new disciples, more disciples and better disciples. The church either takes steps to grow, or it faces deterioration and eventual death.

> *To be a Christian is to believe that we are commanded and authorized to say certain things to the world; things that will make disciples of all nations.*
>
> ~ Rowan D. Williams

This is still the church's God-given task. It is also the challenge that Jesus sets for each one of His disciples – to make more disciples. It is not solely the responsibility of the church body as a whole; it is the responsibility of each one of us. You do this by talking about Jesus every time the opportunity arises. You do this through the spiritual edification of those who are already His disciples. You help followers to be better followers. You do it when you pray for those who are battling a faith struggle. You do it when you pray for missionaries. You help to make disciples when you support missionaries financially and when you help to spread the gospel through reading material, radio and television. You can't evade this command because it is Christ's "Great Commission" to you as a Christian!

Lord, help me to make more disciples for Your kingdom. Amen.

The Three-fold Name

Read Matthew 28:11-20

"Go and make disciples of all nations, baptizing them in the name of the Father and of the Son and of the Holy Spirit." (Matthew 28:19)

Christianity is much more than the awareness of God or faith in Him. It is more than saying, "Yes, there is a Supreme Being!"

It means having a personal relationship with God who came to us in the form of three Persons. Don't worry if you find it difficult to understand the concept of the Trinity. Christianity is about becoming a disciple of the one who came from God the Father and also believed in Him.

We can only know God the Father through God the Son. He shows us the Father who sent Him. But you can only know God the Father and Jesus the Son if the Holy Spirit has worked faith in your heart – faith that Jesus is the

> *God is revealed to us as the Father, Son, and Holy Spirit each with distinct personal attributes, but without division of nature, essence or being.*
>
> ~ James Boyce

Son and that God is His Father and yours. This Spirit works in you like yeast and enables you to know Jesus and to come close to God the Father.

Therefore, the disciples you must go and make are not just people who believe that God exists. They have to know Jesus Christ as their God and they have to be receptive to the work of the Holy Spirit in their lives so that Jesus can live in their hearts. In this way they have to be taught about Jesus and become learners of the Holy Spirit and people of God. Faith must grow in them daily. Christ must mold them and God must become their Father, who loves them and continually works through them.

Father, Son and Holy Spirit, teach me to know You better and more intimately each day. Amen.

Look Back and Be Thankful

Read Ephesians 5:15-20

Give thanks for everything to God the Father in the name of our Lord Jesus Christ. (Ephesians 5:20 NLT)

The middle of the year has come and gone. It is fitting to stop for a moment and consider how the year has been for you so far. Maybe it has been a year of problems and troubles; or maybe it has brought you prosperity, success and achievement. Maybe you had to say goodbye to someone who was very close to you. Maybe there was the birth of a child or the marriage of someone special. Most years our lives are a mix of good and bad.

> *One single grateful thought raised to heaven is the most perfect prayer.*
>
> *~ G. E. Lessing*

Take a few moments today to thank God for all the good things that have come to you from His loving hand. Even if you have had an awful year, there will still be things you can thank Him for. Write them down on a piece of paper. If things have generally gone well, it is just as important to list them so that you don't forget. Include family-related blessings too. Also thank Him if you have profited financially or been promoted at work.

Possibly some of your prayers have been answered; maybe there has been healing in the family; or a small miracle has taken place. If you have grown spiritually in a time of suffering, thank God. If you have advanced in your particular career, it's also something to thank God for. To think earnestly about these things will help you to see your setbacks from a different perspective and you will notice the hand of God in your life.

Loving and gracious Lord Jesus, every year I have endless things to thank You for. Amen.

Chosen to Suffer

Read 1 Peter 2:18-25

To this you were called, because Christ suffered for you, leaving you an example, that you should follow in His steps. (1 Peter 2:21)

In the movie *Fiddler on the Roof*, Tevi, the main character, sings, "If I were a rich man," He asks God, "Would it spoil some vast eternal plan if I were a wealthy man?"

God's "vast eternal plan" has nothing to do with who is rich and who is poor. His plan is the salvation of humankind. To fulfill this plan He sacrificed His Son out of love for the world. Jesus, in turn, appealed to His disciples when He said, "If anyone would come after Me, he must deny himself and take up his cross and follow Me" (Matt. 16:24). By the time Peter wrote our reading for today, many had already died for

> *God whispers in our pleasures, but shouts in our pain.*
> ~ C. S. Lewis

Jesus and many more would follow – including Peter himself.

God has also called you and me – not to a life of peace, power and prosperity – but to a life of self-denial, service and love for others. For some believers this may lead to suffering and even death. To follow Jesus is not a walk in the park. It sometimes includes mockery and rejection. It is sometimes a lonely path on which you must lay down certain things that others take for granted.

Some have taken up the cross by going to a far-off mission field and humbly working for Christ. Others have cared for the sick and helped the poor. Each one of us has a cross to bear. The question is: Do you carry your cross in a worthy manner as you follow the great Cross-bearer?

Give me grace, Lord Jesus, to carry the cross that You have laid upon me, without grumbling. Amen.

Different Spiritual Experiences

Read Galatians 3:21-29

You are all children of God through faith in Christ Jesus. And all who have been united with Christ in baptism have put on Christ, like putting on new clothes. (Galatians 3:26-27 NLT)

Self-created spiritual segregation is an ever-present danger for the Christian disciple. When some people become part of the "new life in Jesus Christ" and become aware of His power and love, they tend to think that the way they received this experience is the only way. With the enthusiasm of their new-found faith they find it difficult to accept that other people also have similar experiences, but in a totally different manner.

The truth is that dedicated churchgoers and zealous evangelists all know about God's power and love that rises above all spiritual borders and makes His Presence a reality in the lives of all believers, regardless of credos and dogmas.

> *Conversion can take many different forms.*
> ~ Billy Graham

When stumbling blocks place other believers outside the reach of God's redemption, due to clashing theological differences, it becomes an obstacle that restricts the flow of the Holy Spirit. It is impossible to live in conflict with fellow Christians and expect the power and love of Christ to flow through you. Stumbling blocks that are set up against other believers are stumbling blocks that are set up against the Master too.

The core of any Christian experience is that the living Christ is accepted in the heart and mind of the believer and that it finds expression through love and service to Him and other people. If this is your experience, be grateful for what you have, but allow others to rejoice in His Redemption even if they have arrived at it in a different way.

Lord Jesus, keep me in harmony with all who love and serve You, regardless of the path they are traveling on. Amen.

The Path of the Lord

Read 2 John 1-13

Anyone who runs ahead and does not continue in the teaching of Christ does not have God; whoever continues in the teaching has both the Father and the Son. (2 John 9)

Many people are confused by the various interpretations of the Word of the Lord. The sad fact is that this state has caused many divisions within the church of Jesus Christ. Our Master's prayer for perfect unity among all believers is ignored by those who regard themselves as authorities and believe that their way of interpreting Scripture is the only way.

The hidden danger is that this attitude provides the breeding ground for the destructive influence of Satan, whose most effective method of attack is from within the church, and not from outside.

> *It has pleased God that divine verities should not enter the heart through the understanding, but the understanding through the heart.*
>
> ~ Blaise Pascal

If you experience uncertainty in this area, it is necessary for you to investigate both the teachings and the teachers. If they are not Christ-centered and grounded on His all-encompassing love, you can be sure that they are not from God and must be rejected.

It's not always easy to understand this issue. It is necessary to pray for God's gifts of wisdom and discernment to enable you, through His Holy Spirit, to arrive at a clear understanding of every situation. In this way you will discover the true teaching of Christ in a new-found way.

Lead me on Your path, Lord Jesus, and grant me a clear understanding of Your teachings. Amen.

The Power of Your Faith

Read Luke 19:45-48

Every day He was teaching at the temple. But the chief priests, the teachers of the law and the leaders among the people were trying to kill Him. Yet they could not find any way to do it, because all the people hung on His words. (Luke 19:47-48)

The Christian faith has been continuously attacked throughout the ages. Cynics have mocked it, and individuals have been persecuted and martyred because of it. Even some people who call themselves Christians have sowed doubt in the minds of others regarding the teachings of Christ and the interpretation of Scripture.

While it is faith that makes all things possible, it is love that makes all things easy.

~ E. H. Hopkins

In spite of all these attacks, the Word of God has remained indestructible. The Truth that Christ brought to light is untouchable, and any attempt by mere people to undermine it can only succeed if Christ's disciples don't accept Him or believe in His teachings.

To play your part in upholding the name of Jesus Christ, it is essential that you maintain a personal and intimate relationship with Him and make sure that your understanding of Scripture is pure and correct.

In this way you will receive strength from the living Christ and you will be able to resist the pressure that is placed on you by those who seek to undermine your faith. Your knowledge of God's Word will give you the ability and assurance to oppose any argument that is aimed against His teachings. For this you need a lot of mercy and firm faith.

Thank You, Redeemer and Savior, that Your Word carries me through in the face of great opposition. Amen.

Praying in the Dark Valley

Read Psalm 102:17-29

The Lord will rebuild Zion and appear in His glory. He will respond to the prayer of the destitute; He will not despise their plea. (Psalm 102:16-17)

Every child of God experiences a time when it is difficult to pray. As believers, we sometimes feel like we are losing grip on the anchor of our lives – the awareness of God's Presence. God, who has always been a reality in our lives, suddenly seems distant and unreal.

Many Christians don't recognize the immeasurable importance that this time can have for them and their spiritual growth. They incorrectly think that God no longer cares about them, that He doesn't hear when they cry out to Him in need and that He won't answer them.

> *Let us advance on our knees.*
> ~ Joseph Hardy Neesima

Times like these require you to trust in the Presence of God and start living in a deeper relationship with Him. You must learn to put your hand in God's hand and to live with Him in the light and especially in the darkness. Then His Presence will be a living and joyful reality. The hour of darkness will pass. Therefore, don't revolt against your inability to pray. Rather determine what you can learn during these times and always hold fast to the truth that God's love for you will never change.

God always listens to your prayers – those you pray in times of sunshine, but also those prayed in the dark valley. He won't scorn your prayer – He will answer you.

Hearer of prayer, help me not to focus on myself and my problems; but to search harder for You and to do Your will until You transform the darkness in my life into light. Amen.

To Not See and Yet to Believe

Read John 20:26-31

Jesus told him, "Because you have seen Me, you have believed; blessed are those who have not seen and yet have believed." (John 20:29)

We usually trust what we can see. If someone tells us something unusual, we suspect that they are misleading us – and no one wants to be misled. Even more so, we don't want others to think that we are fools who can be tricked easily. Therefore, we want to see things for ourselves – because seeing is believing.

This is exactly how Thomas felt after the resurrection. He was no-one's fool. He didn't fall for the other disciples' story that Jesus was alive. But while he was present, Jesus came. This made Thomas look like a fool. The Presence of the risen Lord, the nail marks in His hands and the spear wound in His side transformed Thomas. Darkness changed into light. Skepticism changed into trust. Doubt disappeared and faith, amazement and worship flowed out of Thomas.

Faith to the soul is what breathing is to the body.
~ Thomas Brooks

Thomas probably didn't touch Jesus, or place his fingers in the nail marks or in the wound in Jesus' side. He simply believed and fell at Jesus' feet in worship. But many who saw everything that Jesus did still did not believe. Many in the crowd did not believe. The church authorities and the state did not believe. You might say, "If I was there and saw everything, I would believe!"

Two thousand years later you *can* believe. Millions of people do. Throughout the ages countless people have believed. You can believe because the story of Thomas the doubter sounds sincere and true. Stop for a while and join Thomas in His amazement and submission and declare along with him, "My Lord and my God!"

Gracious Jesus, help me to believe, even when I can't see. Amen.

The Need for a Deeper Love

Read Mark 12:28-34

"The most important one," answered Jesus, "is this: 'Hear, O Israel, the Lord our God, the Lord is one. Love the Lord your God with all your heart and with all your soul and with all your mind and with all your strength.'" (Mark 12:29-30)

No matter how much you might love Jesus Christ, you will always have a feeling of inadequacy when you compare your love for Him with His love for you. No-one can love you as much as He loves you, but this shouldn't prevent you from striving to increase your love for Him.

To accept the challenge of love, you need to meet Jesus regularly in prayer and meditation. You can't love Christ unless your conscious energy is focused on Him and your spirit is in harmony with His Holy Spirit. Both Scripture and the experience of countless disciples tell us that the Master gives Himself in an exceptional way to those who sincerely love Him and faithfully serve Him. It is necessary that you accept His offer and allow Him to fulfill your life. Let your love for Him mature and grow to a sacrifice that is acceptable to Him.

> *People are renewed by love. As sinful desire ages them, so love rejuvenates them.*
> ~ St. Augustine

Even though your love for Him can never compare to His love for you, the fact remains that if you open your life to His gracious influence and His Spirit, and allow His Spirit to work through you, your imperfect love will be touched by His Holiness and He will accept the sacrifice of your dedicated life as evidence of your love for Him and your fellow man.

Faithful Savior, grant that my love for You will increase and grow through the inspiration of the Holy Spirit. Amen.

When Your Faith Is Tested

Read Luke 18:1-8

"When the Son of Man comes, will He find faith on the earth?" (Luke 18:8)

An endless amount has been said and written about the state of the world today. Violence is on the increase and lawlessness and anarchy are the order of the day. The urgent call is being heard more and more that we are living in the last days and that the coming of Christ is at hand. There is nothing more we can do to prevent the decline of society and the destruction of the world.

> *There must be a beginning of any great matter, but the continuing unto the end until it be thoroughly finished yields the true glory.*
>
> ~ Francis Drake

Whether these predictions are true or not, despite the chaos that reigns, we can't reject the standards that Christ has set. The fact that the world is in a desperate condition doesn't give Christians the excuse to stop fighting against the Evil One. We dare not just sit back and wait for the Prince of Peace to come and set the world straight again.

Christian dedication and submission for life and discipleship must be practiced in sunny weather as well as during storms. Despite the Evil One's efforts to undermine the church of Christ, and the tremendous pressure that is mounting against the Christian faith, it will always be your duty to honor the name of Jesus Christ. You must cling to His power and everything He stands for, so that when He does indeed come, you will hear Him say, "Well done, good and faithful servant."

Holy Jesus, if I am tested, strengthen my faith so that I will be able to endure it. Amen.

Love that Heals

Read John 15:9-17

"My command is this: Love each other as I have loved you." (John 15:12)

It often seems as if we are living in a time of great aggression. The media reports incidents of road rage among motorists; violence between sports teams; and mass demonstrations that often turn ugly and get out of control.

Armed confrontations are common in many parts of the world as well as violence and senseless murder. In the business world there is bitterness, hatred and the continuous search for revenge.

The distressing part of it all is that the resulting feelings of aversion eat away at us like a cancer and steal away the fullness of life for which Jesus came. It also robs us of the peace of mind and calmness of spirit that Jesus offers to each of us. He wants us to enjoy the abundant life for which He lived and died.

> *Few things are impossible to diligence and skill. Great works are performed not by strength, but by perseverance.*
> ~ Samuel Johnson

Regardless of the cries for revenge, there is always one way to ensure that you or anyone else enjoy the life that Christ offers. That is to love each other unconditionally – just as the Lord loves us!

That holy love was poured out over us at the cross – it was unconditional and complete. Through this, Christ drew people to Himself and gave them peace. As instruments of His peace, it is our duty to reflect that love and restore peace in our world.

Only through Your love, Lord Jesus, can the aggression in our world be healed. Amen.

Fight Discouragement
in the Power of Jesus

Read 1 Corinthians 15:50-58

Therefore, stand firm. Let nothing move you. Always give yourselves fully to the work of the Lord, because you know that your labor in the Lord is not in vain. (1 Corinthians 15:58)

Discouragement is something most people, if not all, experience at one time or the other. Good intentions are misunderstood; careful plans are thwarted; earnest suggestions are pushed aside; resulting in the temptation to give up. It can happen in your spiritual and secular life, but the frustrations are the same, and it is a well-known fact that discouragement is one of Satan's most popular weapons. He persists, especially with the most enthusiastic people, and his only goal is to undermine Christianity.

> *Develop success from failures. Discouragement and failure are two of the surest stepping stones to success.*
> ~ Dale Carnegie

If you want to fight against discouragement, it is of the utmost importance that you make Christ the center of your life. Before starting any project, first seek God's will in your specific circumstance. Earnestly pray that He will lead you in your decisions and make His will for your life very clear. Move forward then; renewed by the Spirit and strengthened by knowing that God is with you.

You will always face obstacles, as well as people who will try to thwart your efforts. There will be moments when you sense a hint of discouragement. Search for the Master's help to support you and know that what you are attempting to do is being done for and with Jesus. Then you will find that, in Him, it is possible to triumph over all adversities.

Living Savior, I will face life with confidence, knowing that You are beside me. Amen.

It is Never Too Late

Read John 11:1-16

Jesus loved Martha and her sister and Lazarus. Yet when He heard that Lazarus was sick, He stayed where He was two more days. (John 11:5-6)

You, too, have probably also prayed for more time. Perhaps something had to be completed by a certain date and because it was important, you spent a lot of time praying about it. You might have asked God to help you to do something before the due date otherwise it would be too late. And then ... nothing happened.

If you have ever had such an experience, you have probably learned the hard way that you cannot rush God or subject Him to your personal schedule.

When Jesus learned that His friend Lazarus was dying, He did a strange thing. He did not go to support and comfort His friends straight away; He stayed where He was for another two days. When He did eventually arrive in Bethany, He transformed the tragedy of Lazarus' death into an opportunity to glorify God.

> *The time God allots to each one of us is like a precious tissue which we embroider as we best know how.*
>
> ~ Anatole France

There may have been many times in your life when God did not follow your schedule. You prayed fervently but it seemed as if God was too late. But God is never late. His timing is always perfect.

If you love and trust Him, He will let all things work out for your good, in His own perfect time. Instead of demanding from God to act within a certain time frame, you should allow Him to form and polish you according to His perfect will. Then you will live in harmony with Him and have peace of mind.

Forgive me, O Lord, for my selfishness and ignorance. I place my life and my wishes in Your hands and accept Your perfect timing.

Amen.

Cast Away Your Grievances

Read Matthew 18:21-35

Peter came to Jesus and asked, "Lord, how many times shall I forgive my brother when he sins against me? Up to seven times?" Jesus answered, "I tell you, not seven times, but seventy-seven times." (Matthew 18:21-22)

It is very difficult to forgive or to refrain from nurturing ill feelings when you have been wronged or treated unfairly.

When someone scolds or ridicules you, especially in the presence of others, it is almost impossible to forgive them. When you have been treated unjustly, you automatically feel hostile. Your anger reaches boiling point and if it boils over, you create more problems for yourself.

> *When you forgive, you in no way change the past – but you sure do change the future.*
>
> ~ Bernard Meltzer

If you suppress ill feelings, they become an evil, festering sore in your heart, which gradually poisons your thoughts and eventually your entire being.

However difficult it may appear, there is only one way to handle these situations. In your prayers and in your heart, you should continuously confirm that you have forgiven the person who has hurt you. Ask God for grace and strength so that through the Holy Spirit you can forgive as Jesus forgave.

Your forgiveness must not be restricted to your prayers. Jesus' command is, "First go and be reconciled to your brother; then come and offer your gift" (Matt. 5:24). You must go and tell the person who hurt you that you forgive them; only then can you obtain deliverance.

Discipline yourself to forgive those who cause you suffering. Then you can live in peace with God, the person who trespassed against you and yourself.

God of Love, give me the ability to forgive, as You forgave me in Jesus Christ. Amen.

Grow, Grow, Grow!

Read 2 Peter 3:12-18

Grow in the grace and knowledge of our Lord and Savior Jesus Christ. (2 Peter 3:18)

A newly-wed young man wanted to start planting a garden around his new house. He went to an experienced gardener to find out what to do and what not to do. The older man showed him his beautiful garden and explained what the names of the various plants were and how to get them to grow. They came to a certain plant and the older man said, "Years ago I was given a tip about these plants: they grow better if you plant them in the moonlight." "Really?" the young man asked, "Do you always do it this way?" "Oh yes, always. And I talk to them." The young man thought that the old man was kidding him, so he asked, "And what do you say to them?" "I say, 'Grow you wretched creatures. Grow!'" grumbled the older man.

> *All growth that is not towards God is growing to decay.*
> ~ George MacDonald

The apostles give the same advice to believers – just maybe not so explicitly! We aren't told to grow as people in our own estimation or skill. We must grow in grace – God's grace! We must allow God's grace to grow Christ in us.

Allow the Holy Spirit to grow Christ's image in you. Never think that you can stop growing spiritually, however old you might be. Continue to learn more and more about Christ. You can never know Him too well or know too much about Him.

Lord my God, help me, through the Holy Spirit, to never stop growing in Christ. Amen.

Let Christ Be the Referee

Read Colossians 3:12-25

Let the peace of Christ rule in your hearts. (Colossians 3:15)

The referee is one the most important people in a sports game. He must know the rules and how to apply them. His decision must be immediate. Sometimes tensions mount and tempers get out of hand between the players. Then the referee has to intervene, and maintain law and order. Sometimes the referee has to call on another referee to help him make a decision.

The peace that Jesus gives is not only a peace that calms the storm in your heart. He must rule as the other referee does. He is given to you as a Guide in difficult circumstances, where your own preferences, fears and desires can force you to make the wrong decisions. Friends and loved ones can also give you the wrong advice. Rather refer the matter to Jesus. His knowledge is perfect, His wisdom is incredible and His peace can diffuse all disputes.

> *The man who insists upon seeing with perfect clearness before he decides, never decides.*
>
> ~ Henri-Frédéric Amiel

If you are pressured to make decisions that are outside your ability, turn it over to Jesus. You can never calculate the consequences ahead of time because you don't know the future. Let the peace of Christ reign over all your thoughts and trust Him. Know that you are in the best hands!

Lord Jesus, help those who are battling with difficult decisions and let them look to You for the right guidance. Amen.

Called to Peace

Read Colossians 3:12-25

As members of one body you were called to peace. (Colossians 3:15)

Organizations choose teams to achieve certain goals. A commercial firm may send a team to a certain area if it wants to improve matters there. But it will send a completely different team, however, if it wants to clean up a mess.

In the early days of Christianity local groups of believers – or churches – had diverse members. Some were Jews who had converted to Christianity. Others were "heathens." Some were slave owners, while others were the slaves themselves. There were men and women; rich and poor. As a result there were many points of disagreement and sometimes conflict arose. The life of the community was marred by the quarrels that flared up. When Paul encouraged the Christians at Colosse to live in harmony, he reminded them that they were called, or chosen, by God to live in unity and peace with each other.

> *Christ alone can bring lasting peace – peace with God – peace amomg men and nations – and peace within out hearts.*
> ~ Billy Graham

The love that Christ shares is to encourage Christians to live in peace with each other; however much their economic backgrounds differ. It isn't simply a case of "liking" each other. It is a challenge to accept others as children of God and brothers and sisters in Christ.

We are also chosen by God to live in peace. The peace of Christ must not only reign in the depths of your heart, but also in family relationships, church relationships, social relationships as well as in your work situation. You must contribute to unity and hope, just like the Master did.

Lord my God, make me an instrument of Your peace. Amen.

Keep Learning

Read 2 Peter 1:1-10

Grace and peace be yours in abundance through the knowledge of God and of Jesus our Lord. (2 Peter 1:2)

A middle-aged professional man said on one occasion, "When I was young I thought that going to university would teach me everything there was to know about my field of study and that it would be enough for my professional career. Now, fifteen years later, I realize that I am still learning and that my degree was only the beginning of a lifetime of study and growth."

It's the same for the disciple of Jesus Christ. The day you give your life to Christ is only the beginning of a long process of learning about Jesus and growing in Him. You read about Christ in the Bible, or you listen to a sermon about Him. You apply it to your life and work and realize how the Holy Spirit empowers you to a deeper faith and a consecrated way of living. Then you suddenly discover something new about Christ and the process continues. Sometimes life is cruel and you wonder how God can allow certain things to happen to you. But then you discover what it means for your walk with God and you continue again, but on a higher level and with greater strength.

> *What you are must always displease you, if you would attain that which you are not.*
> ~ St. Augustine

Never think that you know everything. No matter how far you have already traveled, there is still another piece of road that you must walk. The riches of Christ are "unsearchable" (Eph. 3:8). However much you might have learned and know about them, you will discover that there are always hidden treasures to be explored and discovered. Therefore, keep learning and allow the Holy Spirit to be your Teacher.

Holy God, lead me daily to new truths about Yourself. Amen.

Who Reigns in Your Heart?

Read Colossians 3:1-15

Let the peace of Christ rule in your hearts. (Colossians 3:15)

Some people have wayward hearts. They are tossed to and fro by stormy passions, jealousy and spite. Others are consumed by anger and bitterness. Many people have a burning desire to take revenge. Others are driven by greed and malice.

Paul knew what it meant to be driven by hatred. On occasion he had been granted permission to kill Christ's disciples, "Meanwhile, Saul was still breathing out murderous threats against the Lord's disciples" (Acts 9:1). Then he met Christ, who replaced his internal conflict with peace, harmony and purpose. In place of the bloodshed he previously sought, he now strived to spread the peace of Christ wherever he went. Christ calmed the tempest in Paul's heart by calling, "Peace, be still."

> *We are not at peace with others because we are not at peace with ourselves, and we are not at peace with ourselves because we are not at peace with God.*
>
> ~ Thomas Merton

Allow the peace of Christ to reign in your heart. Allow Him to speak His words of peace in your storm of rage, revenge and hatred that threatens to take over your heart and life and cause chaos in your thoughts. If you don't find peace here, you might find yourself at war with God, other people and yourself. This might already be the case. Let Christ calm the storm in your life. Let His peace take over your heart and life and calm your passions. Don't be tossed to and fro by hatred and bitterness. Allow Christ to put His strong, calming hand on the steering wheel of your life.

Take over my life anew, faithful Savior, and replace passion with Your heavenly peace. Amen.

September

His Life, Death and Resurrection

God has given us new birth into a living hope through the
resurrection of Jesus Christ from the dead, and into an inheritance
that can never perish, spoil or fade – kept in heaven for you.
~ 1 Peter 1:3-4

Jesus is not a good way to heaven, He is the only way.
~ Anonymous

*J*esus Christ, we worship You as the Life.
Grant that we will awake to the full
realization of Your resurrection glory;
the nearness of Your kingdom,
and the glory of immortality.
Jesus Christ, we worship You as the Light.
Shine in our thoughts so that the
darkness will not mislead us.
Grant that we will walk courageously
through the dark places of this life.
Jesus Christ, we worship You as the Way.
Make us brave enough to follow
wherever You might lead us.
Grant us the assurance that Your
Almighty arms are always underneath us.
Jesus Christ, we worship You as the Truth.
Feed our souls with Your eternal truths
so that we will be more than conquerors.
Jesus Christ, we worship You as the Good Shepherd.
Watch over us so that we won't wander
away from You in stubborn sinfulness.
We pray this in the name above all names;
The name of our Redeemer and Savior;
Jesus Christ!

Amen.

The Message of the Cross

Read 1 Corinthians 1:18-31

The message of the cross is foolishness to those who are perishing, but to us who are being saved it is the power of God. (1 Corinthians 1:18)

A little girl was found in the street, crying bitterly. The constable who found her wasn't sure what to do with her. The only name he could get out of her was "Janet." She didn't know where she lived; she was scared and upset, and didn't even know in what direction her house was. After a few minutes she calmed down and had a moment of clarity. She remembered a monument with a cross that stood in front of her house and she said, "Sir, just take me to the cross and I will find my way home."

The apostles' preaching was aimed at doing just this. They presented the message of the cross

> *The cross is not an isolated, individual aspect of theology; it is itself the foundation of that theology.*
>
> ~ Gerald Hawthorne

to the people they preached to. Their listeners arrived at their spiritual home when they came as far as the cross. It was the message that brought them to repentance and conversion and which opened the path to reconciliation with God.

For anyone without faith, the story of Christ's death is meaningless. For them Jesus is just another good person who paid the price for having the wrong judge. But if you have met God face to face at the foot of the cross it is a totally different reality. Then it is the holiest place in the universe for you!

Heavenly Father, grant that through Your Spirit the message of Your power and love through the cross of Jesus Christ will be heard throughout the whole world. Amen.

Were You There When it Happened?

Read Isaiah 53:1-12

Surely He took up our infirmities and carried our sorrows. (Isaiah 53:4)

When we speak about Jesus' sacrifice we tend to emphasize that He took it upon Himself to have the sins of the world put upon Him and to die for all humankind. However true these thoughts might be, the danger lies in the wording that subtly tempts us to replace "us" with "them" and to see it as a substitutionary responsibility for sin.

Most people shudder at the thought that they could be "sinners" and therefore use words and expressions like "transgression," "weakness," and "shortcoming" in connection with their own disobedience. "Sin" is handled with abhorrence and is reserved for "others."

> *Tell me how much you know about the suffering of your fellow man and I will tell you how much you have loved them.*
>
> ~ Helmut Thielicke

It is true that we weren't alive when Jesus was crucified, but it is important to remember that time can't be measured in matters concerning the kingdom of God. The Lord's time is eternal and for this reason the sins that Jesus carried on the cross have as much significance for us now as they did for the people then. In the concept of eternity the sins for which Christ died are on-going. The result is that, even in our age, our sins are as much responsible for the Master's suffering as the sins in those times.

To live a life of true repentance and conversion, you must allow the reality of the cross to be a continual warning for you to live according to the example and teachings of Jesus and to spare Him the sorrow of your disobedience and sin.

Forgive me, merciful Lord Jesus, for the pain and suffering that I have caused You. Amen.

The Mystery of the Cross

Read Galatians 6:11-18

May I never boast except in the cross of our Lord Jesus Christ.
(Galatians 6:14)

Designed to be an instrument of a slow and torturous death, the cross was dreaded by thousands and despised by the religious Jews. It was used as a method to oppress a defeated nation and as a result was feared, hated and abhorred. It is the instrument that was used for Jesus' death because they couldn't think of anything more physically painful and morally and religiously damning than death by crucifixion.

Yet, Christ transformed His cross. What previously had been an object of ridicule, became an object of worship. People sing, "When I survey the wondrous cross" without thinking that what was once the symbol of hell on earth, has become the symbol of the entrance to a perfect new life.

Jesus lived His life for you – then He gave His life to you. Now He wants to live His life through you!
~ Jacquelyn K. Heasley

One of the most difficult moments of Christ's time on earth was probably when He was confronted with the ghastliness of Golgotha: its pain, apparent overthrow of justice, the atmosphere of increasing hatred, cheap mockery and the blasphemous words that were uttered. He could have avoided it, but He became acquainted with the worst that one person could do to another: He embraced a Roman crucifixion and under impossible circumstances proved that love can triumph.

Christ's triumph on the cross is the triumph of divine love over the worst destructive and evil powers imaginable. Love can triumph even in the worst circumstances and conditions.

Triumphant Savior, Your crucifixion reveals the dominion of divine love over all other powers and influences. We sincerely praise and thank You for this. Amen.

Future Joy

Read 1 Peter 4:12-19

Rejoice that you participate in the sufferings of Christ, so that you may be overjoyed when His glory is revealed. (1 Peter 4:13)

One of humankind's most dynamic powers is envisaging the future and picturing it before it happens. This allows you to dream dreams, to plan ahead and to try and make your dreams a reality.

Because the God of the Bible is a God of promises, He invites His people to look into the future. Jesus taught us to pray, "Your kingdom come, Your will be done." Jesus suffered and died because He could see into the future – to the resurrection and coming glorification. He indicated the way forward to His followers toward His final coming and encouraged them to believe that it could happen any day. And it will! They knew that when He came again it would mean the end of their suffering, tears and pain and that He would bring eternal joy.

> *Taking us through suffering, not out of it, is one of the primary means that the Spirit uses today in bringing us to God.*
>
> *~ Daniel Wallace*

They clung to this prospect while they faced the threat of persecution, lions' dens, burning stakes and painful death. They died with His name on their lips, His cross before their eyes, and His words and promises in their hearts. His love supported them, and His pierced hands held them. Behind them was pain and suffering, before them was greater happiness and joy than anything they had ever known on earth.

Whatever you might have to go through for your faith, just remember: If you accept it in Christ's strength and Presence you will one day receive the crown of glory and live in His holy Presence for all eternity.

Faithful Savior, show me the joy that lies beyond today's suffering.
Amen.

Crazy about Jesus

Read John 10:11-21

Many of them said, "He is demon-possessed and raving mad. Why listen to Him?" (John 10:20)

The fine line between faith and mental confusion is sometimes difficult to determine. Some people become so excited and worked up in their enthusiasm for God, that it may look like they are out of their minds. At the same time, people who are mentally ill can be misled by religious content. Some mentally unstable people become convinced that they are Jesus or the pope, or some other great figure – even God.

There were people who thought that Jesus was going mad when He said that He was "the Light of the world," "the Good Shepherd" or "the Son of God." When He spoke about dying for the sheep – and then rising from the dead – it was too much for some people. But the fact is: Jesus was crystal clear and sober-minded.

> *God has made for us two kinds of eyes: those of flesh and those of faith.*
>
> ~ John Chrysostom

He even healed those who were really mad. For those who were mentally confused, He brought peace. For the lonely, He brought love. For people who were impure, He brought cleansing. For those who struggled with guilt, He offered forgiveness.

For some people, faith in Jesus Christ is just a foolish deception. If you believe in Jesus they would describe you as a bit crazy. Yet, there is an element of irrationality in faith. It can't be reasoned or proved like fixed objects can. But there are few things in life that will help you to stay as sober-minded as when the life and love of Christ fills your heart, life and thoughts. It makes sense to be crazy about Jesus!

Savior, graciously heal those with mental disabilities. Amen.

Right or Wrong?

Read John 10:11-21

But others said, "These are not the sayings of a man possessed by a demon. Can a demon open the eyes of the blind?" (John 10:21)

There are many reasons why people reject Jesus. Some find the miracles too far-fetched. Others think that the Bible is irrelevant for people today. And others find the church full of hypocrites. There are people who are so busy that they never even think about Jesus.

The Bible doesn't only tell us about what Jesus said and did, it also shows us how people reacted to Him. Some were scared of Him and tried to dispute His healings and teachings. Others took an interest and were curious to see what would entertain them next. Others thought that He was a danger to the state. There were those who thought He was the Messiah who had come to lead the Israelites in their revolt against the Roman authorities. There were also those who said, "This is the Son of God; the One who was sent to bring fullness of life." They believed in Him, found life in Him and lived for Him. They logically reasoned that since He could do so many good things, He couldn't possibly be possessed by a demon.

> *Faith is never identical with piety.*
> ~ Karl Barth

You and I must make the right decision; otherwise we will also be proven wrong. You will be right if you listen to Him, react to His invitation and believe in Him – regardless of the questions you might still have about Him. You will be proven wrong if you are too busy, if you enjoy life too much, or if you find no sense in following His lead. If you make the right decision, Jesus our Savior will also get your life right!

Savior, please make my life right with You. Amen.

When You Are Under Attack

Read 1 Peter 2:18-25

When they hurled insults at Him, He did not retaliate; when He suffered, He made no threats. Instead, He entrusted Himself to Him who judges justly. (1 Peter 2:23)

The Christian's life is not always a bed of roses. It can indeed bring about serious disappointments. Believers are often mocked, rejected and hated, and in places where Christians are the minority, they can find themselves in dangerous situations.

On the cross, Jesus endured this mockery as well as the physical pain and agony of the crucifixion. He didn't fight back or predict damnation for those who placed Him there. He quietly entrusted Himself to His Father's righteous judgment. He could do this because He knew that another factor was at work.

> *Against the persecution of a tyrant the godly have no remedy but prayer.*
>
> ~ John Calvin

Beyond Himself and His bitter suffering, and beyond those who were busy crucifying Him, was God the Father, the sovereign Ruler of the universe. Jesus knew that He was in His Father's hands and not in the hands of His condemners. He was certainly not in human hands.

Beyond those who mock and hate you because of your faith, is the same loving Father. He is still the sovereign Ruler of the universe. He holds you in His loving hands. Look beyond the insults and taunts, the mockery and jeering, and see Him who will one day judge fairly over you – and them.

Savior in our suffering, support all who are being attacked because of their faith. Amen.

He Bore Our Sins

Read 1 Peter 2:18-25

He Himself bore our sins in His body on the tree, so that we might die to sins and live for righteousness; by His wounds you have been healed. (1 Peter 2:24)

Sometimes parents step in and pay the fine when one of their children breaks the law. Hopefully the transgressor will recognize his mistake and react to the love of his parents by proving that he has changed his habits. The parent pays the price for the child's transgression.

Christ did something similar when He died on the cross on Golgotha. However you try to explain it, Christ did something there that none of us will ever fully understand. With great thankfulness you can accept that He did it for you and that He did it purely out of love for you. You have to accept and believe that He has dealt with your sin in a way that you could never have and that He makes a new beginning possible for you.

> *By the cross we know the gravity of sin and the greatness of God's love toward us.*
>
> ~ John Chrysostom

However many or few your sins might be, take them to the cross of Golgotha. He knows your sins and is willing to bear them for you. Bring your burden to Him and leave it at the cross. Leave everything at the cross. What He has already done on Golgotha, He can do again within you. Golgotha is not only for Good Friday – it is for every day and every circumstance that influences your life. It will determine how you live – and how you die. How are you living? And how will you die?

Loving Savior, for my sake You endured mockery and scorn. Through this, with Your blood, You accomplished my reconciliation with God. Hallelujah! Amen.

Start Living Right

Read 1 Peter 2:18-25

He Himself bore our sins in His body on the tree, so that we might die to sins and live for righteousness; by His wounds you have been healed. (1 Peter 2:24)

Mark Twain, the humorist, said on one occasion, "It's easy to stop smoking. I've done it a thousand times."

Leaving the past behind is one thing, but starting a new life is something totally different. Past habits exercise a strong hold on what you will and will not do. Feeling like a failure, guilt, and fear of unpleasant consequences can paralyze you to such an extent that you do precisely what you don't want to do.

When you give your life to Christ you bring your sins to Him. Then you leave them there. You don't pick them up and continue to live in sin. The only way that you can get rid of your sin is to open your heart to Christ's love

Sin is sovereign till sovereign grace dethrones it.
~ Charles H. Spurgeon

and allow that love to totally take over your life. Replace the bad things with something good. Erase past mistakes completely and replace them with something new and better in your mind and heart. "Whatever is true, whatever is noble, whatever is right, whatever is pure, whatever is lovely, whatever is admirable – if anything is excellent or praiseworthy – think about such things" (Phil. 4:8).

Develop new and healthy habits; socialize with new friends; form new patterns of behavior; find better things to do and good causes to support. Start living *in obedience to God!* Start living right and keep at it!

Lord and Master, You break the chains of sin and set the prisoner free! Amen.

Healed through His Wounds

Read 1 Peter 2:18-25

He Himself bore our sins in His body on the tree ... by His wounds you have been healed. (1 Peter 2:24)

We all need healing. One of the worst aspects of sickness is the sudden appearance of false healers, "I have the best medicine for your ailment: eat orange peel and onion sauce" (or whatever the concoction might be). These self-appointed healers come in many shapes and sizes. Their advice is diverse, "Try a faith healer;" "Go to my acupuncturist;" or "My friend had the same wound and put saliva on it."

> *Get alone with Jesus and either tell Him that you do not want sin to die out in you – or else tell Him that at all costs you want to be identified with His death.*
>
> ~ Oswald Chambers

Healing is a complex process. And spiritual healing is just as essential as physical healing. Jesus cured people from physical ailments and He healed them internally. He not only touched their bodies; He touched their minds and souls too. Before He was crucified, He healed the sick. After that He became the Wounded Healer and His healing power far surpassed the borders of His earthly life and ministry.

Jesus Christ also offers healing to you. If you have sinned, seek His healing touch. If you are filled with bitterness, allow Him to cleanse your memory and remove the pain and reproach. If you tend to get depressed, allow Him to lift you up. If the relationships in your life are a hopeless mess, allow Him to bring His love to the situation and create calm understanding. If you are physically ill, place yourself in His hands as well as in the hands of your trusted doctor.

Lord Jesus, great Healer, touch the part of my being that most needs Your healing. Fill me with Your life-giving power and save my soul. Amen.

Betrayal!

Read Matthew 26:6-16

"What are you willing to give me if I hand Him over to you?" So they counted out for him thirty silver coins. From then on Judas watched for an opportunity to hand Him over. (Matthew 26:15-16)

Most organizations carefully hide the mistakes and corruption of their members and leaders. It's called "damage control." Political parties are especially inclined to do this, but it also happens in sporting bodies, churches and businesses.

The Bible acknowledges the mistakes and sins of those who play a role in the unfolding story. Judas was one of the worst characters. Since he lived close to Jesus and benefited from all that Jesus said and did, it is especially sad that he "left the team in the lurch." His story is told in stark contrast to the actions of the woman who anointed Jesus. She paid a great price for her love.

> *Believe that as sure as you are in the way of God you must meet with temptations.*
>
> ~ John Bunyan

Judas sold his Master for a price. Judas not only sold his Master; he sold his own soul. These two characters are on opposite ends of the loyalty scale.

You can also react to Jesus with love or rejection – or even with betrayal. No one is safeguarded against the temptation to let Jesus down. Sometimes leaders in the church do it, if not by their words then by their judgmental behavior. Be on guard against this temptation on your spiritual journey. Remember that good leaders are subjected to the same temptations as all of us. Pray for Christian groups who have suffered under the weakness of their leaders, or the frailty of their members. Pray for those leaders you know so that they will not give in to temptation.

Lord my God, help Christian leaders everywhere to live worthy and reflect the gospel purely. Amen.

Drink to the Lees

Read Matthew 26:36-46

Going a little farther, He fell with His face to the ground and prayed, "My Father, if it is possible, may this cup be taken from Me. Yet not as I will, but as You will." (Matthew 26:39)

Sometimes the hardest decision is the right decision. Almost a hundred years ago Captain Scott led a team to the South Pole. One of his teammates was Captain Oates. Oates developed serious frostbite and it was clear that if he survived the expedition he would have to be carried home by the other members of the team.

> *Destiny is no matter of chance. It is a matter of choice. It is not a thing to be waited for; it is a thing to be achieved.*
> ~ William J. Bryan

However, they were so weak and the path was so difficult, that to carry Oates would have endangered all of them. But they couldn't simply leave him behind to die. Oates solved the problem himself. One night he walked out of his tent during a terrible snowstorm and was never seen again.

In the Garden of Gethsemane Jesus battled with the most important decision of His life. Should He try to escape it, or must He accept it as His Father's will: to die for the sins of the world? It was a very difficult decision. But like Captain Oates, He made the right decision. Many other Christian disciples have had to make decisions to give up all kinds of benefits and comforts for the sake of Jesus and the spreading of the gospel.

The Crucifixion confronts you with a tough decision: do you choose Jesus' path with all it might bring, or do you choose "safety first" and think of your own interests? The Christian is faced with many important decisions. Some are big and others are small. But regardless of this, make absolutely sure that you make the right choice instead of taking the easy way out.

Gracious Lord Jesus, help those who have to make a difficult decision today. Amen.

Anguish

Read Luke 22:39-46

Being in anguish, He prayed more earnestly, and His sweat was like drops of blood falling to the ground. (Luke 22:44)

Christianity involves handling the difficult realities of life with courage and faith. In the Garden of Gethsemane Jesus had to battle with the challenge of suffering. Being in great agony He prayed about the path that lay ahead of Him. Before Him was the anguish of the cross and the possibility of death. He had the option to submit Himself or to withdraw Himself. He submitted Himself and His sweat became drops of blood.

> *The bitter herbs of Gethsemane have often taken away the bitters of your life; the scourge of Gabbatha has often scourged away your cares; and the groans of Calvary yield us comfort rare and rich.*
> ~ Charles H. Spurgeon

We mustn't always search for the easy, safe path. Jesus' path is the path of the cross. If you are going through a time of crisis, know that Jesus, your Savior, also went through such a time. If everything is collapsing around you, know that this is precisely what happened to Him.

If your pain becomes unbearable, remember Christ in Gethsemane. If darkness threatens to engulf you, you are never alone. Christ, who knows pain and suffering, is your companion. Because of the darkness around you, you might not see Him, but He is with you the whole way.

Lord Jesus, hold me tight through my time of anguish. Amen.

Darkness Reigns

Read Luke 22:47-53

"This is your hour – when darkness reigns." (Luke 22:53)

There are a great number of "analysts," "commentators" and "authorities" who look at what's happening and then explain how they see things. They identify trends and movements. Sometimes they even dare to predict what will happen in the future. When things are really bad they predict "dark days lie ahead."

It was night-time when the soldiers came to arrest Jesus in the Garden of Gethsemane. He turned to the religious rulers and said, "This is your hour – when darkness reigns." Jesus knew as well as His Father that evil forces were at work in the world. They were at work in the establishments of power and authority where military powers had the upper hand. They worked overtime in the hearts of the crowd who turned their backs on the Light of the World and who would soon cry, "Crucify Him! Crucify Him!"

> *I would rather walk with God in the dark than go it alone in the light.*
>
> ~ Mary Gardiner Brainard

The Evil One was hard at work among the disciples when Judas betrayed Jesus and when Peter denied Him within a few hours.

Darkness is still in control as terrorists descend to murder and maim. It gets out of control when crime, drug abuse and immorality run riot and cripple human life. It reigns when you give Jesus lip service, but allow greed to reign in your thoughts. It rules when prejudice and ignorance cause you to reject people who are different from you.

Sometimes darkness is in control. But when God acts, the light shines through. It happened on Easter Sunday. It shines alone in the darkness, but the darkness has never been able to overcome it. Never!

Faithful Savior, help me to see the light, even in the darkest moments. Amen.

The Crowning of the King

Read Matthew 27:27-31

They twisted together a crown of thorns and set it on His head. They put a staff in His right hand and knelt in front of Him and mocked Him. "Hail, king of the Jews!" they said. (Matthew 27:29)

The events during Jesus' great sufferance reached a climax on Good Friday. The authorities crucified Jesus – an extremely painful form of torture and death. In doing so they unknowingly provided the world with a symbol of love, dedication and sacrifice.

There is much irony in the Crucifixion. One is the scene in front of the governor's palace. The soldiers who were in Palestine to force Roman dominion on Israel thought that this was the occasion for a bit of fun. They made a crown of thorns and put it on Jesus' head. In their eyes He had no authority, yet they mockingly crowned Him as king. They regarded Him with contempt and little did they know that they were elevating Him to a position from which He would reign in a way they could never have dreamed of. For them He was a troublemaker in an outpost of the mighty Roman Empire.

> *Jesus, the Savior, reigns, the God of truth and love;*
> *When He had purged our stains, He took His seat above.*
> ~ Charles Wesley

Today that empire no longer exists. But the King they crowned still reigns in the hearts of millions of His subjects. There are, however, always people who mock and belittle Him. They have no time for Him and scorn the spiritual nature of His reign.

Today you have the privilege of crowning Him in a way those Roman soldiers could never have. You can crown Him as the sovereign King of your heart and life. Become one of His faithful subjects and submit yourself to His kingly rule. Then you will become part of the mightiest empire that this world has ever known – and will ever know!

Savior, expand Your mighty empire to the ends of the earth.

Amen.

The Sealed Tomb

Read Matthew 27:62-66

They went and made the tomb secure by putting a seal on the stone and posting the guard. (Matthew 27:66)

A watch guard has a very difficult task. He has to spend long, lonely hours doing nothing. He has to make sure that nobody who is outside comes in, and nobody who is inside gets out.

The guards who were appointed by Pilate to watch over Jesus' dead body probably thought that it would be an easy task. Surely a dead body couldn't give them much trouble? To try and keep watch over God is an impossible task. All the soldiers in the world couldn't have prevented God from breaking open the tomb if He chose to do it. The guard at Jesus' tomb didn't have the slightest idea that he was simply a pawn in a cosmic drama – because God was ready to do something that had never been done before: to rise from the dead.

> *Christ's empty tomb is the cradle of Christianity.*
> ~ Edmond de Pressensé

The world always thinks that it can stop God. It thinks that it can put Him away, lock Him up and exclude Him. But it can't! God always finds a way to roll the stone away and prevent the guards from stopping Him. He is always fair to the task of the free, sovereign God. Nothing can stop God! Nothing!

Up from the grave He arose,
with a mighty triumph o'er His foes;
He arose a Victor from the dark domain,
and He lives forever with His saints to reign:
He arose! He arose! Hallelujah! Christ arose!

~ Robert Lowry

Everyone Has a Price

Read Matthew 28:11-15

They gave the soldiers a large sum of money, telling them, "You are to say, 'His disciples came during the night and stole Him away while we were asleep.'" (Matthew 28:12-13)

Bribery is as old as humankind itself. It still reigns supreme in business, sport and politics. It eats at society's soul like a cancer.

The guards who were commanded to watch over Jesus' body failed in the execution of their duty. Telling the chief priests about their failure was noble, but then they took the bribe offered to them and lied about what had happened. The religious leaders were more guilty than the guards in this game of deceit. They should have known better. They dished up lies which they enforced through bribery and in this way they also corrupted the guards.

> *Many a dangerous temptation comes to us in fine gay colors that are but skin-deep.*
> ~ Matthew Henry

This twist in the Resurrection tale brings to light the pervasive nature of all human negotiations: the presence of weakness, evil, deceit and corruption. From kings to rich businessmen, politicians, state officials, professional church leaders, sports stars and journalists – this human weakness is a sad fact for everyone.

Try to honestly determine where your breaking point is. Instead of judging the mistakes of the elite, investigate your inner self and try to be honest about the weak places in your own life. Then ask God for the strength and courage to face temptations head on and to overcome them in His power and through His mercy. Pray that you will never be led into those temptations.

Lord Jesus, help those who are under pressure to compromise their integrity. Grant them the courage to stand firm in the truth.

Amen.

Lingering Doubt

Read Matthew 28:11-20

When they saw Him, they worshiped Him; but some doubted.
(Matthew 28:17)

There are many people, even those with an apparently strong faith, who aren't always as strong on the inside as they claim to be. Some look strong and tough, but inside they are cowards. Some people do good things with the sole purpose of benefiting themselves. Some politicians look kind and as if they care about the people they serve – but only until the elections are over.

> *Too often we forget that the great men of faith reached the heights they did only by going through the depths.*
>
> ~ Os Guinness

Some disciples still doubted, even when they gathered on the mountain in Galilee after the Resurrection. They had left Him in His deepest need and probably felt guilty about this. They were real people, some of them quite tough, without any formal training in theology. Those who still doubted were battling with conflicting thoughts and feelings about Jesus Christ.

It might be the same for you. When tragedy strikes it is difficult to understand where God fits into it. When a natural disaster occurs, suffering and human frailty arises, or if there is unfaithfulness to God, your trust in God can take a knock.

There are some people who get through all of this without any doubts lingering in their minds. But even dedicated disciples of Jesus sometimes struggle to keep hold of their faith in the face of adversity, conflict and confusion. If you are struggling, cling to your faith and pray that the confusion and uncertainty will pass. Jesus will surely appear in your struggle and lead you to a deeper faith and a firmer hope.

Savior, when I find it difficult to hold on to You, please hold me tight.
Amen.

His Majesty on the Cross

Read Luke 23:44-49

Jesus called out with a loud voice, "Father, into Your hands I commit My Spirit." When He said this, He breathed His last. (Luke 23:46)

For most of the crowd at Golgotha, it was simply another execution. Yet another criminal had been punished and got what He deserved through a brutal system known as justice. The temple elite were satisfied because this Jesus of Nazareth, with His disruptive influence, had been silenced forever. Little value was given to His wild claims. Now the whole world could see Him for what He really was. At least, that it was they thought.

Yet again, the omnipotence of God was revealed through precisely the Person the priests, scribes and Pharisees attempted to destroy.

> *He came to pay a debt for us that we could never pay ourselves.*
>
> ~ D. A. Carson

Despite the fact that His broken, bleeding body hung on the horrific cross, the Son of God was still in control and triumphed over His enemies. It was He who laid down His life – not they who maintained to have taken it. After Jesus completed everything that God had ordained during His earthly ministry, it was Christ who committed His Spirit into God's hands. Jesus chose where, when and how He would die – not His enemies.

It was Christ who transformed the cross from a dreaded instrument of torture and brutality into a glorious sign of the triumph over evil, sin and death. In this way the cross gives us reason to sing joyfully and not mourn.

My Savior on the cross, I bow in gratitude before Your Majesty.
Amen.

A New Birth

Read 1 Peter 1:1-9

Praise be to the God and Father of our Lord Jesus Christ! In His great mercy He has given us new birth into a living hope through the resurrection of Jesus Christ from the dead. (1 Peter 1:3)

You have probably heard gripping accounts from people about all that God has done in their lives. Some tell of a completely new beginning. Others tell about wonderful answers to prayer, or the miracles that God has performed in their lives.

If you haven't experienced a similar dramatic conversion, or if you haven't had the same success with your prayers, you might be wondering what you need to do to achieve these same amazing results. Why should you be left out of these events? You are probably wondering if there is something you aren't doing right or if some action has disqualified you.

> *God hath given man a short time here upon earth, and yet upon this short time eternity depends.*
> ~ Jeremy Taylor

It is very important to remember that a new life is not something that you yourself can accomplish. It is a gift from God. It comes from "His great mercy." Only He can grant it. Even though it might appear that those who testify seem to have pushed the right buttons, remember that God can't be forced to do things at our command.

Don't be upset or jealous about the spiritual experiences that others have. God works in a unique manner in each person's life. It is all part of God's work of grace and He knows what it's about. Trust Him to do what He knows is right in and through you.

Holy Jesus, use my humble gifts to Your honor and glory. Amen.

He Lives! Today – and Every Day!

Read Luke 24:1-12

"Why do you look for the living among the dead? He is not here; He has risen!" (Luke 24:5-6)

The resurrection of Jesus Christ from the dead makes the Christian faith unique. If this great truth is removed from the New Testament, the gospel loses its redemptive power and simply becomes a beautiful philosophy without any spiritual power.

Christ, the living and eternal One, conquered death and still lives in the world today. His Spirit is available to everyone who acknowledges His sovereignty and opens their lives to His holy influence. Christian disciples today can experience the Presence of the living Christ in their lives just as strongly as the first disciples did more than two thousand years ago.

> *Without the Resurrection there will not be a Christianity – Christianity stands or falls with the Resurrection, and this single factor makes Christianity remarkably one of a kind.*
>
> ~ Steve Kumar

In order to acquire this priceless experience, it is necessary that you exercise a simple and humble faith. According to Scripture, Christ is alive today and He works in the hearts and lives of men and women. If you place Him first, He becomes a wonderful reality in your life. Your whole life is transformed through the knowledge and certainty that He has kept His promise and lives in you.

You should remember, with deep gratitude, that Christ has risen from the dead. He lives today and is waiting to share His life with you. He won't force Himself on you, but when you invite Him into your life, you will come to know the reality of His Presence.

Living Savior, I praise and thank You for this exceptional truth that reminds me once again that You are with me every day. Amen.

Who Are You Looking For?

Read Matthew 28:1-10

After the Sabbath, at dawn on the first day of the week, Mary Magdalene and the other Mary went to look at the tomb. (Matthew 28:1)

Sometimes you don't find what you're looking for because you are looking in the wrong place or looking at the wrong time. On a greater scale, people search for happiness in their career or marriage while they should be looking for opportunities to excel in their work, or to create love and security in their marriage.

Religion is the first thing and the last thing, and until a man has found God and has been found by God, he begins at no beginning, he works toward no end.

~ H. G. Wells

The two women who went to the tomb on Easter Sunday were not looking for the Risen Savior. They were looking for a dead body in the tomb. They wanted to see whether the stone and the guards were still there and whether they could embalm Jesus' body – or so they thought. God often has a surprise in store for us that totally astonishes us. This is the most striking part of the Resurrection story, which confirms the truth of the Resurrection: no one went to Jesus' tomb because they thought they would find Him there alive; they went to see His dead body – and everyone was wrong.

What are you looking for? What are you looking for when you think about God? Someone who will make you happy? Someone who will make you rich? Someone who will make you successful? If this is true, then you are looking for the wrong things. Jesus might do all of these things for you, or He might not do any of them. If you are searching for meaning and sense in your life, peace in your heart, hope for the future, or a faith that will make sense of life's confusion, then you have come to the right place.

Lord Jesus, be the Savior to those who are searching for You today.
Amen.

Fear of God

Read Matthew 28:1-10

The guards were so afraid of him that they shook and became like dead men. (Matthew 28:4)

Fear is an emotion we all experience at one time or another. Even though we regard it as something negative, it plays a positive role in our lives. It prepares us for danger and causes us to act cautiously.

It is ironic that the guards who were placed at Jesus' tomb were scared out of their wits by what happened there. The actual reason that they were there was to fearlessly protect Jesus' dead body. But they had good reason to be afraid. They were overpowered by the One force that was greater than the strength of the Caesar they served – the power of God Himself!

> *All the resources of the Godhead are at our disposal.*
> ~ Jonathan Goforth

Jesus' resurrection proves to us that all the leaders in the world can't compete against the power of God; neither can the highest political authorities. Therefore, it is good to fear God. We must respect His indescribable power because He can overthrow the people and things that appear to be dominating the earth. Through this He can change the world order.

Fear Him who commands the forces of evil, "This far, and no further!" Fear Him who says, "I will destroy the wisdom of the wise; the intelligence of the intelligent I will frustrate" (1 Cor. 1:19). Fear Him because "the weakness of God is stronger than man's strength" (1 Cor. 1:25). Fear Him because He will appear in majesty and power to judge the world at any moment. But not only the world – you and me too.

Almighty God and Father, I tremble before Your power and majesty.
Amen.

Don't Be Afraid

Read Matthew 28:1-10

The angel said to the women, "Don't be afraid, for I know that you are looking for Jesus, who was crucified." (Matthew 28:5)

As beneficial as fear can be, it can also prevent us from becoming effective individuals. We refuse to speak about injustice because we fear criticism. Often, the thing we fear most is change.

The angel at Jesus' tomb said to the women, "Don't be afraid." These are often God's precise words to us. The angels said the same thing to the shepherds in the fields surrounding Bethlehem. The same words were spoken to Mary when the coming of Jesus was predicted to her. And when Jesus walked on the water toward His disciples, He greeted them by saying, "Take courage! It is I. Don't be afraid". (Matt. 14:27).

> *Courage faces fear and thereby masters it.*
> ~ Martin Luther King, Jr.

The angel's words are also directed at you and me. Don't be afraid about the present problems and disorder in the world. It is still God's world and He has no intention of rejecting it. Don't be afraid about future disturbances and chaos; God will eventually enforce His authority on all forms of wickedness. Don't be afraid when your own strength wanes because He will never forsake you or let you down. Don't be afraid of the astounding pace at which things change – with time you will adapt. But in the meantime, trust in the Lord in your confusion and uncertainty. Most of all: don't fear death, because you will be accompanied and protected by Jesus. You can live calmly, full of courage and confidence, because you belong to Jesus. Long ago He rose from the dead and He lives today and every day!

Holy God and Father, You have not given us a spirit of fear, but of love, power and a sound mind. We praise and thank You for this.
Amen.

He Is Not Here!

Read Matthew 28:1-10

"He is not here; He has risen, just as He said." (Matthew 28:6)

Jesus' resurrection is the most astounding event in the history of the world. We approach this event with the same sense of mystery and disbelief which must have surrounded the first Resurrection day.

Matthew tells us that there was an angel at the tomb. He greeted the disciples with the message, "He is not here!" In other words, "He isn't where you laid His dead body. He isn't here where the events of Good Friday took place. He isn't here where the authorities tried their best to lock Him away. He isn't here where the past is buried. He isn't here where your grieving hearts came to mourn. He has risen!"

Perhaps the transformation of the disciples of Jesus is the greatest evidence of all for the Resurrection.

~ John Stott

This is still the message of every Easter Sunday. He isn't among the deceased of the past. He lives and is waiting to meet you on your road through life. He isn't among the memories, losses and problems of yesterday. He lives and moves toward where tomorrow's problems lie in wait; to where you will enjoy courage, vision and strength for the days that lie ahead.

He isn't here where the world thinks they have triumphed over Him. He has victoriously risen, despite the powers of the Evil One and death. He isn't far away from you – He lives and He is available! He is eager to enter the future with you – a future filled with hope, expectations and challenges. Have you met the resurrected Lord Jesus yet?

Savior, help me to enter the future with You. Amen.

Triumphant Jesus!

Read Matthew 28:1-10

"He is not here; He has risen, just as He said." (Matthew 28:6)

Jesus Christ's resurrection, which was confirmed by an executioner, is the greatest event in human history. Jesus removed the burial shroud and revealed Himself to His disciples in His resurrection glory.

This didn't just happen in the gloom of a small room, but in the glow of the open road; in the brightness of the morning sun beside the Sea of Galilee. He came to them and ate with them. He revealed the secrets of the Holy Scriptures to their searching minds. To some He came in the crowds, to others while they were alone. Among His disciples there was no doubt about His resurrection because they met Him unexpectedly at different places.

> *Let us look at the resurrection which happens regularly. Day and night show us a resurrection; night goes to sleep, day rises: day departs, night arrives.*
>
> *~ Clement of Rome*

If Jesus' triumph was limited to a chosen group, it would have still been wonderful. But it doesn't only belong to a moment in history. It belongs to all people of all generations. He who triumphantly walked out of an empty tomb, exists to today. He lives!

Modern hands can't touch Him; human eyes can't see His glory. He isn't able to be perceived in human form – and yet His Spirit speaks to confused individuals, "Peace to you!" And they find peace. In moments of quiet worship the expectant spirit receives the message, "It is I. Do not be afraid!" Then all fear disappears and the certainty and reality of Jesus Christ descends on us: Christ lives today!

Living Lord Jesus, I know You live, because in moments of quietness I feel Your closeness, Your Presence and Your peace. Amen.

The Reality of Christ

Read Acts 25:13-21

Instead, they had some points of dispute with him about their own religion and about a dead man named Jesus who Paul claimed was alive. (Acts 25:19)

After Jesus Christ's crucifixion most people regarded the story of His resurrection as impossible. Even some of His disciples scoffed at the idea. For centuries many Jews rejected the thought that the dead would be raised. Others were unsure about their own position and did everything to deny the fact that Jesus lived.

Today people of other religions still doubt the credibility of the resurrection of the Son of God. This is understandable from those who are not Christians. The tragedy is that there are so many followers of Jesus who only act as if Christ lived and died and that they must honor and worship His memory.

> *It appears that from the dawn of her history the Christian church not only believed in the resurrection of her Lord, but that her belief upon the point was interwoven with her whole existence.*
>
> ~ William Milligan

This approach robs you of the incredible joy of knowing that Jesus lives and that He is your living Savior. The Risen Christ is as much a reality in the Spirit as He was during His earthly existence. He wants to be a part of you through the same Spirit. He wants to be your Mentor, Guide, Traveling Companion and Friend in every situation in your life. Jesus lives! Until you accept this fact unconditionally, your spiritual life will be empty and uncertain.

Invite the Holy Spirit to take total control of your life and to show you which direction to take. Allow Him to work *in* and *through* you. Then you will experience the Presence of the living Christ, which will completely change your whole life.

Living Christ, continue to live in me until my deepest love belongs to You. Amen.

You Will See Him

Read Matthew 28:1-10

"Go quickly and tell His disciples, 'He has risen from the dead and is going ahead of you into Galilee. There you will see Him.' Now I have told you." (Matthew 28:7)

On Easter Sunday every true Christian believer undoubtedly has the desire to visit Jesus' tomb. Then we would apparently believe more easily. We also wish that we could have walked to Emmaus with Him, or have been with the disciples when He met them in the Upper Room.

At the tomb, the women were not only commanded to move quickly, they were also given a promise that they had to convey to the disciples. It was the promise that He would go before them and that they would see Him. And they did!

> *What our Lord did was done with intent, and this alone, that He might be with us and we with Him.*
>
> ~ Meister Eckhart

This promise still stands today. It is part of the gospel message that has been passed down through the centuries. You will see God when you immerse yourself in the pages of the Bible and He walks off the page and into your life, heart and faith. You will see Him when He comes out of the tomb of death and despair and fills your life with hope, faith and expectation. You will see Him when He transforms your empty life into something brilliantly colorful and meaningful. You will see Him when He appears in your ordinary, everyday work and fills it with the glory of His Presence.

You will see Him in the face of someone who needs your love and care; someone who needs your support through the sorrowful and lonely time they are going through. You will see Him face-to-face when you eventually walk through the gates of death, waiting to welcome you when you get to the other side.

Lord Jesus, let me see You ... again and again. Amen.

Go Quickly!

Read Matthew 28:1-10

"Go quickly and tell His disciples." (Matthew 28:7)

Many people think that in order to get "close to God" you need to lose yourself in a mystical cloud and give yourself over to meditation. There is a time and place for quiet meditation and focusing on God, but Christianity is primarily a faith of action.

The angel at Jesus' tomb instructed the women not to be fearful and struck motionless. The angel said to them, "Go quickly!" Or as we might say, "Get a move on!" News of the Resurrection needed to be spread and shared with the other disciples; the people who witnessed the crucifixion; those who saw His miracles and heard His teachings. The women weren't given the luxury of staring in amazement at the empty tomb. There was work to be done and they were called to action. They received the call to be the first people to tell others about the omnipotence of God.

Know Him. Let Him be known!
~ Anonymous

This task is always passed down to every new generation of believers. As a result of God's mighty deed of resurrecting Jesus Christ, our main task is not to get involved in intellectual debates about how it could have happened, but to spring into action. The message is: God has acted; now you must act! You want to continuously remind yourself about every wonderful thing that has happened. The resurrection of Jesus must permeate every aspect of your faith.

Let the certainty that it happened cast off every hint of doubt. Make your faith, perspective and attitude a triumphant resurrection faith that inspires you – and with enthusiasm tell it to others often and soon.

Savior, grant that I will spread Your gospel of love soon. Amen.

Away from the Tomb

Read Matthew 28:1-10

So the women hurried away from the tomb, afraid yet filled with joy, and ran to tell His disciples. (Matthew 28:8)

To abandon something is never easy, whether it be a position you hold or a faith you are connected to. To end relationships can be very painful. To leave the past behind is dangerous because it makes you feel vulnerable. Some people continually live in the past and never move forward.

The women had this astonishing experience at the empty tomb. They went to see the tomb, perhaps to weep there and pour out their sorrow and sadness about Jesus. Instead, they met an angel, received a command from God, and became witnesses of an astounding event. They were asked to accept that He who was dead, was no longer dead, but alive! This meant that they had to leave the tomb, where just a few hours before their hope, desires and devotion had been buried. They had to enter a new world that had only just begun – the post-resurrection world!

> *Look for yourself and you will find in the long run only hatred, loneliness, despair, rage, ruin and decay. But look for Christ and you will find Him, and with Him everything else thrown in.*
>
> ~ C. S. Lewis

It is possible that you also have to leave the graveyard of your past defeats; the place of your disappointments, your sins and failures, your immature dream world of romantic illusions. When you do this you will also know fear and joy; disbelief and excitement.

Ahead of you, Jesus calls you to Life with a capital L. He wants to lead you to it. If you meet the living Christ, you enter a new world where love is stronger than death, where hope triumphs over despair and good reigns over evil.

Savior and Master, help me to leave all my graves of defeat and failure behind and to move on to where You are leading me. Amen.

October

His Path of Hope

If our hope in Christ is only for this life, we are more to be pitied than anyone in the world. But in fact, Christ has been raised from the dead. He is the first of a great harvest of all who have died.
~1 Corinthians 15:19-20 NLT

The word "hope" I take for faith;
and indeed hope is nothing else
than the constancy of faith.
~ John Calvin

*H*oly God of unlimited grace and hope,
the glorious promises in Your Word
ignite an inextinguishable hope in us.
We can continue to hope because You
are our Refuge and Fortress.
You remain the Anchor of our lives,
even when the storms rage and the winds ravage.
Lord Jesus, Your life and suffering,
death and resurrection assure us of hope for an
eternal life with You in the glory of the Father's house.
Holy Spirit of God, Your comfort gives
us hope in the darkest hours of life.
Triune God, through Your grace we
have a firm hope for an eternal inheritance
that You are keeping for us. The wonder of grace!
In this life You hold us safe in Your almighty hands.
You are our hope in life and in death.
Holy Lord Jesus, Your love transforms our hope
into certainty and is our guarantee against despair.
Father, Son and Holy Spirit, keep the flame
of hope alight in our hearts.
In the name of our Savior and Eternal Hope:
Jesus Christ.

Amen.

Start the Day Right

Read Psalm 57:1-12

My heart is steadfast, O God, my heart is steadfast; I will sing and make music. Wake, my soul! Awake, harp and lyre! I will awaken the dawn. (Psalm 57:7-8)

Many people do themselves injustice every day. They wake up in the morning and immediately start complaining which sets the tone for the rest of the day.

When you wake up in the morning, think of all the beautiful things that make the day worthwhile for you. Take pleasure in even the smallest of blessings in life: birds that sing; valued friends; food to eat and clothes to wear. Counting your blessings is a wonderful way to start your day. Decide to have a positive attitude toward everything you have to do today and everyone you will meet.

This day and your life are God's gift to you: so give thanks and be joyful always.

~ Anonymous

Be convinced that God intends only the best for you. Faithfully believe that the good Father will give you self-confidence to face the day with serenity and joy.

Never underestimate the effect of your thoughts in relation to your daily life. Start every day with this unshakable belief, "This is the day the LORD has made; let us rejoice and be glad in it" (Ps. 118:24).

Start counting your blessings from the moment you wake up and your spiritual life will be elevated to a new, unknown level of joy. Then you will be able to meet every challenge of the day.

If you start the day negatively, you only have yourself to blame if your entire day turns out sorrowful and sad. With a positive prayer and the right attitude, every day can be a psalm of praise, and you will be an inspiration to others.

God of mercy, I accept every day as a glorious gift from Your loving hand. Help me fill it with grateful joy. Amen.

Blessed Assurance

Read Matthew 14:22-36

"Take courage! It is I. Don't be afraid." (Matthew 14:27)

Many of the Lord's children have forgotten how to be cheerful and carefree people. We live in a world that is overburdened with troubling things, and people find very little to be cheerful about. They identify with the attitude of the times and forget that, as Christians, they must have the ability to rise above the atrocities of our times.

Christian cheerfulness is not "glittering" naivety that ignores ominous events and shrugs them off as insignificant. Christ commands His disciples to remain cheerful and courageous during distress. This implies that they should acknowledge the fact that things aren't going well, but still have trust in the Lord. Know that in life's darkest hour the flame of hope still burns brightly and clearly. Even when you are afraid and despair stalks you, hold steadfastly to the truth that God is still in control of this earth.

> *Complete happiness is knowing God.*
> ~ John Calvin

Christians should be joyful and at peace because they carry a living hope in their hearts. Even so, this hope should be based on a positive and dynamic relationship with Christ, or else it just wishful thinking. This hope is the mark of the true disciple of Christ.

If you share in the spirit and nature of Christ, you have the joyous assurance that the ultimate victory belongs to Christ, even though it may appear as if evil is triumphing in the world. Then you can face the future with courage because Jesus Christ has conquered the world.

Strong Redeemer, through Your indwelling Spirit I can face the future with joy and peace of mind due to my faith in You. Amen.

The Truth Will Set You Free

Read John 8:31-47

"If you hold to My teaching, you are really My disciples. Then you will know the truth, and the truth will set you free." (John 8:31-32)

This statement is sometimes used to convince a person to tell the truth when they are trying to hide it. However, if the truth was revealed about certain crimes, it wouldn't free anyone – it would in fact put a lot of people behind bars.

The truth that sets you free comes from an intimate knowledge of Jesus. It is this truth that Jesus talks about. Discipleship ends in freedom. When you become a disciple of Jesus Christ, He frees you from fear. You know that your life is now in the hands of the One who calmed the storm. You don't have to be afraid of what is going to happen to you, because you are in His hands – both in life and in death. You are in His company; He holds you firmly.

> *When we lose the right to be different, we lose the privilege to be free.*
> ~ Charles Evan Hughes

Jesus also frees you from your obsession with yourself. This is one of the most important characteristics of the Christian life. You don't have to place yourself in the limelight with everything you think and say. You can now place Jesus first in everything and then other things can follow.

Knowing the truth in Jesus Christ frees you from sin. Paul explains, "Sin shall not be your master, because you are not under law, but under grace" (Rom. 6:14).

If you serve Jesus in a ministry, then you will know this new freedom. The truth is that you are completely free when you submit yourself in love to serve the Master. If you are searching for true freedom, then you must undoubtedly start with Jesus.

Savior and Lord, lead me to the truth that will completely set me free. Amen.

You Can Do It!

Read Luke 9:1-9

When Jesus called the Twelve together, He gave them power and authority to drive out all demons and to cure diseases (Luke 9:1).

There are countless people whose attempts to do something for the Master fail, simply because their heart is not in it. These people's talents are lost because they rely on themselves and their limited reserves. As a result their efforts fail, or worse still; they don't even attempt to try. They not only disappoint the Master, they also rob themselves of the opportunity to savor the joy that comes from serving Him.

> *Give of your best to the Master, give of the strength of your youth; clad in salvation's full armor, join in the battle for truth.*
>
> ~ Howard B. Grose

If you study the Old and New Testaments you will find one common denominator. Not one of the men or women who was called by the Lord had the necessary training or abilities. They couldn't rely on their own strengths or talents to perform the task assigned to them. They were all ordinary, unprepared and simple people.

They had little or nothing to offer in their own strength, but they were empowered by God. As a result they became powerful and effective witnesses for God. The Lord called, they reacted, and He granted them the strength to serve Him.

The Lord has a task for you to perform. If you submit to Him in prayer, seek His guidance and take His hand, He will lead you not only to see what He wants you to see, but through His Holy Spirit He will grant you the abilities you need to undertake the task in His name.

Holy Spirit of God, make my faith strong so that I can live and work to the glory of my Master. Amen.

Searching for God?

Read Luke 17:20-37

"The kingdom of God is within you." (Luke 17:21)

There are many people who earnestly search for fulfillment in their spiritual lives, but all they experience is frustration, disappointment and depression. They search for God in prayer, Bible study and worship, but in spite of their persistence, they maintain that it is impossible for them to find God. As a result, they often become discouraged and unhappy – to such an extent that they run the risk of their faith suffering under it.

If you are sincerely searching to experience God's wonder and glory in your life, you need to realize that He makes His home with you if you love Him and obediently serve Him. As you open your life to the indwelling of the Holy Spirit, God will take over your life, live in you, guide you and support you on your journey through life.

> *If you seek Jesus in all things, you will surely find Him. Likewise, if you seek yourself, you will find yourself – to your own ruin.*
>
> ~ Thomas à Kempis

It is an accepted truth that without Christ you can do nothing, but with Christ nothing will be impossible for you. As St. Augustine once said, "Without God, we cannot; without us, God will not."

When you enroll in service to Christ and allow His Holy Spirit to serve others through you, your search will come to an end. The living Christ will live in you and grant you the fullness of life which He came to make available to us.

Heavenly Father, lead me daily in Your loving way. Teach me to live faithfully and sincerely. Amen.

The Word of the Lord

Read Hosea 1:1-9

As for God, His way is perfect; the word of the LORD is flawless.
(2 Samuel 22:31)

Do you speak to the Lord? And does the Lord sometimes speak to you? It is possible that you have received a special message from God. On the other hand, you might feel jealous of people who claim that they have received messages while you have not received any. But be careful, because not everyone who *claims* that God has spoken to them really heard from Him.

Nevertheless, our God is a God who speaks. At the beginning of creation God said, "'Let there be light', and there was light" (Gen. 1:3). When God spoke, it was always a word of action. In the same manner, He spoke to the prophets, of whom Hosea was one. This meant that when the prophet spoke to the people, or to kings and princes, he brought God's message and not his own. This is why the prophets spoke with authority. Their authority came from God. They weren't trying to sell themselves. God didn't speak to them for the benefit of their own spiritual enrichment, but to get His message across to the people.

> *The first duty of love is to listen.*
> ~ Paul Tillich

God might be speaking to you. He can do it in any place and at any time. He might give you a message to give to someone else, or He might speak directly to you in order to lead you onto His path. He might speak to you while you are reading the Bible, while you are praying, while you are reading the newspaper or during a conversation with other people. He might call you when are busy worshiping Him or even while you are doing nothing important. But when God speaks to you, you will certainly know it!

Lord Jesus, Savior, grant that my ears will be open when You speak to me. Amen.

God of Comfort

Read 2 Corinthians 1:1-11

Praise be to the God and Father of our Lord Jesus Christ, the Father of compassion and the God of all comfort. (2 Corinthians 1:3)

Some people who refuse to believe in God claim that believers create a God and then use Him as a crutch to lean on. In times of problem and difficulty they can't handle the situation so they rely on a God to see them through.

Christians mustn't feel distressed about this point of view. A fact of life is that we get hurt and sick. In such circumstances all wise people turn to their physician so that they can get healed as soon as possible. Trouble is also a normal part of life and it appears in unexpected places. We turn to other people for help. There is nothing wrong with turning to God for spiritual help. One of His self-appointed roles is to provide comfort. While He is the Lord and requires obedience, He is also our Comforter. He is the God of all compassion and gives us courage in every situation.

> *No affliction nor temptation, no guilt nor power of sin, no wounded spirit nor terrified conscience, should induce us to despair of help and comfort from God!*
>
> ~ Thomas Scott

When we are sick, He touches us with a healing hand. When we wander away from Him, He calls us to return to Him time and time again. When we are despondent, He fills our lives with new hope. When we have nothing, He is our all. When we are exhausted, He grants us rest. When we fall or fail, He tenderly picks us up. When we are hopelessly lost, He always finds us again. What do people who don't have God to comfort them do in their darkest hours of testing?

Loving Savior, comfort all Your children who are involved in one or other tense situation. Amen.

You Will Never Walk Alone

Read Jeremiah 1:1-12

"Do not be afraid of them, for I am with you and will rescue you,"
declares the LORD. (Jeremiah 1:8)

The Christian disciple can be absolutely certain of one thing: he will never walk alone. In spite of all opposition, God promised Jeremiah that He would be with him and protect him. Jeremiah needed protection because he had made enemies in high places.

God also promises to be with you and me, however terrible the dangers or problems might be. He is there to protect you if you face physical danger as well as when you face danger of another kind, like financial danger, economic instability, and job uncertainty. God is with you through it all.

> *Be Thou a bright flame before me, be Thou a guiding star above me, be Thou a smooth path below me, be Thou a kindly Shepherd behind me, today – tonight – and forever.*
>
> ~ Colomba of Iona

God is with you when you have to handle emotional trauma. If you are robbed of your spouse, rejected by those you love, or overwhelmed by loneliness – God is always near and He will never leave you in the lurch. If you fear that you are going to lose your health or even your healthy mind, you can be assured that God is holding you in His almighty hands. If it appears that political disorder is going to destroy everything you have lived and worked for, God is always present to keep you standing and to support you.

If the thing you fear most was to happen and death came knocking on your door, God would be there to lead you to the eternal residing place of His glory.

Thank You, heavenly Father, that no matter what I might go through,
You are always there to hold me tight. Amen.

Spirit of Love

Read Romans 5:1-11

Hope does not disappoint us, because God has poured out His love into our hearts by the Holy Spirit, whom He has given us. (Romans 5:5)

People all over the world can testify of their love for Jesus Christ. These people differ in nationality, tradition and culture. Nevertheless, they bear witness to the love and faith in Jesus Christ who died on the cross 2,000 years ago. They are convinced that He is still alive today. How is this possible? They've never seen Him. His earthly ministry lasted about three years and the reports on that are rather fragmentary.

The secret of His unique attraction does not lie in some theological formula or religious organization – regardless of how important these things may be in the right context. But Jesus promised to grant His Spirit to everyone who accepts Him and confesses that He reigns all over the earth.

> *When led of the Spirit, the child of God must be as ready to wait as to go, as prepared to be silent as to speak.*
> ~ Lewis Sperry Chafer

Through the ages He has kept His promises. He said that His Spirit would live in every person who loves Him and serves Him. Many modern followers believe that this experience with the living Christ is valid and true today.

If you want to stand on the sideline, remember that Christ can convert your life. A new, unparalleled strength will take possession of your spirit. It will enable you to do the things that are pleasing to God and will reassure you of Christ's life-changing presence in your life.

If you have the Spirit of Christ in you, you will know the reality of His holy Presence. Love for Him will radiate from your heart and life.

I praise You, Lord, that I can experience the power of Your living Presence through the work of the Holy Spirit. Amen.

Sun-kissed Mountaintops

Read Micah 4:1-5

"Come, let us go up to the mountain of the LORD. He will teach us His ways, so that we may walk in His paths." (Micah 4:2)

Some of Christ's most committed disciples experienced dark moments during their spiritual pilgrimage. All of us experience both prosperity and adversity in life. The prosperous moments pass by in the blink of an eye while the dark moments seem endless. Then the gray clouds of depression and discouragement descend on us. Our view becomes obstructed and we fail to see the Living Christ.

Beautiful light is born of darkness, so the faith that springs from conflict is often the strongest and the best.

~ R. Turnbull

It is here that Micah's advice is uplifting. For every problem in life there is but one answer: return to God.

There is no reason to stay in the dark. Fix your eyes on the mountaintops, then your road through the dark valley will not seem so long.

Persevere in prayer and focus on the goodness of God. Strengthen your daily walk with the Master. Perseverance and enthusiasm during the difficult moments of life will guide you through the darkness. Then you will see the sun-kissed mountaintops of the Lord's grace.

There is no other path to God and His power than through Jesus Christ, prayer, meditation and Bible study. It will give you courage in the dark and enable you to sing songs of praise, even in the darkest night. God's grace will make you glad again. You then move out of the dark depths with a stronger faith and a complete trust in your God.

Light of the world, I thank You that You shine in the darkness of my life. Even though I go through dark depths, I will not be afraid because You are with me. Amen.

Achieving Happiness

Read Proverbs 16:20-33

Blessed is he who trusts in the LORD. (Proverbs 16:20)

Happiness is the one thing that all people anxiously seek. Yet it seems to constantly escape most people. That is why Henry David Thoreau said, "Happiness is like a butterfly: the more you chase it, the more it will elude you, but if you turn your attention to other things, it will come and sit softly on your shoulder."

We often forget that happiness is something that comes from deep inside when our spirit is in harmony with God. With God at the center of our lives, it is possible to find lasting happiness, even in the most trying of times.

Many people seek happiness in material things. To put your trust in earthly possessions is to elevate things that are destroyed by moths and rust to the highest level. Such people often find out too late that they do not own their possessions, but their possessions own them. Matthew 16:26 says, "What good will it be for a man if he gains the whole world, yet forfeits his soul?"

> *Three grand essentials to happiness in this life are something to do, something to love, and something to hope for.*
> ~ Joseph Addison

Others think that breaking free from rules and regulations brings happiness. They lead a wild life, only to discover that this leads to disaster. One should guard against confusing freedom with immorality.

You can also seek happiness by isolating yourself from the world and living only for yourself. Eventually you'll come to a point where you are lonely and unfulfilled beyond measure. Love finds its highest fulfillment in service to others and this service is a requirement of happiness.

A life where God has complete control is a life of true happiness and inner peace.

Lord, I know that through You alone can I find true happiness.

Amen.

Seek Beauty

Read Philippians 4:2-9

Whatever is true, whatever is noble, whatever is right, whatever is pure, whatever is lovely, whatever is admirable – if anything is excellent or praiseworthy – think about such things. (Philippians 4:8)

Most people are aware that the world around them is becoming sordid and polluted. This is no surprise in light of the shocking newspaper headlines.

Appalling attitudes and immoral lifestyles are taking the limelight. Decency has been replaced by arrogance and insolence to such a degree that everything civilized and lovely is under the constant threat of destruction. The kind heart finds this sorrowful and disconcerting.

> *Beauty is but the sensible image of the infinite. Like truth and justice it lives within us; like virtue and the moral law it is a companion of the soul.*
>
> *~ George Bancroft*

If you share this perspective, you should guard against being influenced by negative inclinations. Beware of yielding to the temptation to accept that this degradation of values is now the norm and standard of modern society.

You should rather try to look past the filth and squalor of the world. Look at the things around you and find the beauty in them. Seek the glory of our Creator God in the songs of birds; in the breathtaking miracle of dawn and dusk, the majestic mountains; the ebb and flow of the tides and the abundant life that surrounds you.

Listen to soothing music and contemplate the good things still present in the world today. Then you will experience the peace of God that surpasses all comprehension.

Lord, help me remove the ugliness in this world. Let it be replaced with beauty and goodness through the help of the Holy Spirit. Amen.

Admitting God's Presence

Read Jude 1-25

Keep yourselves in God's love as you wait for the mercy of our Lord Jesus Christ to bring you to eternal life. (Jude 21)

Salvation, God's free and undeserved gift to man, is one of the cardinal principles of the Christian faith. There is nothing you can do to earn God's love; He gives it freely to everyone who is willing to accept it.

It is often said that what you receive for free is not as appreciated as much as something that has been earned through effort and exertion. Can God's love ever be earned?

His love for you is complete and perfect. The only obstruction that may prevent you from experiencing a deeper awareness of His love is your inability to receive it.

> *There is a God, not a dead one, or stuffed one, but a living one, who with irresistible force urges us towards more loving.*
> ~ Vincent Van Gogh

The necessity to deepen and enrich your spiritual life is a responsibility you have to accept if you want to experience a meaningful relationship with God through Jesus Christ. The Father has already given you His love and nothing can detract from that. Whether you utilize this gift or not depends entirely on you.

Remaining aware of God's love requires prayer, Bible study, meditation and quietly waiting on the Lord's Presence.

Your fellowship with God should result in your whole life being immersed in Christ's Presence. Your sanctuary and quiet time become your driving force, enabling you to cope with the demands of life. The Master is with you all the time, it is your responsibility to admit and confess His Presence in every situation in life.

O mighty God, love and thanksgiving flow spontaneously from my inner being when I rejoice in Your undeserved love. May Your love always flow through me. Amen.

Compassion

Read Matthew 9:32-38

When He saw the crowds, He had compassion on them, because they were harassed and helpless, like sheep without a shepherd. (Matthew 9:36)

Compassion and pity are the outstanding characteristics of the unique personality of Jesus Christ. These were the core of His message, His life and His greatness, and not an indication of any form of weakness.

Scripture tells us that ordinary people enjoyed listening to Him and they traveled great distances on foot to hear Him speak. His words reveal the depth of His wisdom and knowledge of human nature.

You may call God love, you may call God goodness. But the best name for God is compassion.

~ Meister Eckhart

Nevertheless, the way in which He spoke these words did not only touch the minds of people but also their hearts. They could feel His love for them and reciprocated it back to Him.

The eternal Christ is alive, and His compassion for people is just as real today as it was when He walked the roads in Palestine. While we read the gospel and rejoice in the undying truths of what He told us, love for Him is generated in our hearts because of His love for us.

If life has disappointed you; if you have failed and been overwhelmed by despair; if you don't know where to turn for courage, strength and inspiration, then remember the compassion and empathy of the living Christ. He is with you in your distress through the power of His undying love. Get up and purposefully start building a new life for yourself. Christ cares for you; He understands you and gives you courage and strength.

I thank You, Lord Jesus, for the joyful knowledge that even when I am abandoned and alone, I am an object of Your compassion and sympathy. Amen.

Joy Replaces Grief

Read John 16:17-33

"Now is your time of grief, but I will see you again and you will rejoice, and no one will take away your joy." (John 16:22)

If we are absolutely certain that we are children of God, it is our sure guarantee that we can break through the barrier of pain and sorrow. We can then come to quiet waters where there is peace – no matter how stormy the way might have been.

This is the certainty that grief is finite. Christ accepted that it was the will of His Father to lead Him to Golgotha because it lead to a greater joy.

It is not God's will for us to remain untouched by grief, even Christ Himself cried at the grave of Lazarus, but the Lord doesn't want grief to deprive us of our peace.

There is a liberating joy in the knowledge that our faith and trust in God have withstood the test of personal grief and loss.

> *In this world, full often, our joys are only the tender shadows which our sorrows cast.*
>
> ~ Henry Ward Beecher

The truth is that in our earthly existence we will never be guaranteed freedom from grief. God Himself does not promise this to His children. What He does promise us, though, is His peace.

Time heals all wounds. God leads His faithful children to new levels of acceptance and greater understanding of their grief. The greatest peace in life is not born out of superficial experiences, but from the deepest pain and sorrow.

It is as though we see God better through a veil of tears, and then grief can serve a holy purpose in our lives, "Consider that our present sufferings are not worth comparing with the glory that will be revealed in us" (Rom. 8:18).

I thank You, the Word that has become flesh, for Your assurance that if I sow in tears I will harvest with joy. I exult in Your peace.

Amen.

When Only Hope Remains

Read Jeremiah 17:9-18

Let my persecutors be put to shame, but keep me from shame.

(Jeremiah 17:18)

You might have endured deep sorrow, been overwhelmed by great difficulties or experienced a disaster. You might have consoled yourself with the thought that it would all soon be over. You might have prayed for light in that dark moment and trusted God to send you a blessing to balance things out. You may have tried to negotiate with God. But sometimes the dark cloud doesn't disappear and the sun simply won't shine. Disaster continues without ceasing.

> *All human wisdom is summed up in two words – wait and hope.*
>
> ~ Alexandre Dumas

In Jeremiah's deepest darkness he prayed that God would destroy his persecutors and save him. God usually answered when Jeremiah prayed. The prophet pleaded with God, but there was no answer, only silence. God didn't speak comforting words, or offer a message of hope or a promise to help. God didn't even reprimand him for his vengeful thoughts. There was no light at the end of the tunnel; only endless darkness.

This sort of experience might sound familiar to you. If you aren't used to it don't think that it will never happen to you – irrelevant of how dedicated you are to God. One disaster can follow on top of another. Hostile circumstances can continue without end. But God was with Jeremiah in the darkness, just as He has been with countless other people. He will also be with you. Jesus promised to be with us until the very end of the age (see Matt. 28:20). Just stay on the right course – Jesus Christ is with you!

Faithful Master, hold me tight in Your love, even when there is no light in the darkest of tunnels. Amen.

Singing in the Storm

Read Jeremiah 20:7-18

Jeremiah was definately in a storm [handwritten]

Sing to the LORD! Give praise to the LORD! He rescues the life of the needy from the hands of the wicked. (Jeremiah 20:13)

It's easy to praise the Lord when things are going well. If you achieve success or prosperity, or if you enjoy happiness, health and love you feel like glorifying God with a song of praise.

Jeremiah wasn't prosperous, successful or happy. Even though he was obedient to God, he was hated by the people and their leaders. Inside he was torn and tortured by his doubt. Despite his loneliness and despondency, he could still sing a song of praise to the Lord. He could also call others to do the same. He firmly believed that God was good, despite his own personal situation.

> *The shepherds sing; and shall I silent be? My God, no hymn for Thee?*
>
> ~ George Herbert

The worse the situation you find yourself in, the more necessary it is to praise God. You might not *feel* like it. (You might rather feel like running away *probably* and weeping.) But praise God instead, because it will help you to focus on Christ and not on yourself. It will remind you that in the past you received many blessings and you will hear God's promise to rescue you. It will lift your spirits and in the end you will *want* to shout for joy and sing to the glory of God.

Through all the changing scenes of life, through joy and sorrow, let me sing Your praise with my mouth and heart, O Lord my God!

help me to open my heart and let you in, open my mind to the vastness of your love for me, open my ears to hear the Holy Spirit in all that I do. when things go awry hold me tight so I can't try to bolt and run away. let me be at peace with you to know that you will help me through the course, you've got my back, you've got me under your wing of protection. if I'm having trouble at all, help me not to make others miserable, but to show love and compassion to someone else. Don't let me dwell on my troubles. In Jesus' name. Amen Amen.

There Is Still Hope

Read Jeremiah 23:1-8

"The days are coming," declares the LORD, "when I will raise up to David a righteous Branch, a King who will reign wisely and do what is just and right in the land." (Jeremiah 23:5)

We all hope for a better future. We yearn for rulers who will exercise true justice and wipe out poverty. We hope that wars will only be part of history. But in the reality of life, it never works out precisely like this. As a result, we lose heart, and even, all hope.

Jeremiah prophesied during the reign of a bad king. The king was disobedient to God and brought misery on his people. Jeremiah knew that there was no hope as long as this king was on the throne. But Jeremiah looked further. His firm faith in God told him that in the future this king would be dethroned and destroyed. God would break the present checkmate and establish a king who would be wise, honest and fair. Jeremiah believed God's promise and looked forward to a better future. He hoped in the Messiah and this hope kept him going through the terrible times in which he lived.

> *Every blade of grass, each leaf, each separate floret and petal, is an inscription speaking of hope.*
>
> ~ Richard Jefferies

Christians also hope for a future without war, poverty and sickness. They believe it because God promised that His kingdom would come. No matter how bad the world is, how corrupt and weak its rulers might be, how unfair the social system is within which we live and work, Christians keep hoping because they know that God is capable of intervening and setting up a new and better order. Because they hope, Christians roll up their sleeves and work toward that better world. Are you doing your part?

Faithful Savior, prevent me from being overwhelmed by the injustices in this world. Help me to hope in a new order according to God's will. Amen.

To Hope for Freedom

Read Jeremiah 31:18-25

This is what the LORD Almighty, the God of Israel, says: "When I bring them back from captivity, the people in the land of Judah and in its towns will once again use these words: 'The LORD bless you, O righteous dwelling, O sacred mountain.'" (Jeremiah 31:23)

Many people aren't free because they live under a strict political system. Some are doomed to live in dire poverty because of the poor economic conditions which don't allow them to develop. Others are slaves to alcohol and drugs, or trapped in the web of guilt, sex, slavery or emotional dependence.

Jeremiah conveyed God's promise to free Israel when they were captives in far-off Babylonia. Far from home, they probably dreamed of their freedom and return to Jerusalem.

> *When you say a situation or a person is hopeless, you are slamming the door in the face of God.*
>
> ~ Charles L. Allen

The promise that Jeremiah conveyed to them was later fulfilled. They returned, but not to the happiness they expected. Life was difficult and times were hard.

In the end, true freedom is only found in Jesus Christ. Spiritual freedom is not a product of political or economic circumstances. It is an internal freedom that many people have known, even if their outward circumstances were undesirable and they were oppressed. You can experience spiritual freedom if you submit yourself to Jesus Christ's reign and become His humble servant. Then you will be free from guilt, fear, reluctance and the damage that has been done to you through a very poor self-image.

Christ will set you free – free to live, to grow, to praise Him and to serve others. You will be freed to truly become a child of God. He will enable you to leave dangerous habits behind and to replace your despair with hope.

Lord my God, bless those who aren't free today. Grant them a hope for freedom and fulfill this hope in their lives. Amen.

The Transforming Power of Christianity

Read Revelation 21:1-8

He who was seated on the throne said, "I am making everything new!" (Revelation 21:5)

Wherever you look, you see things that need to change. Racial tension and industrial unrest occur worldwide. Thousands die daily from starvation. These are just some of the symptoms of a sick world that is crying out for healing.

It is right that the moral message of the gospel be heard in all these situations and that the church of Christ speaks out where evil reigns. But when we oppose social and political evils, we have to remember that the Christian ethic can't be forced on a non-Christian world with any hope of success.

> *If you are looking for an example of humility, look at the cross.*
>
> ~ Thomas Aquinas

Basic Christianity is first and foremost a God-to-man relationship. If you dare to pray for a society where people are treated like Christ would treat them, you need Christians who are filled with the Holy Spirit and who are willing to serve their fellow man with love.

The primary task of the Christian church is not to solve political and social problems, even though we must be concerned about these issues. The church's primary task is to introduce people to Jesus Christ so that their lives can be lived according to His will.

When the transforming power of Jesus Christ is revealed in the lives of the Master's dedicated disciples, the world will see His glory and people will be attracted to Him.

Loving Savior, grant that Your beauty, peace, power and love will be revealed in my life. Amen.

Dark Days

Read 2 Corinthians 4:7-15

We are hard pressed on every side, but not crushed; perplexed, but not in despair; persecuted, but not abandoned; struck down, but not destroyed. (2 Corinthians 4:8-9)

Sometimes your life journey is cruelly disrupted by problems that arise. Not one of us is safeguarded against difficulties, and Christ never promised that the Christian's voyage through life would be smooth sailing on a calm ocean.

If we approach our problems with a positive attitude, God can use them to motivate us to serve Him more effectively and to approach our fellow man with greater compassion. This is the positive approach about which Paul speaks to us today.

Learn to take your every problem to the Bible. Within its pages you will find the correct answer.

~ Billy Graham

When you are going through difficult times, wait in silence, trust God and find out through prayer if He is trying to teach you something. Do not allow problems to control your life. Guard in particular against panic, however great your dismay may be. God is greater than any problems you may experience.

Every problem poses a different threat to your spirit. Some problems appear dramatically out of nowhere, while others creep into your thoughts and life quietly and subtly.

Without a sincere and living faith that enables you to triumph over your problems, the way ahead will be impossible.

Faith in the goodness of God and in the sure knowledge that He has a purpose for your life will enable you to face the future with confidence. Nothing can separate you from the love of God that is in Christ Jesus our Lord (Rom. 8:39).

Merciful Lord, provide me with the strength and courage to face each day's problems head on. Your unfailing love transforms the darkness in my life into Your light. Amen.

Create Hope through Christ

Read Isaiah 35:1-10

Say to those with fearful hearts, "Be strong, do not fear; your God will come, He will come with vengeance; with divine retribution He will come to save you." (Isaiah 35:4)

There are people who don't realize their potential because they are timid and afraid. They possess the ability, but when the test comes they draw back. Many people who could deliver a good report about themselves in their chosen sphere of life, fail due to this weakness in their character. This often leads to a feeling of inferiority and inability, which makes the feeling of inferiority increase.

He who lives in hope, dances without music.

~ George Herbert

The Christian should never suffer in this way. As a child of God, you have the promise that His Son, Jesus, will continually be your companion and friend through life. He has undertaken to help you and to carry your burden of guilt, responsibility and suffering with you. You have His word that He will never forsake you or let you down.

With the promise of divine support and the assurance that the Son of God is with you in every situation, you can live your life full of certainty and without fear.

With You, Savior and Master, I can face life with confidence.

Amen.

Do Not Be Dismayed

Read Matthew 28:11-20

"I am with you always, to the very end of the age." (Matthew 28:20)

Sorrow and grief come into our lives suddenly, unexpectedly and unannounced – radically changing things. Where first there was understanding and love shared, there is now only a gaping void that can only be understood fully by those who have been down that path themselves.

Sorrow comes to us in many forms but it is most commonly cause by the death of a loved one. When a person you loved, cared for and had a relationship with is no longer there you feel completely isolated. But realize that you only weep for yourself because your loved one is safely with the Lord. Let that be a comfort and consolation to you.

God does not require you to follow His leadings on blind trust. Behold the evidence of an invisible intelligence pervading everything, even your own mind and body.

~ Raymond Holliwell

There are other sorrows just as bad as death and sometimes there are sorrows even worse. When someone brings great shame on a family we usually hear, "Death would have been better!" There can also be dreadful suffering because of physical disability, a child's deformity or terminal illness – all which we are powerless against.

It is in such circumstances that we lift our tearful eyes to the mountains and hear the voice of the God of love saying, "Do not fear, for I am with you; do not be dismayed, for I am your God. I will strengthen you and help you; I will uphold you with My righteous right hand" (Isa. 41:10).

Loving Lord Jesus, I come to lay my sorrow and grief in faith at the foot of the Cross, in the quiet trust that You will comfort me. I thank You for that. Amen.

Make the Most of Your Faith

Read 1 John 5:1-11

This is the victory that has overcome the world, even our faith. Who is it that overcomes the world? Only he who believes that Jesus is the Son of God. (1 John 5:4-5)

It might sound strange, but many people don't handle their faith with the respect that it deserves. They might go to church and give a reasonable account of what they believe, but their faith lacks the motivation that could empower their daily lives. They are religious without any knowledge of the benefits of a living faith.

The result of this unfortunate situation is that while the living Christ waits to share the riches of His grace with them, they refuse to accept it and live incomplete and lukewarm lives. If you consider what God, through Jesus Christ, is waiting to share with you, and you realize the poverty of your faith, then you know that you have not dealt justly with God's grace.

> *The secret behind getting more faith, is to get to know God more.*
>
> *~ Lester Sumrall*

The greatest token of thankfulness you can show the Master is to gratefully accept everything that He offers you. His love, peace and strength are gifts that are shared to make your life fulfilled and happy. Above all, His Holy Spirit will come to dwell in your life and will transport you to the peak of certainty in your faith.

This experience is not given to disciples who refuse to get involved with the life of Jesus Christ. It is achieved through prayer and the study of Scripture. Those who accept the challenge of this faith receive the fullness of the living Christ in their lives.

Living Savior, I dedicate myself anew to You so that I might experience a full and satisfying faith. Amen.

Hope for a New Heaven and Earth

Read Isaiah 65:17-25

"Behold, I will create new heavens and a new earth. The former things will not be remembered, nor will they come to mind." (Isaiah 65:17)

The year is speeding to a close and another year already looms ahead. If you look back on the past year you will be reminded of things that happened and are now a part of history.

It's difficult to let go of the past, and it gets more difficult as you grow older. And yet, the Bible presents a God that not only creates, but who constantly recreates. He isn't caught in the past, even though you might be.

As beautiful and valuable as the things of the past might be, and as holy and sacred as our traditions might be, they are all in the process of being forgotten. God is busy creating a new heaven and a new earth – and possibly a new church and new people for Himself. He is still busy moving beyond our visual field and sometimes even beyond our imaginations. When Jesus came, He was beyond the imaginings of the people of His day.

Don't fear change; embrace it.
~ Anthony D'Angelo

In a matter of months we will be entering a new year. We must be thankful for the things we leave behind – much of it is evil and everything is transient. Be happy about what lies ahead: a new creation, a new heaven and new earth that Christ will establish when He comes again. Don't stop hoping.

Lord, my God and Father, help me not to cling to the past, but to look to the future with the hope of Your new heaven and new earth.

Amen.

No More Weeping or Sadness

Read Isaiah 65:17-25

"I will rejoice over Jerusalem and take delight in My people; the sound of weeping and of crying will be heard in it no more." (Isaiah 65:19)

What is your honest wish for the future? Good health to overcome your illness; a steady job to overcome your unemployment; or the healing of a broken family? Of one thing you can be absolutely certain: the future will bring the same mix of success and failure, good and poor health as in previous years.

You can, and should, be positive and trust God to keep His promises in the future. The prophet didn't know what the future would bring, but he knew his God. Despite the history of his people, which was filled with disaster, misery, defeat, and even slavery – and was mixed with recovery and prosperity – he still dared to look forward and envision the rebuilding of Jerusalem.

> *There can be no kingdom of God in the world without the kingdom of God in our hearts.*
> ~ Albert Schweitzer

He believed that the best was yet to come and he dreamed of a time when God would put an end to their suffering, pain and sorrow. It is still a good idea to dream and to hope for better times from God's hand. We dare not limit it to Jerusalem.

This theme is discussed in the book of Revelation. It is one aspect of the great gathering of souls around God's throne. The message is clear: There will always be weeping and sorrow on earth. But in heaven, God will wipe the final tears from our eyes. What an indescribable prospect!

Savior, help Your children to wipe the tears from their eyes and to wait in expectation for the coming of Your kingdom. Amen.

Renewing Tradition

Read Romans 12:1-8

Do not conform any longer to the pattern of this world, but be transformed by the renewing of your mind. Then you will be able to test and approve what God's will is – His good, pleasing and perfect will. (Romans 12:2)

Tradition serves as an anchor and compass, which is why it should not remain static. It should be open to the demands of the present and continuously develop with every generation.

Upholding tradition for the sake of tradition will only lead to stagnation and alienation from the rest of the world. You cannot walk into the future if you are facing the past.

Renewal is therefore not foreign to tradition. In fact, tradition offers the only basis for true renewal. Without the basis of renewal, every renewal constructed is just a form of opportunism.

> *Human beings, by change, renew, rejuvenate ourselves; otherwise we harden.*
>
> ~ Johann Wolfgang von Goethe

The renewal of tradition is not only necessary because of the demands every new period brings, but it is also a calling on man's life. As a calling, renewing tradition can only take place on the pure and fixed principles. Principles are those things that help us to distinguish between what is important and what is not; what should be preserved and what can fall away.

Naturally, the principles that we use to distinguish between issues are only contained in Christian beliefs. This enables a person to distinguish between what tradition should be adhered to and what tradition can be adapted or disregarded altogether.

New times bring new demands. New demands can only be evaluated in the light of the eternal principles of God's Word in which His purpose for our lives is revealed.

Almighty Father, give me the wisdom to distinguish truly, so that I can live for those things which really matter. Amen.

The Will of God

Read Mark 14:32-42

"Abba, Father," He said, "everything is possible for You. Take this cup from Me. Yet not what I will, but what You will." (Mark 14:36)

Few people can say with absolute honesty that they have never acted impulsively. Human nature is inclined to rush into things, to make rash decisions and to follow certain behavior without thinking about it properly and without the necessary preparation or planning. The reason for this is that we follow the desires of our hearts and rely on our own abilities – often to our detriment when things go wrong.

Jesus taught us how to make decisions, even in crisis situations. A shining example of this is Jesus' prayer to His Father in the Garden of Gethsemane when He was in deep anguish. Jesus fully and unconditionally trusted in God's wisdom and will.

> *I have held many things in my hands, and I have lost them all; but whatever I place in God's hands, I still possess.*
>
> ~ Corrie ten Boom

God knows better than you do what is in your best interests and what will bring the greatest good for you in the end. Whatever decision or problem you face, first take it to God in prayer. Be sensitive to the Holy Spirit and allow Him to lead you. In this way you will experience peace of mind and joy that comes from knowing that you are living and hoping within God's will.

Lord and Master, I trust You to lead me in all things every day.
Amen.

Solace in Tears

Read Psalm 56:1-13

Record my lament; list my tears on Your scroll – are they not in Your record? (Psalm 56:8)

Tears provide release and cleanse an anguished spirit. Shakespeare said, "To weep is to make less the depth of grief."

Crying also prevents sorrow from developing into despair. If we never cry, we'll lose out on inner healing. Christ Himself stresses the benefit of tears, "Blessed are those who mourn, for they will be comforted" (Matt. 5:4).

Tears are not only shed by the weak, but also by the strong, since tears can also arise from love, tenderness and compassion. Washington Irving says, "There is a sacredness in tears. They are not the mark of weakness, but of power. They speak more eloquently than ten thousand tongues.

> *The soul would have known no rainbow if the eye no tears.*
> ~ John V. Cheney

They are messengers of overwhelming grief, of deep contrition, and of unspeakable love."

In His compassion God sees our grief, and through our tears He provides us with something bigger than our grief. Through the tears of Jesus Christ, God sanctified our tears. Jesus was godly enough to resurrect Lazarus and human enough to weep with the mourning. He was powerful enough to remove the cause of their tears, yet human enough to shed tears Himself.

Thank God for the healing, delivering and purifying power of sincere tears. They ease grief, bring acceptance and eventually lead to joy. In addition, we also have God's promise that there will be an end to our tears. John speaks of the new heaven and earth and says, "He will wipe every tear from their eyes" (Rev. 21:4).

O, Holy Comforter, I thank You that I can find solace through my tears; they make my grief bearable and bring me closer to You.

Amen.

In the World, but Not of the World

Read John 16:25-33

"In this world you will have trouble. But take heart! I have overcome the world." (John 16:33)

The mystery of Jesus Christ becoming flesh is that the Redeemer became one with all people at all times. He mingled with all types of people and called them His friends. He was never exclusive in His relationships with others.

The meaning of Christ's incarnation is that God became human in Christ and came to live among people. He came to share in their experiences and understand their problems, in this way He wanted to guide them to a meaningful relationship with God the Father.

You give me Your shield of victory, and Your right hand sustains me; You stoop down to make me great.

~ Psalm 18:35

Strange as it may appear, the Christian needs the world in order for his faith to be fully revealed. Jesus knows everything about the world and its temptations, fears and cruelty: all the sinful factors. He does not withdraw from them into peaceful isolation. Do not fear the problems and the difficulties of the world. Even if we are not of this world, we are inevitably in the world. Jesus states unequivocally that His followers will experience difficult times, but He has also promised never to leave or forsake us. That is why we can persevere courageously to give our testimony in a corrupt world – Christ has already gained the victory.

Christ does not call His disciples to a solitary life protected from the onslaught of the evil in the world. He does promise us that we, as His faithful witnesses, will gain the victory.

I praise and glorify Your name, my Lord and God, that I may gain victory over sin and corruption through the power of Your Holy Spirit in me. Amen.

A God Who Stands Far Away

Read Psalm 10:1-18

O Lord, why do You stand so far away? Why do You hide when I am in trouble? (Psalm 10:1 NLT)

One of the worst aspects of trouble is the feeling of helplessness, loneliness and the powerlessness to do anything about it. It feels as if there are invisible people working against you, trying to get you down. You feel lonely because it seems that the whole world has turned against you.

If you have ever felt like this, you are perfectly normal. The psalmist also felt like this and so have millions of others through the centuries. The psalmist was surrounded by wicked people who wanted to destroy him. They were shrewd crooks and made life very difficult for him. He felt that God, who should have defended him and destroyed the villains, had hidden Himself when he needed Him most.

> *So long as we imagine it is we who have to look for God, we must often lose heart. But it is the other way round – He is looking for us.*
>
> ~ Simon Tugwell

The psalmist was busy learning the most difficult lesson that anyone can learn: that trouble is normal. So powerful is evil and so widespread is corruption that anyone who thinks that it should be different is living in a fool's paradise. Yet, the psalmist didn't lose his faith in God. He appealed to God to come out of His hiding place and to do something about the evil and difficulty that he had to deal with.

You should also remember that no matter how difficult life gets, God only hides Himself for a short time. He probably wants you to search for Him in the darkness so that you will know without a shadow of a doubt that He still loves you and will bless you again soon.

Help me, Lord Jesus, to search for You until I find You. Amen.

November

His Path of Faith

Dear friends, let us love one another, for love comes from God.
Everyone who loves has been born of God and knows God.
Whoever does not love does not know God, because God is love.
~ 1 John 4:7-8

Love is invisible – it cannot be seen or measured,
yet it is powerful enough to transform you in a moment,
and offer you more joy than any material possession could.
~ Barbara de Angelis

*H*oly Lord Jesus our Savior of love,
We praise and thank You that through
Your coming to our world we have
come to know God as the God of love.
He loved us so much that He sent You so
that we could come to know Him as
the God of everlasting love!
Glorified Savior, through Your life we know what love truly is.
We know it unshakably through the example You set for us:
no matter how hopeless the situation might seem;
however irreconcilable the estrangement might appear;
however horrific the trespass might be –
God-given love can always overcome it.
Teach us, Lord Jesus, to love as You loved –
unconditionally and for all time.
Make our love holy; refine and purify it,
even if it is through fire.
Let our love glow brighter so that we will be a
reflection of Your holy and divine love in our world.
In the name of Him who leads us to love,

Amen.

Faith in the Unseen

Read Hebrews 11:1-10

Faith is being sure of what we hope for and certain of what we do not see. (Hebrews 11:1)

For many people, faith is a mystic and supernatural phenomenon that seems far removed from the hard and practical reality of everyday life. Although they wish to have more faith, they are deeply conscious of their ignorance as to what faith really is. "If I could just have faith," they sigh.

Others are continually pleading with God for more faith, but in spite of their efforts, their faith is still ineffective. We must realize that faith is an integral part of human nature. Most people use their faith in a negative way and therefore incorrectly.

People believe in their incapability to attain a high goal; they believe the endless fears that obstruct their view; they believe in failure rather than success. It is not a question of receiving more faith, but of putting the faith we already have to positive use.

> *I believe though I do not comprehend, and I hold by faith what I cannot grasp with the mind.*
>
> ~ St. Bernard of Clairvaux

When Christ says, "You must have faith in God!", He is commanding His followers to live in a constructive and positive way. Anyone can believe in "someone" or "something" but without faith in the victorious Christ, no one can be saved.

Faith is necessary in our spiritual lives. Without it, it is impossible to live in true fellowship with God. Faith is complete, unconditional trust in God. The glorious result of Christian faith is the definite certainty of God's living presence. When faith gives you the certainty that God loves you, all the other things in your life fall into place.

I thank You, Spirit of God, for making me sure of my faith. Let me see the invisible every day, to the glory of God the Father. Amen.

What More Can We Believe?

Read 1 John 4:7-21

We know and rely on the love God has for us. (1 John 4:16)

An all-important question is: "What do you believe in?" Some people storm through life and only believe in aggression. Others trust in their ability to outwit people. Many believe in their family relationships or their earthly possessions. There are people who think their honesty will get them through. Then there are those who believe in their own hard work and dedication.

These are all useful things, but they will let you down sometimes because they are human-based and focused on personal abilities. When you have tested God's love, you will discover that only there you are on solid ground. You trust in something outside of yourself and your own abilities. You are no longer dependent on any human being. Humans are fallible and fragile.

> *God loves us, not because of what we are, but because of who He is.*
>
> ~ Anonymous

If you believe in God and trust Him, you place your trust in an Almighty Source – the most powerful Source in the whole wide world – the love of God! This love has been here from the beginning and will be here until the end.

It is available to both the strong and the weak. It is there for you in both success and failure. It helps you when things go wrong and empowers you when all is going well. When everything else fails, God's love is still there. Nothing in the whole of creation can separate you from the love of God. Jesus, our Savior, leads us to this exceptional love.

Lord Jesus, everything fades next to the love of God. Through You I trust in this love. Amen.

Drive the Evil Spirit Out!

Read 1 John 4:7-21

There is no fear in love. But perfect love drives out fear, because fear has to do with punishment. The one who fears is not made perfect in love. (1 John 4:18)

Fear is an evil spirit that creeps up on us and outwits us. It haunts us and follows us; it nullifies our best efforts and prevents us from attempting great things. It causes us to surrender to the things we most strongly resist. It is at the same time a defense mechanism and a stumbling block.

The people in biblical times feared God. He was the sum-total of all the unknown powers that could embitter a person's life. If you were guilty, you were scared of His power to punish. Before people learned that God is love, they feared His disapproval when they trespassed His commands.

> *Everything comes from love, all is ordained for the salvation of man. God does nothing without this goal in mind.*
> ~ Catherine of Siena

Jesus' coming opened the floodgates of God's love. Because Jesus loved people, they discovered that God loved them. Therefore, they began to love themselves and others. They were no longer bound by fear because they knew that they were in the grasp of a mightier power.

You need not fear God any longer, although you must obey His commandments because you love Him. You needn't fear yourself any longer because you know that you have been made whole through His perfect love. You no longer need to fear the future because it is under the God of love's sovereign authority and control. You needn't fear His final judgment because His crucified Son has redeemed you. You need never fear again because you are held by the compassion, love and grace of the God of love. And His love is perfect!

I thank and praise You, Lord Jesus, for teaching me that God's perfect love drives out all fear. Amen.

Spiritual Confusion

Read 2 Chronicles 20:18-30

Have faith in the LORD your God and you will be upheld. (2 Chronicles 20:20)

We live in a period of spiritual awakening and the Spirit of God is working across the entire world. Humankind is becoming increasingly aware of spiritual values. There is a search for God and for truth that has been seldom observed in previous generations.

This desire for spiritual values has resulted in various interpretations of the doctrines of Christ. There are many secular teachings that create confusion in non-Christian communities and even among Christians.

At the beginning of every act of faith, there is often a seed of fear. For great acts of faith are seldom born out of calm calculation.

~ Max Lucado

What you say in defense of your faith is important. But still more important is the place you give to Christ Himself in your life. You should love Him more than the doctrines and theories about Him. The core of our Christian belief is after all based on the love we have in Christ.

Outraged propagandists may argue and perhaps confuse you about what you should believe. Unless their testimony is inspired by the love of Christ, He is not the center of their focus and you should not trust what they say.

When you are confused by strange and new doctrines, keep your spiritual eye on Jesus, your Guide. Allow Him to renew and strengthen your faith through the Holy Spirit. You'll have a wealth of noble tradition and a life filled with joy and tolerance through the working of the Holy Spirit. Your faith then rests in Christ and His Spirit will protect you against confusion in your spiritual life.

Savior and Friend, You are the foundation of my faith. I praise Your glorious name. Amen.

Do You Love or Do You Demand?

Read 1 Corinthians 13:1-13

These three remain: faith, hope and love. But the greatest of these is love. (1 Corinthians 13:13)

Life on earth is a question of give and take. It seems that the majority of people practice the "take" while the minority "give." Strangely, those who "give" seem to be the happiest of all.

Unfortunately, some people demand things that can't be given. Love can't be demanded, it must be earned. Physical birth doesn't give parents the right to demand that the child love them. Love cultivates love, and if the child is nurtured in love, he reacts with love.

All God can give us is His love; and this love becomes tangible – a burning of the soul – it sets us on fire to the point of forgetting ourselves.
~ Brother Roger

Elderly people, who are usually compassionate and friendly, often become prey to self-pity and instead of giving love, they set unrealistic demands. If they would only develop the spirit of love and remember those who serve them, then they would never have to demand love because all their needs would be joyfully fulfilled.

Many of the beautiful things that enrich our lives come from ordinary people who have learned to love others. Even though their love is often sacrificial, it is surpassed by the joy they experience through the offering they bring. Someone who loves his fellow man expresses that love through care and kind-heartedness. Those who are inspired by love and serve others share with the world the love that fills their hearts.

People who set demands receive monetary benefits, but those who give in the Spirit of love have discovered the blessing that God has reserved for them.

Savior of love, I want to give the best to others in the spirit of love. Help me to achieve this through Your Spirit. Amen.

When Viewpoints Collide

Read 1 Corinthians 13:1-13

But the greatest of these is love. (1 Corinthians 13:13)

Unfortunately there are many dedicated Christians who find it difficult to be polite and friendly toward other Christians who don't have the exact same beliefs as them. As long as they stay within the narrow context of their Christianity they are full of grace and kind-heartedness, but if they find themselves in an unfamiliar Christian fellowship, they become very critical and uncomfortable.

When a person feels like this, it is in reality a reflection of the small-mindedness of their faith and the narrow-mindedness of their point of view. It is a silent confession that their religious faith is only as high as their denominational walls. Their faith isn't great enough in understanding or strong enough in love to bridge the gap created by theological differences.

> *If thou knowest the whole Bible, and the sayings of all the philosophers, what should this profit thee without the love and grace of God?*
>
> ~ Thomas à Kempis

A dynamic and living faith is grounded in God's holy love for you and your love for God. From this double-sided chord of love your love for others is determined. This is the central teaching of Jesus Christ and any faith that lacks this dynamic of holy love ·is certainly not from God. High-sounding creeds and the value of rituals can never compensate for the lack of holy love in the church of God.

What a wonderful church would we be and what a wonderful ministry and witness would we have if unbelievers admiringly said, "Look at how these Christians love each other." It would be a place without opposing beliefs; where arguments would cease and love would bloom.

God of love, through Your grace and power I will make love the determining power of my faith. Amen.

Christian Growth

Read John 15:1-17

"Remain in Me, and I will remain in you." (John 15:4)

Now is the time to begin a new spiritual challenge. Perhaps your spiritual life has become a cumbersome burden to you. Maybe you are not experiencing the enthusiasm and dynamism you enjoyed previously. Then it is time to take some time out and prayerfully seek the reason for this.

It is undoubtedly true that when your faith loses its splendor and the reality starts fading, it is because you have turned your eyes away from Christ. Perhaps you are focusing on something which may be good in itself, but ultimately is inadequate in satisfying your deepest longing and need.

> *Faith is a living, daring confidence in God's grace, so sure and certain that a man could stake his life on it a thousand times.*
>
> ~ Martin Luther

Faith that has Jesus at the center is alive and sparkling. Jesus does not ask you to be faithful to a dogma or a specific religious code, but to be primarily devoted to Him.

He places an important premium on His relationship with you and your personal relationship with Him. The miracle of His mercy is that He has given us His Holy Spirit to fill our lives so that He can manifest Himself through us. If we place Him first, all other things will fall into place. — *not necessarily our agenda — but His will for us. Things or situations that are better for us*

The uninformed would perhaps think that such unconditional surrender speaks only of an overdose of piety that will rob life of its energy and excitement. Such people only have a vague concept of the Master.

He has come to give life, abundantly and richly! This is the inheritance of those in whom He lives, and who in turn remain in Him.

Indwelling Lord Jesus, come and live in me through Your Holy Spirit. May my life reflect You. Amen.

Less Effort and More Faith

Read Psalm 37:1-11

Commit your way to the LORD; trust in Him. (Psalm 37:5)

Most of the time we create the problems we experience in our Christian lives. We build dividing walls where there is none; we feel distant from God even though He is close to us; we debate the characteristics of faith, but seldom try to apply them in practice.

It is exciting to prove that faith in God is an attainable proposition. For a while you may have struggled with a problem. You may have tried every possible solution and as a last resort, you started praying.

> *Faith is a reasoning trust, a trust which reckons thoughtfully and confidently upon the trustworthiness of God.*
>
> ~ John R. Stott

This prayer was different from all the others. When you prayed before, you were already planning in your mind how to find the solution in your own strength.

You prescribed to God how matters should progress. Now you are praying because you are desperate and drowning. All crutches have been removed and you have to totally depend on the Lord.

The action of total surrender to God in complete faith will give you a feeling of relief and freedom. You will have a new spirit of expectation. You will wait on God to act when you have become deeply conscious of your own inability.

To be able to wait during this period – be it long or short – you should joyfully subject yourself to the perfect will of God. Then you will make an exciting discovery: God acts in your best interests in His incomparable way.

The way in which God works and the ease with which He does it, are often amazingly simple. Just let go – and let God!

Savior, I joyfully give my life to You completely. I ask that only Your perfect will be done in my life. Amen.

Dark Days

Read 2 Corinthians 4:7-15

We are hard pressed on every side, but not crushed; perplexed, but not in despair. (2 Corinthians 4:8)

No human being is without problems. At some time the smooth passage of our lives is cruelly disturbed. Upsetting influences drive away our inward peace and serenity. Yet suffering can serve a purpose.

Maybe you have traveled selfishly along the highway of life for a long time and have become self-centered. Or perhaps you have become insensitive to the distress of those who are less privileged than you are. Suffering can suddenly make you aware of the problems around you.

God uses trials to motivate you to serve Him with greater commitment and show your fellow man more understanding.

> *Conviction never so excellent, is worthless until it coverts itself into conduct.*
> ~ Thomas Carlyle

When you are tested, wait on the Lord. Never allow trials and tribulations to conquer and rule your spirit. Whatever happens, remain in control of the situation and do not become upset. — *have self control* ←

A tried way of triumphing over problems is to have faith of such quality that it will enable you to conquer your doubts and fears.

Faith in the goodness of God, and the certainty that He has a purpose with everything in your life, will enable you to face the future confidently. This will strengthen the conviction that nothing can separate you from the love of God.

Heavenly Father, grant me the mercy to learn from my tribulations and to change problems into tokens of mercy. *Amen.*

*Make Prayer a Way of Life

Read 1 Thessalonians 5:12-28

Pray continually. (1 Thessalonians 5:17)

The great benefit attached to putting aside time for prayer and quiet meditation is undeniable. Rich spiritual blessings flow forth from such times of prayer: inner peace; spiritual strength; determination and purposefulness. They form anchors in life and are founded in those quiet moments spent alone with the Master. This gives meaning to life.

It should be clear to every Christian disciple that true prayer is infinitely more than saying your prayers, which usually consists of a few quick moments where a string of requests are mumbled. When prayer is used to satisfy God or prevent unpleasantness, it becomes a mere safety mechanism or superstition.

> *Do not always be wanting everything to turn out as you think it should, but rather as God pleases, then you will be undisturbed and thankful in your prayer.*
>
> ~ Abba Nilus

True prayer is a relationship with life; an attitude that overshadows the nuances of every day. The ordinary humble tasks that have become routine, can become hallowed by regarding them as practical prayers to the glory of God.

During those moments, when your thoughts are not occupied by a specific task you can focus on the Master. He is your ever-present Traveling Companion through life. Wherever you are, you can know that you are in His Presence and that you can talk to Him as a friend.

The power and beauty of prayer lies in its simplicity. Even though traditional prayer has its place in our worship, it is the heart-strengthening childlike prayer to God that makes Him a living reality in your life.

* *I thank You, my Redeemer, that I can develop a living and practical prayer life through the help of the Holy Spirit. Amen.*

Stay with the Essential Issue

Read Luke 9:57-62

He said to another man, "Follow Me." (Luke 9:59)

Jesus continually discussed the deep truths of God with the priests and teachers of the Law at the temple and synagogue. From a young age He was able to stand His ground with even the most knowledgeable men, and a small number became His secret disciples.

Jesus spoke to the ordinary people but never discussed abstract theological issues. He made His appeal on a one-to-one basis. It was always, "Follow Me," "Come to Me" or "You are My friends." He personalized the relationship between Himself and the ordinary people. Later they would try to write about this personal experience and that is how the Christian creeds and dogmas were formulated. But to

> *The reason for loving God is God Himself and how He should be loved is to love Him without limit.*
>
> ~ Bernard of Clairvaux

experience Christ in your heart is a prerequisite for all dogmas and theories.

Very few people have been won over for Christ through theological debates. It is when the living Christ is presented in simplicity and power that He is accepted as Redeemer and Savior and faith becomes living and glorious.

You must have dogma if you want to give an account of the faith that is within you, but make sure that you keep your life focused on Jesus. This isn't possible without sincere love.

I thank You, Lord Jesus, that my faith is grounded in You and not in theological arguments. Amen.

Travel Light

Read Matthew 6:25-34

"Do not worry about your life, what you will eat or drink; or about your body, what you will wear. Is not life more important than food, and the body more important than clothes?" (Matthew 6:25)

Are you one of those people who cannot throw anything away? Worthless items are saved because you think you may need them one day. In time, this hoarding becomes a real problem, if not for you then for the people who must sort through all your belongings when you are no longer here.

It is probably safe to say that if you have not needed an item during the last year or so, you will never need it. Discipline yourself and get rid of redundant items that have become useless to you. Maybe someone else could possibly use them.

> *The present is never our goal: the past and present are our means: the future alone is our goal.*
>
> ~ Blaise Pascal

To do this you will probably have to fight the hoarding desire that you have developed over the years. You may be in a situation where you have collected everything that you could get your hands on and now you have no more space.

Perhaps you have become so burdened and impeded with non-essentials that you are chained to the material world. These things may seem like treasures to you, but they bind you to the past in such a way that you can hardly see the future.

Rid yourself of these non-essential items and allow the Holy Spirit to determine what you should value. Then you will understand the value of the present and move freely with self-confidence into the future. This also applies to any obsolete and useless spiritual red tape you may have.

O, Holy Spirit, help me to free myself from the past and to reach out to the future so that I can win the prize in Jesus Christ. Amen.

Be Patient with One Another

Read Colossians 3:12-17

Therefore, as God's chosen people, holy and dearly loved, clothe yourselves with compassion, kindness, humility, gentleness and patience. Bear with each other and forgive whatever grievances you may have against one another. (Colossians 3:12-13)

People today are impatient and in a hurry on almost every aspect of life: on the road, in our speech, in our church meetings, in our communication – everywhere and all the time. There is more to Christian patience than simply waiting quietly. The original word is sometimes translated as "long-suffering."

The Christian actively embraces the suffering, problems and difficulties that accompany discipleship. Some manage to turn them around for good. The wise Christians realize that enduring certain setbacks can lead to positive gains. Jeremiah said, "It is good to wait quietly for the salvation of the LORD" (Lam. 3:26). Those who learn to wait quietly find that their deliverance comes from God.

> *Be as patient with others as God has been with you.*
> ~ Anonymous

Patience also involves bearing with others' mistakes and weaknesses. It handles the aggression of those who resist the faith. On one occasion a drunkard stumbled out of a bar in London while an evangelist was busy preaching. The drunken man walked up to the preacher and knocked him down with his fist. After the preacher had stood up and dusted himself off, he said to his attacker, "God bless you, brother" and continued with his sermon. How much of that kind of patience do you and I have?

Jesus, my Savior, give me the kind of patience that loves until the end. Amen.

Christ Works in Miracles

Read John 2:1-11

"Do whatever He tells you." (John 2:5)

The first miracle Jesus performed on earth was at a wedding. In the same way He wants to make a miracle of love out of every marriage today.

He is intensely interested in our personal happiness – this is such a simple yet breathtaking truth. He guides us to each other; He ignites the love in our hearts. He knows that it is not good for people to be alone.

> *The miracles of Jesus were the ordinary works of His Father, wrought small and swift that we might take them in.*
> ~ George Macdonald

He does not only undertake to accompany us during the wedding ceremony, but also for our whole wedded lives. He remains the Good Shepherd for the entire journey of life.

He never forces Himself on us. He does not randomly intervene in relationships or force open doors. That is why it is essential for us to invite Him in.

Like He did at the wedding feast in Cana, Christ gives a new sparkle and effervescence to ordinary, everyday things. Water becomes wine in His hands.

It is so easy to fall into a soul-destroying rut in your marriage. But Christ can rekindle the spark of true love and adventure in your relationship.

The definite and irrefutable condition for divine miracles lies in the words Jesus' mother spoke to the servants at the wedding, "Do whatever He tells you." Obedience to His will as revealed in His Word assures us that every marriage can become a miracle in His loving hands.

I thank You repeatedly, living Master, for the continuous miracle of love You work in my life every day. Amen.

Faith Will Carry You Through

Read Hebrews 11:30-39

[The prophets] who through faith conquered kingdoms, administered justice, and gained what was promised. (Hebrews 11:33)

Many people worry themselves sick about the future. It seems as if there is unrest and disruption throughout the world and people always ask, "How much longer can it continue like this?" Even if this attitude is understandable, it eventually leads to depression and despair. And that worsens the situation. Then people ultimately lose hope and bow before what they regard as the inevitable.

> *The ultimate ground of faith and knowledge is confidence in God.*
>
> ~ Charles Hodge

Throughout the centuries the world has been filled with conflict. Humankind has experienced every imaginable form of danger, hardship and catastrophic disaster. Through greed and lack of involvement, cravings for honor and man's digression has caused or contributed to every disaster on earth.

Nevertheless, history proves that there has always been a core group of believers who have trusted God. By His mercy they overcame stumbling blocks and were rewarded for their steadfast faith.

However dark and disastrous your circumstances may appear, place your trust steadfastly in God. Hold on to the certainty of the risen Savior who triumphed over the world.

Despite the anxiety and panic in the world, you should continue to believe in the irrefutable fact of a loving and almighty God who can create order from chaos. He will protect everyone who trusts in Him. It is still God's earth, despite the fact that the world seems to believe the opposite.

Finisher of my faith, I place my complete trust in You under all circumstances and at all times. Amen.

The Spirit of Love

Read Colossians 1:1-8

He has told us about the love for others that the Holy Spirit has given you. (Colossians 1:8 NLT)

Someone once said, "Selfishness makes everything a burden; love makes everything a delight!" Love is the core ingredient of our Christian lives. Almost all the great heroes of the faith were known for their love. It is, however, something that is easy to talk about, but not so easy to perform. We are selfish, proud and greedy by nature. To love means to be selfless, humble and generous.

How do you become a loving and friendly Christian instead of selfish and unpleasant? It doesn't just happen and it also doesn't come about by struggling and worrying. It doesn't result from being disciplined and it can't just be produced. In the Christian sense of the word, you start to love when the Holy Spirit takes possession of you.

> *Not where I breathe, but where I love, I live.*
>
> ~ Robert Southwell

Much has been said in recent times about how the Holy Spirit empowers Christians. A lot has been said about speaking in tongues, miracle healings and other gifts. Much less has been said about the fruit of the Spirit, yet the primary result of the fruit of the Holy Spirit in your life is the desire to overcome your natural selfishness and to love others.

When the Holy Spirit possesses you (you don't possess Him!) He ignites your life with love – both for God and your fellow man. This is not a sentimental, soppy love, but an inner feeling of goodwill. God takes possession of your deepest heart and fills it with the same love that Jesus, our living Redeemer, had for people.

Lord my God, through Your Spirit fill my heart with powerful, outgoing, caring love. Amen.

Healing for a Sick World

Read 1 Corinthians 14:1-8

Follow the way of love. (1 Corinthians 14:1)

It would be interesting to find out how much time and effort it has cost to find cures for all the world's troubles. International, national and local organizations and institutions have been formed and an enormous amount of time and effort has been sacrificed by well-meaning people in an effort to alleviate poverty, to reduce suffering, to maintain peace and to bring an end to violence and aggression.

As commendable as these objectives might seem, there is only one solution to all the world's ailments, and that is obedience to Christ's command, "You must love as I have loved you" (John 13:34).

You might think that this is an oversimplification of a complex issue and that it can never be im-

> *The hunger for love is much more difficult to remove than the hunger for bread.*
> ~ Mother Teresa

plemented on a worldwide scale as a practical cure for a sick world. But it is not only possible; it is the only way to peace and stability in a torn and hurting world.

But it must start with the individual – with you and me. Love must be rooted in our personal relationships before we can grow in it and bear fruit in international affairs. In the same way that you demonstrate Christian love to your fellow man, this attitude must be spread until the world is restored to the perfection of God's creation.

Lord Jesus, help me to follow Your example by spreading the medicine of love to this sick world. Amen.

The Loving Father

Read Psalm 37:23-40

I was young and now I am old, yet I have never seen the righteous forsaken or their children begging bread. (Psalm 37:25)

People often doubt the depth and authenticity of God's love. It happens especially when they or someone they know is going through a difficult time or when they experience adversity. When a tragedy occurs, God's love is often questioned and this can easily lead to an attitude that will damage one's spiritual life and allow doubt to enter one's mind and heart.

It is exactly in these situations that you need to draw from the reserves of your faith so that you can firmly impress God's endless love for you in your mind. If this was not the case, Jesus would have died in vain. Take note of Scripture and read about those who abundantly received the saving and supporting grace of God's love in the midst of disaster and distress.

> *Love is life. All, everything that I understand, I understand only because I love.*
> *~ Leo Tolstoy*

Take time to be alone with the living Christ. Feel how His strengthening power takes control of you and banishes all fear and doubt from your mind and replaces it with certainty and trust. These alone are the fruit of a life grounded on Jesus and His love.

Believe in the all-encompassing love of God and you will live on victor's ground through Jesus Christ and His love.

Thank You, Lord Jesus, that You will never let us down. Amen.

Exceptional Love

Read 1 Peter 2:11-17

Show proper respect to everyone: Love the brotherhood of believers, fear God, honor the king. (1 Peter 2:17)

We all use the word *love* very loosely and vaguely. It means different things to different people and even different things for the same person, depending on the context.

Why should Christians show exceptional love to fellow believers? Because they are aware of a unity with other Christians that is different from ordinary relationships. It is a "special relationship"; they are bound together "in Christ" even though they might demonstrate different forms of discipleship. Some are Catholics, others are Pentecostals, others are Protestants, yet Christ is everything for all of them and therefore they are bound together because they are bound to Christ.

> *The supreme happiness in life is the conviction that we are loved – loved for ourselves, or rather in spite of ourselves.*
> ~ Victor Hugo

He replaces their selfish isolation with love. The love He grants is not the world's love – it is God's kind of love. It cares, shares and gives. It is the kind of love that makes a person mature.

Other Christians need your love. Some are lonely, or they have problems and troubles. They depend on the extra reserves God has given them. God's love is at work in you and you have been called to share it with them. God wants to love them through you and in the process He will make you a more loving person.

Holy Master, make me sensitive to the problems other Christians face and show me how I can help. Amen.

Live Together as a Family

Read 1 Peter 3:1-12

Finally, all of you, live in harmony with one another; be sympathetic, love as brothers, be compassionate and humble. (1 Peter 3:8)

We know that there are different types of love. We also know that the word *love* is sometimes twisted in today's culture to mean *sex*. But Christians must love one other like members of a family love one another. They must support each other in various endeavors; participate in sport together; and try to understand each other.

Brothers and sisters help each other when one of them is in need. They rejoice in each other's

> *To love another person is to help them love God.*
> ~ Søren Kierkegaard

joys and feel each other's pain. They share in one another's victories and successes, and sympathize with one another's losses and disappointments. Naturally, they quarrel sometimes, but they soon make up again.

This is how we should care for each other as Christians. It isn't a soppy kind of care, but a powerful and sensitive action. Many Christian groups speak about love and feel good when they hear stories of sacrificial love. But those who make a difference are those who act like family for those who need love. They make it a practice, as Jesus expects us to do. You can only love like this if you allow Jesus' love to enter your heart and life and take possession of you. This love crowns all other kinds of love.

Thank You, Lord Jesus, that You bind us together like a close-knit family who truly love each other. Amen.

The Greatest Life Experience

Read Ephesians 3:14-21

May you experience the love of Christ, though it is too great to understand fully. Then you will be made complete with all the fullness of life and power that comes from God. (Ephesians 3:19 NLT)

It's difficult to determine precisely what has been the greatest experience in one's life so far. Some regard the moment they met their spouse as their greatest experience. Others will remember thrilling moments that caused great excitement, fulfillment and satisfaction in their lives. These times stand out as peaks on the level plains of our lives and we remember them with gratitude.

If you treat your spiritual path with the earnestness it deserves, you will remember that moment when God's love became a wonderful reality to you. It might have come with dramatic suddenness, or it gently dawned on you like

> *When I have learnt to love God better than my earthly dearest, I shall love my earthly dearest better than I do now.*
> ~ C. S. Lewis

the rising sun. You cherish that moment when God became a living, personal Presence in your life.

At that moment divine love entered your life and was revealed in your life you became aware that you possessed the nature of God because God is love, and to express love is to let God express Himself.

The realization that God loves you and fills you with His Spirit is an unforgettable and great life experience that becomes richer and more meaningful as the years pass. God's Spirit filling your spirit is not a once-off occurrence. It is a moment by moment participation in the divine nature through prayer, Bible reading, meditation and positive testimony through the love that you extend to the world.

Holy God, the privilege of knowing You through Jesus Christ, and of living in Your Presence, is the greatest experience in my entire life.
Amen.

Love in Action

Read Colossians 1:3-14

We always thank God, the Father of our Lord Jesus Christ, when we pray for you, because we have heard of your faith in Christ Jesus and of the love you have for all the saints. (Colossians 1:3-4)

It has been said that you can tell if someone is a Christian by the way he loves. This is sometimes true, but not always. Sometimes Christians are better known by their judgmental attitudes, pride, petty fighting and insensitivity toward human suffering.

The people Paul wrote to were new Christians. For them it meant they had to give up one religion for another. This meant more than simply changing religious systems; it meant a complete change of heart.

> *To be loved for what one is, is the greatest exception. The great majority love in others only what they lend them, their own selves, their version of them.*
>
> ~ Johann Wolfgang von Goethe

To become Christians they had to open their hearts and lives to the love of God in Christ Jesus. In this way they became channels of God's love. They couldn't keep it to themselves, but had to give it away to others. They couldn't only receive God's love; they had to give it too. This probably meant that they sent money to the poor people in Jerusalem.

We can also become instruments through which God reaches people. You can do this by supporting missionary work or offering to help at a soup kitchen; or visiting hospitals and old-age homes to carry Christ's comfort there. By visiting inmates in prison you can become a vehicle for God's love. This is Christian love in action.

Lord Jesus, keep me from only talking about love and not performing deeds of love. Amen.

Our Christian Duty Is to Love

Read Psalm 133:1-3

How good and pleasant it is when brothers live together in unity!
(Psalm 133:1)

Through the centuries the world has experienced the tragic consequences of disunity. Instead of being one in the Spirit of Jesus Christ, as the Master prayed, various groups and denominations argue about relatively less important dogmas instead of uniting together in a fight against the Evil One. War, civil unrest and acts of aggression and terrorism are busy shaking the foundations of society. It seems as if these terrible acts are on the increase instead of diminishing.

A variety of reasons have been given as the cause of this disunity and unrest, but the root cause of this evil is the rejection of the Master's command to "love one another as I have loved you." It seems that, above all doubt, obedience to this command will solve all the problems facing humankind in these turbulent times.

Love has power to give in a moment what toil can scarcely reach in an age.
~ Johann Wolfgang von Goethe

The starting point is not on an international level, but with you. The ordinary Christian is called to love; to show compassion, understanding and tolerance; to forget pride and preconceptions and to be sympathetic toward the views of those who think differently.

The smallest pebble that is thrown into the pond sends ripples across the whole pond. Your single act of Christian love can send ripples across the length and breadth of the earth. Your Christian duty is to do exactly this.

Christ of love, help me to be united with my fellow believers so that I can obey Your command. Amen.

The Power and Importance of Love

Read 1 Peter 4:7-19

Above all, love each other deeply, because love covers over a multitude of sins. (1 Peter 4:8)

We sincerely wish that we could forever erase the bad things we've done and that we could get another chance to do the good things we should have done, but didn't. We wish that our mistakes and failures wouldn't hamper our growth to maturity.

You *can* make up for your mistakes and shortcomings; don't allow them to hold you back. Love – deep love – God's kind of love "covers a multitude of sins." God so desires you to be filled with His love that He is willing to forget your sins if you will only allow Him to spread love through you. A word of encouragement, an act of compassion, a prayer for a struggling soul, a gift of love in a difficult situation. God is excited when He sees you do such things, especially when you persevere in them. These are the most important things to Him in the whole world.

Only love enables humanity to grow, because love engenders life and it is the only form of energy that lasts forever.

~ Michel Quoist

Strong, deep love can also accomplish other things. If you love earnestly and persevere in it, your life will be so filled with love that you will not have the time or inclination to sin.

Love drives sin out of your life because its effect is so powerful that it begins to transform your life, personality and actions. It doesn't only have benefits for those receive it, but also for the one who gives it. It also changes you. Isn't it time that you also start loving unconditionally?

Savior of love, let me never slacken in my love for others. Amen.

Growth through Pain

Read John 15:1-8

November 25

"He cuts off every branch in Me that bears no fruit, while every branch that does bear fruit He prunes so that it will be even more fruitful." (John 15:2)

God often uses pain and sorrow to teach His children important lessons. By doing so He also strengthens our character and gives us the opportunity to grow spiritually. Sorrow is a fruit and God does not allow this fruit to grow on branches that are too weak to carry it.

Christ tells us that God is the great Gardener who lovingly prunes His children. The right pruning methods result in vines, shrubs and trees that grow better and bear more fruit.

In our lives there are many in-fertile shoots: bad habits; wrong thoughts and sinful inclinations.

The more we grow in grace, the more glory we bring to God.
~ Thomas Watson

Therefore the pruning-shears of God are sometimes required.

Our heavenly Father is a Master Pruner. He knows all about our shortcomings, His pruning promises growth and abundant fruit. Under the tender care of the Gardener, the wounds heal and new life bursts out everywhere.

He who has learnt to carry his cross will find peace. You will be a conqueror and you will stand strong in this world. Christ did not come to make all pain disappear but to teach us to bear it with dignity and to glorify Him through it.

Then you have become a participant in Christ's suffering on behalf of the whole world. It is through the positive contributions of those who have experienced suffering and pain that this world becomes a better place to the glory of God.

Father of abundant grace, help me to accept the pain in my life as part of Your loving pruning. Enrich me through Your healing mercy so that I can bear abundant fruit. Amen.

Unshakable Trust

Read Romans 12:9-21

Be joyful in hope, patient in affliction, faithful in prayer. (Romans 12:12)

When everything seems to be going wrong for people, they are often tempted to act in either one of two ways. They can either be completely overwhelmed by their problems and collapse under the pressure, or they can try impulsively to solve them in their own strength. The Lord has promised never to forsake or leave you. The Scriptures tell us time and again of how God kept His promises. It is therefore imperative that you trust Him completely on your journey through life. You cannot hurry God or prescribe to Him. He has His good time and method. His timing is always perfect.

> *He rides at ease whom the grace of God carries.*
> ~ Thomas à Kempis

Even if you find it difficult to understand in your present confusion, you must accept that God sees the overall picture of your life. He is all-knowing and all-seeing. Your faith in Him must be of such a quality that you will unshakably trust His promises and abide obediently by His judgment.

When trying times cross your path, place your burdens in His care and on trusting in Him. Seek the guidance of the Holy Spirit to teach you to wait patiently on the Lord. Ask Him for the discernment to see His answers to your prayers.

God wants you to experience only the best and the most beneficial, and if this takes place in strange and roundabout ways, you should continue believing and trusting steadfastly. Those who stand steadfast in affliction, receive God's most precious gifts from His treasury of mercy.

Lord and Father, I find peace of mind by trusting You completely. Keep me steadfast through my faith in You. Amen.

God's Unfailing Love

Read Psalm 13:1-6

I trust in Your unfailing love; my heart rejoices in Your salvation.
(Psalm 13:5)

We all need something to hold on to when things get too difficult for us. At such times some people think about their loved ones and persevere for their sakes. Others look beyond the present pressures and dream of peace and rest. Some think about their previous successes while others look past the pain and think about the work that still needs to be done. Many buckle under the pressure but some turn to God.

David knew both prosperity and adversity. As a shepherd he fought against wild animals. He survived Saul's persecution when his life was threatened. Through all his bewildering experiences he knew that he had one steadfast source of strength – God's love. It carried him through the worst experiences, but also through the best life could offer him. His own strength often failed; his health failed; his hope weakened; his friends deserted him; he knew defeat – but God's love never let him down.

> *To stop God from loving me would be to rob Him of His Godhead, for God is love no less than He is truth.*
> ~ Meister Eckhart

We can also trust in God. However low you've sunk in the mire of sin; however foolishly you've acted; however overwhelmed you've been through unmanageable circumstances; however lost you've felt – you can always rely on God's love for you. Christ, who tasted death and rose from the dead, is the perfect embodiment of God's unfailing love. Whatever the situation is you have to handle, Christ has already been through it. He will never let you down. Find Him and cling unflinchingly to Him!

Thank You, Savior and Redeemer, that I can depend on Your unfailing love. Amen.

Everything for the Good

Read Romans 8:28-39

We know that in all things God works for the good of those who love Him, who have been called according to His purpose. (Romans 8:28)

When our lives are on the verge of being destroyed by problems, sorrow or affliction, we find it extremely difficult to believe that God can and will make all things work out for the good of those who love Him. Even if only a little hope remains, it is sufficient for God to fulfill His plan for our lives. We can never lose so much that God cannot create something good out of what remains. There is no loss that God cannot compensate for.

Such is hope, heaven's own gift to struggling mortals, pervading, like some subtle essence from the skies, all things both good and bad.

~ Charles Dickens

God is so much greater than our comprehension. His omnipotence is not limited and His love is infinite. How will we, with our limited ideas, ever completely understand His perfect plan for our lives if we do not have a burning faith in our hearts?

After overwhelming sorrow or disappointment it may sound inappropriate to say that God can make it work out for our good. Yet believing this is an integral part of our healing and solace. If it were not for this Christian hope, we would all have broken hearts. Hope for tomorrow is today's inspiration.

For those who love God this is the most glorious knowledge: God wants only the best for us and He wants everything to work out for our good. Silent and solid trust in God sets His power free on our behalf. Out of our love for Christ, good is born.

Great Comforter, thank You for the promise that everything will work out for me according to Your will. Amen.

Faith Like Little Children

Read Matthew 18:1-5

"I tell you the truth, unless you change and become like little children, you will never enter the kingdom of heaven." (Matthew 18:3)

If investigating everything is part of your personality, there will always be questions that require answers. While you study facts about God, nagging questions trouble you and you can end up feeling isolated. You seek, discover and demand answers that nobody can give. You become more and more frustrated. You may even feel inclined to abandon the Christian faith due to its demands. The confusion caused by conflicting religions and convictions is self-inflicted. But admitting that God exists is the simple foundation on which to build your faith.

> *A great man is one who has not lost the child's heart.*
> ~ Mencius

To say with conviction, "I believe in God," is to identify yourself with the greatest life-giving Power in the entire universe. If such a declaration is sincerely and honestly applied to your life, it will make God a reality for you.

Although you may have doubts about God, He does not have any doubts about you at all. He sees and knows you for what you are and what you can become. He expects you to share your life completely with Him through a childlike faith. Then your life will be abundant.

Master, my faith in You is simple, but my trust in You is very real. Strengthen my faith through Your Holy Spirit. Amen.

Growth through the Truth

Read Ephesians 4:1-16

Instead, speaking the truth in love, we will in all things grow up into Him who is the Head, that is, Christ. (Ephesians 4:15)

It is a glorious and unsurpassed truth that faith in Jesus Christ saves you from sin. This is the starting point of the gospel. But the growth process should start in your life after you have accepted Christ as your personal Savior and Redeemer.

If you don't think growth is necessary or important, it will not be long before your spiritual experience will be shipwrecked on the stormy seas of disappointment and despair. There must be growth and development, or else your spiritual life will diminish and die.

> *It is truth alone that capacitates any soul to glorify God.*
> ~ John Owen

There are many resources that God has made available for us to improve our spiritual growth. But we should take care that the aids don't become goals in themselves. Fellowship with believers is necessary, but fellowship that is not centered around Christ serves no constructive purpose.

A study of the Bible will be a source of continuous inspiration and guidance, but the purpose should always be to point the disciple to Christ and to glorify Him. Good deeds and charitable work undoubtedly produce favor with God, but these are only the results of our acquaintance with Jesus Christ and can never take the place of our faith in Him.

There can only be spiritual growth if your main objective is to reflect the image of Christ more and more. It should be at the heart's desire of every believing Christian disciple. In this way your spiritual life becomes more than emotion and it demands of you your very best for the Most High.

My Lord and Redeemer, let Your Holy Spirit take possession of me in such a way that I will live solely for Your glory. Amen.

December

His Path of Love

"For God so loved the world that
He gave His one and only Son, that
whoever believes in Him shall not
perish but have eternal life."
~ John 3:16

The love of Christ is like the blue sky,
into which you may see clearly, but the real
vastness of which you cannot measure.
~ Robert Murray McCheyne

*H*oly God and Father of our Lord Jesus Christ,
who is also our loving Father through His merit:
We praise You for sacrificing Your Son out of love for us.
We praise You for Advent which reminds
us of His joyful coming to earth.
We praise Your name for yet another time of family joy,
excitement and happiness.
We bow in gratitude before You for all the
blessings that accompany our celebration of Christ:
for the strengthening of family and friendship bonds,
for rest, peace, books and music.
Heavenly Father, our celebration of Christ reminds
us once again of Your immeasurable love; a love that
doesn't depend on whether we deserve it or not.
May Your love drive us to love You and
our fellow human beings in return.
Grant, Lord Jesus, that the wonder of love
and goodwill will remain in our hearts
throughout the new year.
May it fragrance our homes and
from there spread out to others.
May the birth of the Christ child
influence our entire lives for good.
Holy Jesus, make this season a true celebration
of You in our hearts, homes and in the world.
We pray this in the name of the
Child of Bethlehem, Our Savior.

Amen.

Rest in God's Love

Read Psalm 66:5-20

Come and see what God has done, how awesome His works in man's behalf! (Psalm 66:5)

Human thoughts and emotions can be very inconsistent. A sudden change in emotion can cause you to feel joyful the one moment and sad the next. In a surprisingly short space of time you can change from being hopeful to hopeless; strong to weak; positive and self-assured to uncertain and indecisive. Your whole approach to life can change through events, personal success or crisis – even through weather conditions. It's easy to feel depressed on an overcast day.

> *The God of the Christians is a God of love and consolation: He is a God who fills the soul and hearts of those whom He possesses.*
>
> ~ Blaise Pascal

Throughout your life and in every conceivable situation you may find yourself in, it is necessary to strive to find and maintain a measure of stability in order to handle each day's demands and challenges. In the face of the uncertainty in the world today, you need to hold on to one or other firm hope so that you can find peace of mind.

To achieve this goal just look around you and take note of the incredible wonder of God's creation. Absorb the beauty of nature, music and art; be amazed at developments in science.

But, above all, remember that God has revealed His love for you through the sacrifice of His Son on the cross at Golgotha. Hold unflinchingly to this truth and find peace of mind.

Jesus, Source of true love, visit us with Your salvation and let us rest in Your love. Amen.

God Has Been Good to Me

Read Psalm 13:1-6

I will sing to the Lord, for He has been good to me. (Psalm 13:6)

A wise person once remarked that most people are as happy as they decide to be. But many people are not happy at all. They complain about the economy; politics; the cost of living; the world's problems and the weather. They even complain about complaining!

Our Scripture reading for today was written by David – and he had first-hand experience of trouble. It came at him from all sides; and some he brought upon himself. He also knew sickness. Despite all the things he could have complained about, he still testified of God's goodness, which was so good that he could sing and rejoice about it.

> *God, who needs nothing, loves into existence wholly superfluous creatures in order that He may love and perfect them.*
> ~ C. S. Lewis

We can also sing about how good God has been to us. Or we can complain about problems that have come upon us. You must decide. It is, however, far better to rejoice over God's goodness. View your problems from the right perspective. Behind every problem is a God who lovingly cares for you; who provides for you, redeems you and sincerely loves you.

God was good to David, Jesus, Paul, Peter and John. He was good to those who were martyred for their faith in Christ. He loves the believer who loves Him. He loves you too. He gave you life and health; He has saved you from dangerous situations, and has continually surrounded you with His protective love. He has given you hope and salvation. God has been good to you – sing about it!

Give thanks to the Lord, for He is good; His love endures forever! Psalm 106:1

The Power of Humility and Love

Read Zechariah 9:1-10

See, your King comes to you, righteous and having salvation, gentle and riding on a donkey, on a colt, the foal of a donkey. (Zechariah 9:9)

We live in an age of aggression – this is the opinion and experience of many people. There seems to be a lot of evidence to support this viewpoint when we consider recent international and ethnic conflicts.

This, however, goes much further when we consider the aggressive attitudes of opponents in business and sports. There is an increase in aggressive behavior on our roads. The higher percentage of interpersonal aggression also bears witness to this disturbing fact.

When the corn is nearly ripe it bows the head and stoops lower than when it was green. When the people of God are near ripe for heaven, they grow more humble and self-denying.

~ John Flavel

The people were in an aggressive mood when Jesus entered Jerusalem on Palm Sunday. They had waited for the promised Messiah who they thought would be a powerful warrior who would lead them in a mighty revolt against the detested Roman authorities. Instead, they found the Lord riding into Jerusalem on the back of a donkey. For that period in history a donkey was the appropriate means of transport for a peaceful and loving leader.

Jesus' humility and love won the struggle against aggression at that period in time. Through His followers, the same *can* and *will* happen today too.

Jesus, humble Savior, continue with Your sovereign task and rule in my life in glory. Amen.

Imprisoned for Christ

Read Colossians 4:1-9

Pray for us, too, that God may open a door for our message, so that we may proclaim the mystery of Christ, for which I am in chains.

(Colossians 4:3)

Through serving Christ, some people become involved in activities they would never otherwise have pursued. Mother Teresa became world famous through serving the poor and suffering on the streets of Calcutta. Billy Graham became a household name through the massive gatherings he held in the name of Christ. Dietrich Bonhoeffer, a German theologian, became a martyr when his faith led him to become an accomplice in an attempt to assassinate Hitler.

> *The golden rule for understanding spiritually is not intellect, but obedience.*
> ~ Oswald Chambers

The apostle Paul was a zealous Pharisee who became a missionary for Christ, which landed him in prison. He then used his time in prison to write letters with instructions and encouragement to the churches he had planted. The gospel he spread brought freedom to thousands, but caused the loss of his own freedom. And yet, out of that prison cell, came incredible teachings which have led the church and individuals throughout the centuries.

You never know where discipleship to Christ might lead you. It takes some people to the ends of the earth. For some it leads to great accomplishments in music, prayer, writing and teaching. But you can't prescribe to Christ where He must lead you. You must open yourself up to Him. His calling may not lead you to fame – more often it will lead to isolation, poverty and loneliness. The key is always obedience to Him, without thinking about the consequences – even if your obedience leads you to a prison cell!

Savior and Master, help me to obey You, despite the cost. Amen.

The Comforting Love of God

Read Jude 17-25

Keep yourselves in God's love as you wait for the mercy of our Lord Jesus Christ to bring you to eternal life. (Jude 21)

Even though the Christian believer has the glorious promise of eternal life, the death of a loved one leaves a painful wound in your heart when you have to get over the shock and work through the reality of the loss. Even though you can rejoice in the fact that those who have died in the faith have gone on to receive their reward in God's eternal kingdom, what do you do with the loneliness in your life in the meantime?

When the Master prepared His disciples for His return to His Father, He poured His peace over them. At the same time He gave His comforting Holy Spirit so that God's all-encompassing love could fill their lives on earth, until His love would lift them up into God's kingdom in heaven.

I was not born to be free. I was born to adore and obey.

~ C. S. Lewis

This same peace and love is Christ's wonderful gift to you. Trust in Him and open your life and heart to Him; allow Him to show you where to serve; offer your love and compassion to others so that the living Christ can work in and through you for the good of His people. In this way you will remain in the neverending embrace of God's love. He will lead you through your disappointments until you enjoy God's glory in eternity.

"Breathe, O breathe Thy loving Spirit into every troubled breast! Let us all in Thee inherit, let us find the promised rest." Amen.

Thankfulness

Read Colossians 3:5-17

Be thankful. (Colossians 3:15)

There are people who find it very difficult to show their gratitude. They also find it difficult to *feel* grateful. They fear that they will then be obligated to acknowledge that they owe the person they are grateful to.

Many of our Christian experiences are born out of the gratitude we feel toward God for what He has done for us. The Christians in Colosse were encouraged to be thankful. By hearing the gospel and believing in Jesus, God lead them out of heathenism and idolatry into a healthy, living and loving way of life. They were also placed in a loving, truthful and forgiving Christian fellowship. In short: they received salvation through Christ and were filled with God's Holy Spirit. There was so much for them to be grateful for.

> *This day and your life are God's gift to you: so give thanks and be joyful always!*
>
> ~ Jim Beggs

We also have so much to thank God for. He provides for your daily needs, however meager it is at times. Thank God for your health and safety, for your family and faithful friends and all the other good things that God has provided for you. Be especially thankful for the salvation through Jesus Christ that you now experience. Thank Him for your Bible, your church, and your pastor. Be thankful for all the help God gave you when you were in trouble and experienced crises, or when you were upset or depressed.

Thank God that He has forgiven your sins and restored your peace with Him. Be thankful that you can look forward to renewal on the other side of this life in the Eternal Father's house with Jesus Christ.

Gracious Father God, besides all the other gifts You grant me, please grant me the gift of a thankful heart. Amen.

One Path to Wealth

Read Colossians 3:5-17

Let the word of Christ dwell in you richly. (Colossians 3:16)

Many people are obsessed with money. They think about it day and night. Everything they do is measured against what it will cost them or how much they will gain. They haven't mastered money; money has mastered them.

There are many forms of wealth. In Charles Dickens' famous *A Christmas Carol* the miser, Scrooge, had a lot of money, but was miserable and nasty to others. His clerk, Bob Cratchit, who could barely make a living, had a loving family that he valued far above all Scrooge's treasures. He was by far the richer of the two.

> *God only, and not wealth, maintains the world; riches merely make people proud and lazy.*
>
> ~ Martin Luther

Paul considered his new life in Christ as his greatest asset. He often wrote about the "riches in Christ." When you hear about Christ and He speaks to you it is a source of wealth that you can draw on and cherish. If you regularly meditate on God's Word you are connected to an immeasurable source of wealth. If that same Word remains in you, it will enrich you more than any gold mine can. Spiritual wealth does not erode through inflation. Unlike a gold mine, it doesn't have a limited lifespan.

As a believer in Christ it is important to realize the different forms of wealth you have access to. Knowledge, wisdom and health are all valuable. So are your family, friends and fellow believers. Let Christ's words lead you in determining which type of wealth you will regard most highly.

Holy Savior, help me to appreciate spiritual riches so that I will not desire things of no eternal value. Amen.

Does God Listen to You?

Read John 9:24-34

We know that God does not listen to sinners. He listens to the godly man who does His will. (John 9:31)

A Jewish man went to the Wailing Wall every day for twenty years to pray to God. Someone noticed this and asked how it felt to always pray there. He replied, "It feels like I'm praying to a wall." It's possible that sometimes your prayers to God also feel like this.

The early Israelites believed that the only way to get to God was through living a good and God-honoring life. "God doesn't listen to sinners" was the common wisdom of those days.

> *Prayer requires more of the heart than of the tongue.*
>
> ~ Adam Clarke

Jesus proved that this is not true. God does listen to sinners! Every person is a sinner and God does listen to prayers, so He listens exclusively to sinners. He listens especially to those who know that they are sinners and who bow before Him in repentance and humility. Righteous people, good people and strong people don't have more of a hold on God than anyone else.

The fact is that God longs to hear your prayer, whether you are a hero of the faith or a sinner; young or old; well educated or uneducated. He rejoices in hearing your prayers, whether you pray with confidence or find it difficult to put a sentence together. God does not prefer the eloquence of those with a gift for speaking. God rejoices in receiving your prayers, even if they are blundering and simple utterances that are confused and mixed up. Whatever your situation, "pray without ceasing."

Lord Jesus, teach me to pray! Amen.

No Condemnation: Only Love!

Read Romans 8:1-11

Therefore, there is now no condemnation for those who are in Christ Jesus. (Romans 8:1)

It is surprising how many people live their whole lives terrified of God's condemnation. They live under a cloud of despondency and are convinced that God is waiting to punish them for every little faux pas.

To maintain such a view of God makes your religion a burden. It creates a destructive attitude toward life because you can't appreciate what is good and beautiful if you are scared of the One who created all beautiful things.

It is love, not fear that brings out the best in you. This is one of the things Jesus demonstrated and taught. If you live in fear of condemnation, you can't possibly

> *Jesus came treading the waves; and so He puts all the swelling tumults of life under His feet. Christians – why afraid?*
>
> ~ St. Augustine

give your best or grow to spiritual maturity. Fear might prevent you from doing certain destructive things, but it is only love that will remove the desire to do them. In this context Christ no longer condemns you, but He requires your faithfulness through the dynamic power of love.

When you have been freed from deadly fear through Christ's love and mercy, your view of life expands. You realize what you can become while, through the power of Jesus, you undergo a deepening of your love for Him. You are gloriously freed from all destructive fear of condemnation.

Thank You, Lord Jesus, for freeing me from all destructive fear and for the gift of Your indescribable love. Amen.

And After Death?

Read Acts 16:25-34

Believe in the Lord Jesus, and you will be saved – you and your household. (Acts 16:31)

Throughout the history of humankind there have been those who have had little or no idea of what awaited them after their physical death. There have been some bravados who pretended not to care about the future; while others have vehemently denied that there is any future after death. Most people are confused and unsure and as a result of their uncertainty, they are afraid.

For Christians, the glorious truth of eternal life was confirmed when Jesus rose from the dead after His crucifixion. Through His victory over death He brought redemption and eternal life for all who believe in Him and accept Him as Lord of their lives. The empty tomb forever confirms the power of God's love over the grave – a love that brought hope to those for whom Jesus died.

> *Death is as the foreshadowing of life. We die that we may die no more.*
>
> ~ Herman Hooker

If you are looking for reassurance that God is in your life, believe in His promises. Accept Jesus Christ as your Savior and Redeemer; open your heart and life to Him so that His Holy Spirit may come and live in you. Dedicate yourself to Him anew and be assured that the Risen Savior will banish all fear and uncertainty. Your inheritance will then be eternal life in His kingdom.

Savior who grants eternal life, without You I cannot live; without You I dare not die. Amen.

Waiting for the Messiah

Read Luke 2:25-35

At that time there was a man in Jerusalem named Simeon. He was righteous and devout and was eagerly waiting for the Messiah to come and rescue Israel. (Luke 2:25 NLT)

Children wait impatiently for Christmas to arrive. We have all experienced that kind of excitement at one time or another. When the occasion finally arrived we could hardly believe that it was real. Not everything we are so impatient for comes as surely as Christmas. People buy lottery tickets and wait for their "lucky day." That day never arrives for most people. Others wait for poverty to be alleviated and find that that day is being delayed.

God's people wait longingly for Him. Sometimes He comes quickly and unexpectedly. In other situations He prolongs His

Faith takes up the cross, love binds it to the soul, patience bears it to the end.

~ Horatius Bonar

coming and keeps His disciples full of anticipation, sometimes for very long periods. Simeon was an elderly man and was typical of many dedicated people in Israel who looked forward to the coming Messiah.

When God finally sent His Son, many didn't recognize and accept Him. But Simeon was not one of them. He patiently and humbly obeyed the promptings of the Holy Spirit and welcomed Jesus. He knew that the long wait was finally over. He glorified God through his reception of the Holy Child.

There is something deeply moving in the picture of this elderly man welcoming the small Child, in whom He recognized God's greatest Gift. Don't become impatient if you are waiting for God to fulfill His promises. No calculation or textual research will hasten His coming. He will come in His own time. Wait patiently for Him and trust Him completely.

Christ-Child, help me to wait patiently for Your coming. Amen.

To Die in Peace

Read Luke 2:25-35

"Sovereign Lord, now let Your servant die in peace, as You have promised." (Luke 2:29 NLT)

Death is not a topic we like to think or talk about. We don't like to use the word *dead*, but rather use euphemisms like *passed away*, *called to higher service* or *departed from this life*.

After welcoming the Christ-Child and praising God, the elderly Simeon prayed a beautiful prayer to God that is known as the *Nunc Dimittis*. Simeon walked with God and lived a life of dedication, faith and hope.

The insight of the Holy Spirit enabled him to see that this Child was God's Promised One, and for this reason he was ready to die. He accepted life from God's hand and was now ready to die "in peace."

> *God buries His workmen, but carries on His work.*
>
> ~ Charles Wesley

See how Simeon addresses God, "Sovereign Lord ... Your servant." Mary reacted in the same manner when the angel announced that she would bring God's Son into the world, "'I am the Lord's servant,' Mary answered, 'May it be to me as you have said'" (Luke 1:38).

God's servants accept both their calling to serve and their calling to stand aside of their service in the same faithful and obedient manner. They know that they are God's servants in life and in death. All that they desire is the privilege of being obedient to Him. They are not afraid to die because they know that they are in God's loving hands – both in life and death.

Holy Lord and Master, thank You for teaching us to die in a worthy manner. Amen.

Jesus' Influence

Read 2 Corinthians 5:11-21

If anyone is in Christ, he is a new creation; the old has gone, the new has come! (2 Corinthians 5:17)

Religion is like a magnet for people who like to argue. They can quote a Scripture verse out of context and waste precious time by giving it a meaning it was never intended to have. Religion can become so philosophical that it loses its significance for the average person.

A meaningful religious faith must always lead to practical results. It is of little value to tell people to love God if you do not demonstrate it through your love for others. To emphasize the therapeutic benefits of forgiveness is certainly not enough. It is

> *Busy yourself with keeping your mind in the Presence of the Lord.*
> ~ Brother Lawrence

essential that you reach beyond the theory and apply forgiveness in practice.

You might be a dedicated follower of Jesus Christ, but if your spirit is petty and narrow-minded your faith counts for very little. It is when you live in the Presence of your Lord that you reflect something of His merciful and radiant personality, and that you bless everyone you come into contact with. Then they intuitively know that you walk with Jesus. They are then blessed through you.

No one can effectively argue against a positive and living faith. When dishonest people become honest; when lives are transformed through Christ's love; when homes that were horrific become heavens, there can be no argument against the influence of the living Christ on people's lives.

Savior and Lord, grant that the greatest argument I can give for my faith will be the quality of my daily life. Amen.

Do Not Be Afraid!

Read Luke 1:26-38

The angel said to her, "Do not be afraid, Mary, you have found favor with God." (Luke 1:30)

Many people's lives are ruled by fear. There are people who are afraid of other people; of the future; of loneliness; of financial need; or ill health. Nearly everyone is afraid of death.

Mary was afraid because she didn't know why the angel was visiting her. She was completely flustered. But then the angel said, "Do not be afraid, Mary."

God had a task for Mary that would require much courage, commitment and emotional strength from her. It was a huge role, an important position and a difficult task to which God called her.

> *Courage is doing what you are afraid to do. There can be no courage unless you are scared.*
>
> ~ Eddie Rickenbacker

We need to hear that message again and again: Do not be afraid! It is often repeated in the New Testament. Christ says to you today: Do not be afraid! Don't be afraid of your declining health; or the state of the world's economy; or the increase in terrorism; or the rise in crime; or the spread of diseases; or worldwide hunger.

Some of the things you fear might never happen to you. Some might happen, but not on the catastrophic scale you fear. Some will happen, but humanity has the incredible ability to solve problems.

Above all the things we fear is an almighty God who is in ultimate control. He finds favor with you and He sincerely loves you. You can trust in Him and peacefully continue with the task you have been called to perform.

Father God, grant that Jesus' example will give me renewed courage for each day. Amen.

J-E-S-U-S!

Read Luke 1:26-38

You will be with child and give birth to a son, and you are to give Him the name Jesus. (Luke 1:31)

People today are inclined to name their children after movie stars, sports heroes or any other popular celebrities. A girl's name is often chosen because it sounds pretty, and a boy's because it sounds strong.

In biblical times a name often indicated the hope that the parents had for their child and what he or she would become. Family names were also carried down. The name *Jesus* means "Savior." It focuses on Jesus' role of redeeming humankind. He came to save completely. His redemption incorporated the forgiveness of sin, but it also included healing, holiness, renewal, joy, the fruit of the Spirit, love and hope.

> *The name of Jesus is, in my mind, a joyous song, in mine ear a heavenly sound, in my mouth honey-full sweetness.*
> ~ Richard Rolle

Jesus is the most beloved name in the entire universe. It means different things to different people. When you are lonely, it means friendship and love. When you are depressed, it means joy. When you are afraid, it means courage. When you are sick, it means healing. When you are guilty, it means forgiveness. When you have fallen, it means restoration. When you are in the midst of trouble, it means light in the darkness. When you die, it means life on the other side of the grave.

It is the name most of us use for God – and this is correct. Without Jesus, we would never have known God.

Jesus, Jesus, Jesus sweetest name I know. Fills my every longing, keeps me singing as I go. My Savior and Redeemer. Amen.

The Human Savior

Read Romans 1:1-7

The Good News is about His Son. In His earthly life He was born into King David's family line. (Romans 1:3 NLT)

Through the centuries there have been many great men of God. Some of them were prophets and others were saints. Some were very dedicated and others sacrificed themselves for others in God's name. There were great teachers among them.

These were all people who were sent by God. In other words, they were ordinary people who God used in extraordinary ways. Jesus was also fully human. He had the same physical form as all the others. He ate and drank, worked and slept. He sometimes got tired and searched for the rejuvenation of solitude. He prayed and received strength from God.

Jesus was God and man in one person, that God and man might be happy together again.

~ George Whitefield

In biblical times a person's identity was confirmed, through the naming of his parents, not by a number or reference in a central register. This could be extended by naming the great-grandparents. Jesus is described as being "born into King David's family line."

Only a person who was fully human could save us. He had to experience our fears, temptations, loneliness and sorrow so that He could give us life in all its fullness (John 10:10). By becoming fully human, Jesus raised the standard because He was the perfect person. Through this He gave a new quality and dimension to human life. He made it what God intended it to be. Are you what God intended you to be?

God of mercy, help me to be more and more like Jesus. Amen.

Son of God!

Read Romans 1:1-7

He was shown to be the Son of God when He was raised from the dead by the power of the Holy Spirit. He is Jesus Christ our Lord.
(Romans 1:4 NLT)

You might sometimes ponder and marvel at the fact that the life of a Galilean carpenter, who lived more than two thousand years ago, still receives the admiration and worship of millions of His followers. What was it about Jesus that drew people to Him? Why were so many lives changed by the impact of His life and teachings?

Jesus was far more than an ordinary person. He was not only fully human, but fully and perfectly God. He was more than a man called and empowered by God because many prophets were called by God in this way. Jesus was the Son of God. He came from God and He was God. When

> *After 1,900 years, Jesus Christ still counts for much more in human life than any other man that has ever lived.*
>
> ~ William R. Inge

He rose from the grave it was the final confirmation that it was God who had come to earth. It confirmed His dominion over the forces of evil. It proved that He triumphed over death!

The gospel of God, the gospel of Jesus Christ, and the gospel of the Bible is always the good news of the resurrection. Because Jesus rose and triumphed you can also triumph over temptations. Through Jesus' resurrection we have the hope that life is stronger than death. Because He lives you can know joy instead of sorrow, hope instead of despair, peace instead of confusion. You don't receive these blessings by taking part in some or other spiritual gymnastics. They come to you as God's gift through His triumphant Son – Jesus Christ!

Savior and Master, fill my whole life with Your resurrection power.
Amen.

A Son Is Given

Read Isaiah 9:1-6

To us a Child is born, to us a Son is given. (Isaiah 9:6)

The birth of a child is an occasion of great joy. The parents are congratulated and the baby is showered with gifts and wonderful wishes for the future. A whole new time of love and excitement is born for the world.

When Jesus was born in Bethlehem, He fulfilled the age-old dream of the birth of a Child who would do what no earthly person could do. But this Son was different. He wasn't just anyone's Son – He was God's Son! No human child was capable of fulfilling the hope of humankind, but God's Son was! He was God's gift to humankind. He was God's gift of obedience. No other person was ever completely obedient to God before.

> *Wherever the Father is (and He is everywhere) there the Son is, and wherever the Son is, there the Father is too.*
> ~ St. Cyril

If people want to be obedient, they must overcome their human inclination to be disobedient. They can't accomplish this unless they trust in the Son of God. God's Son also gives them God's love. God's kind of love doesn't come from the human heart, which is corrupted by much self-love. But these weak and errant hearts can be filled with Christ's love.

Christ lives in those who believe in Him and His love can transform them. God's Son is also God's gift of true and perfect humanity. It is only through Jesus Christ that human nature reaches its highest point. Those in whom Christ lives achieve the fullness that they are capable of achieving.

These are God's gifts in Jesus Christ: obedience, love and humanity. Pray that these gifts will grow to maturity in your life during this festive season.

Father of mercy, let Your Son be revealed in my life more and more.
Amen.

The Coming Kingdom

Read Isaiah 9:1-6

Of the increase of His government and peace there will be no end. He will reign over His kingdom, establishing and upholding it with justice and righteousness from that time on and forever. (Isaiah 9:7)

If you think that the world is in a terrible condition, you are probably right. It has always been this way. It is not a sign of the end times – it is completely normal. But the important question is, "Will it ever get better?"

Despite the fact that the Old Testament prophecy about a coming Messiah has been fulfilled in Jesus Christ, the world is still afflicted by poverty, oppression, starvation, greed, war, crime and terrorism. As a Christian, do you bravely attempt to balance the list of bad things with a list of good

> *Our heavenly Father never takes any earthly thing from His children except He means to give them something better.*
> ~ George Müller

things? Or do you despairingly give up in defeat and ask God to destroy the world because it is so evil? Rather do what the Hebrew prophets did. They hoped and dared to dream of a new world where God would reign supreme.

They painted a glowing picture of a world where God would reign. In a certain respect their dreams were unrealistic – because they could never be fulfilled. Yet in another sense they were realistic. Their hope was grounded, not in the abilities and merits of earthly leaders, but in the power of God's saving and renewing love. This is the only way of looking at the future in a way that will give us true, deep and lasting hope.

However deep the world might have sunk in the mire of sin, you must still expect the great kingdom of God. Hope and pray for that time when God's power will be revealed, when peace will reign and when righteousness and justice will triumph.

Lord Jesus, rule over this world and my heart with Your loving and just hand. Amen.

Great Joy!

Read Luke 2:8-20

The angel said to them, "Do not be afraid. I bring you good news of great joy that will be for all the people." (Luke 2:10)

The thought of inviting Christ into their lives fills many people with feelings of unworthiness and reverence and it causes them to tremble. The concept of the responsibility that they connect with Christianity causes feelings of fear and anxiety. Many people turn away from Jesus because they simply can't determine the benefit of following Him.

The situation today is no different than it was on the night of Jesus' birth. In the same way that the angel spoke to the shepherds and brought them "good news of great joy," the living Presence of Christ in you is confirmation of the greatest joy that you will ever

Jesus accepts you the way you are, but loves you too much to leave you that way.

~ Lee Venden

know. The coming of Jesus Christ into your life is the good news of the Christian faith. Remember that when the angels appeared to the shepherds, the angel announced the birth of the Savior and the good tidings of great joy that would be for all the people.

If the living Lord Jesus Christ offers Himself to you so graciously in exchange for your dedication to Him, don't allow fear or unworthiness to rob you of the great privilege of knowing Him as your Redeemer, Savior, Master and Friend. Accept Christ into your life and experience the great joy that the angel heralded for all people.

Holy Christ-Child, I humbly and gratefully open my heart to You.
Amen.

Prince of Peace

Read Isaiah 9:1-6

He will be called Wonderful Counselor, Mighty God, Everlasting Father, Prince of Peace. (Isaiah 9:6)

We usually refer to Christmas as a season of peace and goodwill. The song of the angels was indeed a message of peace. Our conflict-ridden world desperately needs this message more than any other message. It is ironic that with all our developments in technology, international organizations, and instant communication, we are just as plagued with war as previous generations.

The Old Testament prophet dreamed of a Messiah who would be a "Prince of Peace." The Hebrew understanding of peace was far more comprehensive than ours. While we have a slightly negative association with peace (the absence of war and conflict) the people in biblical times thought about peace in a beautiful and positive way. It was much more than the absence of conflict. It was more in line with what we see as prosperity. Peace was to continue toiling the soil, gathering the harvest, building families, developing societies, and worshiping and glorifying God. Peace was well-being, progression, and the promotion of good health and happiness.

> *When we are unable to find tranquility within ourselves, it is useless to seek it elsewhere.*
> ~ François de La Rochefoucauld

During Advent time we again celebrate the coming of Christ to this world. *Christ* is the Greek word with the same meaning as the Hebrew word *Messiah,* which means "Anointed One." God's Anointed One is coming again as the Prince of the greater peace, the peace that heals broken people, builds families, strengthens societies, encourages love and promotes well-being. Won't you consider how you can promote this peace during Advent time and throughout the whole year?

Loving Savior, let peace reign supreme and let the entire human race strive toward it. Amen.

Where Does Your Knowledge Lead You?

Read Ephesians 3:14-21

May you experience the love of Christ, though it is too great to understand fully. Then you will be made complete with all the fullness of life and power that comes from God. (Ephesians 3:19 NLT)

It is a proven fact that many Christians are dissatisfied with their faith. It is not that they have become antagonistic or aggressive toward those things that used to be holy to them, but with changing circumstances and unfavorable attitudes they have become indifferent to their spiritual lives. Christianity has progressively lost its attraction for them and they no longer acknowledge Christ's reign in their lives.

> *Believers who have the most knowledge, are not therefore, necessarily the most spiritual.*
> ~ John Newton

How is it possible that a once pulsating Christian faith can fade away until it eventually becomes a mockery of its initial glory? There could be many reasons for this: neglecting fellowship and worship; the inability to develop a constant prayer life; superficial Bible reading and study; and the challenge of peer pressure. These are just a few things that can lead to spiritual numbness.

A famous philosopher once stated that it is possible to know precisely what Christianity is about without being a Christian. There are many people who study the content of the faith, who know all the church's dogmas and who can passionately debate a theological issue, but whose lives reflect nothing of the beauty of the living Christ.

To experience the fullness of a living and positive faith, you need to consecrate yourself to Christ. Then you can rise above all the theories of religion. When knowledge leads to consecration, it serves a valuable purpose, but when it simply remains static knowledge, it is a failure.

Savior, grant that my knowledge of You will lead me to a deeper appreciation of Your divine character. Amen.

Rich in All Things

Read 1 Corinthians 1:1-9

I always thank God for you because of His grace given you in Christ Jesus. For in Him you have been enriched in every way – in all your speaking and in all your knowledge. (1 Corinthians 1:4-5)

There are different ways in which a person can become rich. Most people strive for material wealth and some see this as the sole purpose in life. Others dedicate themselves to acquiring academic knowledge and attain degree after degree. Some of them become authorities in their chosen field of study. There are people who become rich in friendships and they build an extensive circle of friends whom they can depend on at all times. Then there are people who become rich in "treasures," things they collect that have artistic or historical value.

> *The rich in this world cannot be made useful for the Lord, unless their riches have been cut out of them.*
>
> ~ Hermas

The Corinthian converts were rich in a completely different way. They possessed spiritual wealth – they had many spiritual gifts, like prophecy, healing, speaking in tongues, wisdom and miracles. The Holy Spirit worked in them in these dramatic ways, not for their own glorification, but so that the church as a whole could be enriched. Paul had much to say to this specific group of Christians about their disunity and boasting. And yet, they were spiritually rich.

You can also be blessed by God, despite your shortcomings. He makes you rich in love, faith and hope. He might fill you with praise and prayer and a deep gratitude toward Him for this grace. He might have blessed you with healthy family bonds and probably also an exceptional church family.

Don't envy other people's worldly riches. Cherish the true riches God has graciously blessed you with.

Lord Jesus, with Your love in my heart I am extremely rich. And for this I praise and thank You. Amen.

No Room – But God Was There

Read Luke 2:1-7

*She gave birth to her firstborn, a Son. She wrapped Him in cloths
and placed Him in a manger, because there was no room for them in
the inn. (Luke 2:7)*

The accommodation could have been better, but it was all the
inn-keeper could offer them. The welcoming party for God's Son
was small and socially unimportant, but the shepherds had sincerity that was inspired by a heavenly vision. The Caesar's decree
caused an uprise, but it undoubtedly brought about the reunion
of family members that would not have otherwise come together.

> *Abide with me! Fast falls the
> eventide; the darkness deep-
> ens: Lord with me abide!*
> ~ Henry F. Lyte

In the midst of this joyous activity
the Prince of Peace was born. God
accepted the best the inn-keeper
could offer and the shepherds'
worship gave Mary and Joseph
the deep contentment of knowing
that their Child was born among their own people.

One of the Holy Father's wonderful character traits is that
He is always constructive in the midst of destruction. In every
situation that seems hopeless, He always brings a glimmer of
hope. In the darkest moments of life, He drives the darkness
away. God is never overwhelmed by circumstances or conditions.
Those who trust in Him inherit this holy optimism. There is no
situation where God is not present or cannot help.

When everything looks hopeless and you want to give up,
don't give in to fear or despair. Positively confirm that God is
present in the situation and that He is your loving Father and
guide. Never fear because God is always with you and He brings
His wisdom and light to brighten your situation – if you will
only allow Him to.

*Heavenly Father, I thank You through Jesus Christ that You are
always there when I need You the most. Amen.*

A Son Is Born!

Read Isaiah 9:1-6

To us a Child is born, to us a Son is given, and the government will be on His shoulders. And He will be called Wonderful Counselor, Mighty God, Everlasting Father, Prince of Peace. (Isaiah 9:6)

Our world is inundated with problems. There is a huge disparity between the poor and the rich. There are threats of nuclear war; terrorism; drug smuggling; human trafficking; sickness, disease and overpopulation.

The Hebrew prophet Isaiah had exceptional insight. In the midst of social injustice, political unrest and economic uncertainty, he told the people of his time, "The answer to all these problems lies in the birth of a Child." He listened to God, studied the world around him and then made the shocking announcement that the human race was in such a mess that only someone outside the situation had any hope of saving it. The prophet said, "We need a Messiah to help us with this mess. Only God can provide a Messiah!" Seven hundred years after this prophecy, a Son was born – God's answer to humanity's problems.

> *A world of nice people, content in their own niceness, looking no further, turned away from God, would be just as desperately in need of salvation as a miserable world and might even be more difficult to save.*
> ~ C. S. Lewis

Today we rejoice in His coming. It brings hope to a world that is sick of despair. They yearn for salvation of souls entrenched in sin; the healing of the bodies and minds of sick people, joy for those who experience sorrow. Jesus' coming is a challenge. He doesn't remove our problems but He equips us to face them and shows us the direction we need to move in. Christmas reminds us of our personal responsibility towards the world.

Savior and Redeemer, show us how to solve the problems in our world. Amen.

To God Be the Glory!

Read Luke 2:8-20

The shepherds returned, glorifying and praising God for all the things they had heard and seen, which were just as they had been told. (Luke 2:20)

It's hard to imagine what the shepherds must have thought and felt when the angel of God brought them the wonderful news. In the merciless world in which they lived and worked, a Savior was born. These simple people were chosen by God to be the first to hear "the good news of great joy." They quickly hurried to Bethlehem to witness this miracle for themselves, and our reading today says, "The shepherds returned, glorifying and praising God for all the things they had heard and seen, which were just as they had been told."

> *Christ alone can bring lasting peace – peace with God – peace among men and nations – and peace within our hearts.*
>
> ~ Billy Graham

Even in our day and age we have Jesus' assurance of salvation and hope. Scripture assures us that He came so that we could have life and have it to the full (John 10:10). He sacrificed His own life so that we could be reconciled with God. So marvelously great was and is Almighty God's love for humankind.

We have not only heard of this great act of love, but we can testify to it in our own lives: God's love is greater than human thoughts and the heart of the Eternal God is amazingly compassionate.

After a blessed Christmas it is only fitting to return to everyday life with praise and worship to the God of love we have once again heard and experienced.

Holy God, we honor You. We worship and praise You. We thank You for Your unending love. Amen.

Get Your Priorities Straight

Read Luke 2:25-39

*When Joseph and Mary had done everything required by the Law of
the Lord, they returned to Galilee to their own town of Nazareth.*

(Luke 2:39)

The Christian faith requires absolute obedience to God, but how
often is this requirement faithfully kept? Everything we have,
even life itself, belongs to the Lord who has graciously entrusted
it to us. We must practice good and faithful stewardship over
what He has given us. But do we acknowledge Christ's sovereignty over every aspect of our lives?

True stewardship involves all our material possessions; our
time; our entire being. What you
undertake must be done in the
name of God if you want to be
faithful to your high calling in Jesus Christ.

> *Lord, we do not mind who is
> second, as long as Thou art
> first.*
>
> ~ W. E. Stangter

You are indebted to Him for
everything you have and everything you are, and as a result, He
must enjoy priority over your life and daily activities. This means
that you must first satisfy God before you think about yourself
– however difficult and uncomfortable this might seem. He has
redeemed you, and through your acceptance of Jesus Christ,
He has not only become your Father and Friend, but also your
Savior and Redeemer. Therefore everything in your life must be
subordinate to His will.

If you call on the help of the Holy Spirit and allow Him to
guide your thoughts on your journey through life, you will have
the desire to subject yourself to God's will. His Presence and
Companionship then become more real to you.

*Savior and Redeemer, in thankfulness I consecrate myself anew to
You and accept Your rulership over my life with absolute obedience.*

Amen.

Jesus, Our Example and Role Model

Read 1 John 3:1-10

Dear friends, now we are children of God, and what we will be has not yet been made known. But we know that when He appears, we shall be like Him, for we shall see Him as He is. (1 John 3:2)

It is human nature to copy other people. A teenager will try to copy the facial expressions of an older person. A child will laugh because an adult laughs, even though he doesn't understand the joke. We dress like our sports heroes and celebrities and copy their hairstyles. Even in adulthood, some people take on a leading figure in their profession as their role model.

Jesus Christ is the only role model for Christians. The Spirit works His fruit into our lives, "love, joy, peace, patience, kindness, goodness, gentleness, faithfulness and self-control" (Gal. 5:22-23). All these qualities are found in Christ. Those who excel in these qualities are more Christ-like than those who don't have them. But these qualities don't all come at once or in equal measure, sometimes it takes years for the Spirit to bring them all to maturity.

> *More like Jesus would I be, let my Savior dwell in me; fill my soul with peace and love, make me gentle as a dove.*
>
> ~ Fanny J. Crosby

But even the youngest believer in whose life Jesus has begun to take form is on his way. To get an idea of what you will be like when the grace of God's work of love is completed in your life, you need to look at Christ. You certainly won't be less of the person you are now. Your personality won't be erased. You will, indeed, be more characteristically yourself and possess your own personality and character more than ever before. What is left uncompleted on earth, will be completed in heaven. Christ is our Savior and role model in this life.

Lord, help me through the Spirit to be more like Jesus every day.

Amen.

Strong to the End

Read 1 Corinthians 1:1-9

He will keep you strong to the end, so that you will be blameless on the day of our Lord Jesus Christ. (1 Corinthians 1:8)

The Christian's earthly journey is a marathon and some people make it through to the end. Others fall by the wayside. To journey with Jesus requires not only grace, but perseverance.

For most of His disciples it means a bumpy ride rather than a smooth, uninterrupted progression. If you have given up or are considering it, our reading today is especially for you.

It was difficult for the early Christians to believe. They were surrounded by a variety of strange beliefs. They were continually spurred on to deny their faith and return to their old ways. It was impossible for the Christians to worship the Roman Caesar, but it was demanded from them as a social requirement. At times they were persecuted and this made life very difficult for the Christians. They always feared that they would backslide.

It is not the going out of port, but the coming in, that determines the success of a voyage.

~ Henry Ward Beecher

On the other hand these Christians lived with the strong expectation that Jesus would return in their lifetime. Paul encouraged the believers in Corinth to trust that Christ would grant them the strength and ability to persevere. Had they depended on their own strength, many of them would never have survived.

We also need Christ's strength to persevere until the end. If you have given up for some reason, start again and allow Christ to empower you for the long journey ahead and start traveling at His side.

Savior on our journey through life, we pray that today You will grant Your power and grace to those who are battling to persevere until the end. Amen.

Face the Future with Hope

Read Isaiah 65:17-25

"Behold, I will create new heavens and a new earth. The former things will not be remembered, nor will they come to mind." (Isaiah 65:17)

As we approach the end of this year it is helpful to meditate on the way in which our faith helps us to view the world. You might have good reason to be optimistic or pessimistic. This will probably depend on your plans for the future or disappointments you experienced in the past. But try not to focus on your own circumstances and instead think about God – the God of the Bible and the Father of our Lord Jesus Christ.

> *When considering the creation, the how and the when does not matter so much as the why and the wherefore.*
>
> ~ R. de Campoamor

We have hope for the future because, despite the fact that He is the God of unlimited resources and incredible initiative, He is the God of renewal and recreation. His work of creation continues endlessly, even if you are caught in the past. He is the God of the future because He comes to us in the future He continually creates anew. His actions were breathtaking in the past, and He is still busy planning a new heaven and a new earth.

Revelation ends with a glorious dream of God's great future and even there He creates a new heaven and a new earth. God is never finished and He continually creates new things. He creates new generations; He makes people new creations. Out of the destruction and decay of the past, He creates new things and new people. Look for God's creativity in the world around you in the new year.

Holy Spirit of God, grant that I will always face the future with hope. Amen.

Jesus Is Coming!

Read Revelation 22:6-21

"Behold, I am coming soon! Blessed is he who keeps the words of the prophecy in this book." (Revelation 22:7)

People have tried to predict Jesus' second coming for many centuries. Much publicity has been given and much preparation has been done, but the end result of all of these predictions has been anti-climax, disappointment, disillusionment – and unbelief. Even followers of the Resurrected Jesus tried to find an answer, only to find that God alone knows when that day will come.

In many cases the predictions about Jesus' second coming have forced people to get their lives in order. They keep themselves busy with this and try to overcome their transgressions and shortcomings in the hope that they will meet the great Master. This is commendable, but when the predicted date comes and

> *We must never speak to simple, excitable people about "the Day" without emphasizing again and again the utter impossibility of prediction.*
> *~ C. S. Lewis*

goes without anything happening, people relax because they think the urgency is no longer there.

Because Jesus said that no one except the Father knows the date, it is essential that you live in such a way that you are always ready and willing to receive Him. There are constant opportunities to improve your life. Make a habit out of living according to God's commandments, live close to Christ, and make certain that when He comes again, you will be ready to receive Him with thanksgiving and worship.

Savior, following Your example, I will live in such a way that I will be ready to welcome You with thanksgiving when You come again.
Amen.